UNDERSTANDING GLOBAL NEWS

A Critical Introduction

Jaap van Ginneken

SAGE Publications
London • Thousand Oaks • New Delhi

First published 1998. Reprinted 1999, 2002, 2003

First published as *De schepping van de wereld in het nieuws: de 101 vertekeningen die elk 1 procent verschil maken* by Bohn Stafleu Van Loghum, Houten/Diegem 1996.

SAGE Publications Ltd
6 Bonhill Street
London EC2A 4PU

SAGE Publications Inc.
2455 Teller Road
Thousand Oaks, California 91320

SAGE Publications India Pvt Ltd
32, M-Block Market
Greater Kailash – I
New Delhi 110 048

British Library Cataloguing in Publication data

A catalogue record for this book is available from the British Library

ISBN 0 7619 5708 1
ISBN 0 7619 5709 X (pbk)

Library of Congress catalog number 97–061880

The Sheffield College
Hillsborough - Learning Resource Centre
(0114) 260 2254

Typeset by Mayhew Typesetting, Rhayader, Powys
Printed and bound in Great Britain by Athenaeum Press Ltd., Gateshead

UNDERSTANDING GLOBAL NEWS

17.99

Fata Morgana. 1: Mirage <suddenly – like a *fata morgana* rising out of the desert clouds – houses, trees and people materialized – Joseph Wechsberg>; esp. one with marked displacement and distortion. 2: Something insubstantial or illusory . . .

Webster's *New International Dictionary*

CONTENTS

PREFACE

....

This is a book about the 'social construction' and 'social representation' of world affairs by North American and Western European media, which also shape news definitions on other continents. First, here are a few remarks about what this book is and is not meant to be.

AUDIENCE   The book is aimed at several audiences at once: students at university level in communication and the humanities; students of professional schools in journalism and social work; teachers at secondary schools; but also at professionals and volunteers working in the field of world affairs, and at an educated public in general.

LEVEL   The book should be accessible to everyone with a secondary education or a high-school diploma. It shuns unnecessary abstractions and jargon, and tries to provide concrete examples and illustrations.

SUBJECT   The book is an introduction to the subject of world news, and in particular to 'Western' news about 'non-Western' countries and peoples and issues. It seeks to understand why this news is as it is by integrating findings from a wide variety of disciplines.

APPROACH   The approach is primarily conceptual: the book reviews the various 'universal' mechanisms which have been identified as playing a role in this context, and attempts to identify some of the 'missing links' between them. On the one hand it refers to the major theoretical approaches which have been proposed; on the other hand it refers to the major research projects which have been carried out, but without going into minute detail.

POINT OF VIEW   The author's point of view is 'middle of the road', disagreeing with the proposition that journalism (or science) is (or can be) unproblematically factual, neutral and objective. But he also disagrees with the proposition that they are intentionally controlled or slanted. This is the exception rather than the rule.

AREAS COVERED   Analyses relate primarily to the major US media and news organizations, which exert a huge influence abroad. But it also discusses examples from Great Britain, France and some smaller European countries.

FOLLOW UP The book provides ample suggestions for further study: possible illustrations from everyday media practice, individual research projects, more theoretical literature. Thus it can easily be used as a stepping stone for more advanced levels, in combination with other material.

The writing of this book was supported by a small grant from the Netherlands 'Third World Communication' Foundation and the National Commission for Information about Development Cooperation. I particularly thank Mr Barend de Ronden of the Foundation and Ms Jodie Ermers of the Commission for their help and patience. The project was encouraged and supervised all the way by Cees Hamelink, Professor of International Communication at the University of Amsterdam, who also lectured at the International Institute of Social Studies in The Hague.

The manuscript was read by a sample of colleagues; researchers and lecturers in communication departments and journalism schools, current and former journalists with experience in international newsgathering, and others: Piet Bakker, Jan van Beek, Teun van Dijk, Eric Haas, Manon Louwerens, Christ'l de Landtsheer, Connie van der Molen, Karel Roskam, Peter Sluiter, Joost Smiers and Nico Vink. I am very grateful that they were willing to take time to comment on an early draft of the manuscript and to suggest various improvements. Needless to say, they cannot be held responsible in any way for remaining judgements or controversial statements.

Jaap van Ginneken,
Villeneuve Loubet/Amsterdam,
May 1997

1 INTRODUCTION

The only feeling that anyone can have about an event he does not experience is the feeling aroused by his mental image of the event . . .

For it is clear enough that under certain conditions men respond as powerfully to fictions as they do to realities, and that in many cases they help to create the very fictions to which they respond . . .

For certainly, at the level of social life, what is called the adjustment of man to his environment takes place through the medium of fictions. By fictions I do not mean lies. I mean a representation of the environment which is in lesser or greater degree made by man himself.

Walter Lippman, 'The world outside and the pictures in our heads'[1]

Is it easy to report the simple truth about plain reality? Or is what we see before our eyes largely determined by what we carry between our ears? Is the measure we take of things inevitably determined by the yardsticks we employ? Take something very basic such as maps: are such views of the world determined by world-views? If so, does this also extend to elementary language and categorizations, or even statistics and numbers? Do we inevitably frame places and people in ethnocentric ways? Is it possible to have news without views? Or do we judge the world 'out there' by the world 'in here', by mental representations continuously built and rebuilt through social processes?

Although a social scientist by training, I have spent large chunks of my life as a journalist, working for a wide range of daily and weekly newspapers, radio and TV broadcasters. My roles included those of foreign correspondent and roving reporter. I carried out assignments in some forty countries outside Western Europe and North America, in Africa, Asia and Latin America. Many things went right, but many things went wrong too. Today, most of my work is as a communication analyst and author. This is an appropriate time to make up the balance sheet and try to identify things I learnt the hard way: the many traps eagerly awaiting a Westerner bringing non-Western news. No matter what one does, one remains tied to one's own perspective on the world, in many ways which are counter-intuitive, because everyday experience of the ordinary world seems so self-evident and unproblematic.

Let us begin with some very concrete examples. For one trimester each year, I teach seminars on media and intercultural communication within the international Access programme at the Faculty of Political,

Social and Cultural Sciences of the University of Amsterdam. Occasionally, I also lecture on this subject at the Institute of Social Studies in The Hague, the Training Center of Radio Netherlands, and other places. Some students in these various English-language programmes may come from Holland itself, but the vast majority originates from other countries all over the world. In recent years, I have often started such courses with a little mind game, an exercise to demonstrate both the universality of ethnocentrism and its specificity.

Each student gets three blank pieces of paper and a thick, dark, felt-tipped pen. I start the stopwatch and give them three minutes (or five) – but no more – to draw a map of The Netherlands: their tiny host country at that point in time. After that, they have three more minutes to draw a map of Europe, and after that, three more minutes to draw a map of the world. It is an unfair game, of course. Three minutes are not nearly enough to gather your thoughts, recognize the traps, and produce a more or less correct map. The students are pushed to make flagrant mistakes and gross distortions.

The interesting fact is not so much that they make mistakes but which particular mistakes they make and how these mistakes vary with nationality and personal history. Dutch students render their own country in a very characteristic shape. They are never surprised to see that their maps match each other in great detail. They are surprised, however, to learn that their foreign colleagues do not have the faintest idea about even the approximate shape of their host country. Most render it as a simple blob, without any characteristic shape at all.

Similarly, the map of Europe posed few problems to most European students, but there were several snags. Students from the British Isles often had a less articulate view of 'the Continent'. Non-Scandinavian students drew Norway, Sweden and Finland as three near-identical protrusions in the north. Northern students detailed those southern countries where they had been on a holiday. Even though most of these exercises took place after the fall of the Berlin wall and the Soviet Empire, all Western European students persisted in drawing 'Europe' as if it did not extend beyond Berlin, whereas Eastern European students usually made it three or four times as deep: up to and including the Ural Mountains. Students from Latin America accentuated the Iberian peninsula, and students from Catholic countries accentuated Italy (although they sometimes reversed the characteristic boot shape).

Most revealing, though, were the world maps: their idiosyncrasies as well as their similarities. As an illustration I reproduce and comment on half a dozen of these world maps here (Figure 1.1), as they were printed next to an article I wrote on the subject for a psychological magazine. A Palestinian map (upper left) has the major part of the world consisting of the continents of Eurasia and Africa, which

Figure 1.1 *The mind game. World maps drawn by students from: Palestine (upper left), Japan (upper right), Holland (centre left), Brazil (centre right), the US (bottom left) and Indonesia (bottom right).*

seem to be entangled in a very confusing way. The Middle East is at the centre. The Gulf, the Saudi peninsula, the Red Sea and the delta of the Nile river are all very prominent. The Americas are quite marginal. The Japanese map (upper right) was drawn by someone who had studied in Great Britain before. It has Japan at the centre, but depicts the two island groups on either side of the Eurasian continent, which – by an interesting slip of the pen – is marked with the label 'Europe'.

A Dutch map (centre left) has the Netherlands in the middle of the universe, and not nearly as small as it might seem to others. The Great Dike and the Zuiderzee/IJsselmeer inlet can easily be recognized. All other European countries are grouped around it. The Greek isles, Israel and its Arab neighbours are prominent. The former Dutch colony of Surinam (next to Guyana on the northern coast of South America), and the 'Netherlands' Antilles in the Caribbean, can easily be recognized as well. Half of the Americas, Africa and Asia have fallen off the map. By contrast a Brazilian map (centre right) makes the Americas much more prominent. The three North American countries are identified individually. The label for South America coincides with Brazil itself. The Spanish-speaking Andean countries look shaky in contrast, as does Africa. It seems to identify Portugal as the only individual country on the European continent; the E (and the form on which it is stamped) might identify either España or Europe. Italy is a small protrusion. The rest of the Eurasian continent is identified with the 'ex-USSR'.

A US map makes the Anglo-Saxon world seem extremely prominent, from the US and Canada, via Britain, to Australia and New Zealand. Latin America has shrunk, and Latin Europe has disappeared. Those countries with which the US was at war 'since the war' have also become invisible, from Korea, China and Vietnam to Iran and Iraq. An Indonesian map in turn has the island archipelago in a rather central position, halfway between the 'Hindia' (Indian) Ocean and the Pacific Ocean. Asia dominates the map and Australia is also very large.

The mechanisms in all these cases are basically threefold. The first concerns centrality. There is a tendency to place one's own country in a central position, at least, in a more central position than it would be in others' maps, and to group the rest of the world around it. Simultaneously, there is a tendency to make other countries and, indeed, entire continents peripheral. To conceive of one's own country as peripheral seems a very weird thought. The second mechanism concerns volume. There is a tendency to enlarge the surface of one's own country, to inflate it disproportionately in comparison to others. Simultaneously, there is a tendency to deflate other areas considered as irrelevant. The third mechanism concerns articulation. There is a tendency to render one's own country in great and characteristic detail, and to reduce other countries and continents to shapeless blobs. On the one hand, this is a very 'logical' result. On the other hand, it also betrays the collective narcissism with which we are all imbued.

But there is more. Apart from the idiosyncrasies of each nation, most of these maps from all around the world also had certain basic features in common. There was a general tendency to inflate the 'developed' countries of North America and Western Europe and to deflate the 'developing' countries of Asia, Africa and Latin America (except for the continent the student originated from). There was a general tendency to identify the former and present 'great powers', such as the (ex)-USSR and the USA. Great Britain and Ireland were often identified, as were Australia and New Zealand, and sometimes Canada. Students from former colonizing and formerly colonized countries often gave more weight to each other than to others.

Mental maps

The point is, of course, that all these are 'mediated' views of the world; they are not based on direct observation. Until the recent launching of manned spacecraft, no one had seen the world and the world map with his or her own eyes. Maps, for all their claims to physical exactness, are cultural productions. They map relevant places, distances, features of the land- and seascape. Mark Monmonier, author of *Maps with the News* and *How to Lie with Maps*, sums up:

> Not only is it easy to lie with maps, it's essential. To portray meaningful relationships for a complex, three-dimensional world on a flat sheet of paper or a video screen, a map must distort reality . . . To avoid hiding critical information in a fog of detail, the map must offer a selective, incomplete view of reality. There's no escape from the cartographic paradox: to present a useful and truthful picture, an accurate map must tell white lies.

The makers of maps often put their own city, country or reference points at the centre. Gradually, it dawned upon geographers and map-makers that the earth was not flat but round. In 1492 the first globe was produced, but the problem was how to render the surface of the global ball on paper. Peel an orange any way you want, and try to flatten its skin: you will always have to cut and force and damage it. The Mercator projection of 1569 was the best-known for centuries. It was originally a sea-farers' map, but it distorted the land masses and it did so in a somewhat ethnocentric way, which basically stayed with us for centuries to come.

The world map with which we are most familiar today does two things. On the one hand, it enormously inflates the territories closer to the poles, that is to say, precisely those 'northern' continents and countries which came to dominate the modern world: the US with a huge Alaska, Canada and a huge Greenland, Western Europe and a huge Scandinavia, Russia in Eastern Europe and Asia with a huge Siberia. On the other hand, it enormously deflated territories closer to the equator: Latin America, Africa and Australia, for instance. Only recently have other projections tried to correct for this. A well-known alternative is the Peters projection, which keeps volume constant, by compensating for width with height and vice versa. This produces a world map which seems compressed in the north and elongated around the equator. More recently, Professor Robinson of the University of Wisconsin has worked out a compromise map for the authoritative US National Geographic Society. It retains some of the northern delusions of grandeur, but reduces them to a more realistic scale.

It has meanwhile been pointed out that apart from the pure volume of continents and countries, Western ethnocentrism also emerges in other features of the best-known world maps. The northern countries are at the top: they are implicitly depicted as superior to the southern countries on the map; some say they 'dominate' them. The most developed countries are usually depicted on the upper left side of the paper, which gives them a kind of primacy in those countries reading from top to bottom, and from left to right.

Most world maps also have the Atlantic at their centre, with North America in the upper left and Western Europe in the upper centre. Some world maps, however, have the Pacific at their centre with Western Europe in the upper left and Japan in the upper centre. Australians often proposed to reverse this entire pattern, and put Australia on top of the world. There is no need to add that there is no 'natural' order saying that one territory is at the top and another at the bottom, one territory to the left and another to the right. It is a completely arbitrary choice, made by and in the most developed countries to suit their view of the world. It came to be experienced as natural though, even to such an extent that space photographs of the earth are now usually depicted with the same conventions – which further seems to naturalize this world view.

The same holds for the geometric grid which was projected onto the earth's surface to indicate an exact location by a combination of horizontal and vertical degrees. The numbering of the latitudes has a certain objective foundation, once we know that the earth has poles and turns around an axis. By contrast the meridian is a purely subjective invention, since there is no natural zero point. The British took the Greenwich (London) observatory as the centre of the universe and ultimately succeeded in having this view adopted worldwide. The French produced the standard metre (litre, kilogram) and ultimately succeeded in having their metric system adopted worldwide as well. Even describing the location of an event in such purely mathematical terms, therefore, literally means looking through a Eurocentric grid.

Even the hour of the day, and the well-known reference point of Greenwich Mean Time or GMT, implies a Eurocentric perspective, and in more subtle ways than we realize at first. Primacy is once again in Europe, in Great Britain, in London. Putting the date-line (date-change line) at the opposite end of the globe implies a dark midnight in the Pacific and a clear midday in the Atlantic. Saying something happened in the year so-and-so, furthermore, automatically introduces a very specific yardstick and cultural perspective. The arch-event, the reference point is made the birth of Jesus in the year zero of Western civilization: at the height of Roman civilization, halfway between the prelude of ancient Greek civilization and the follow-up of medieval Christian civilization.

This is not to say that this yardstick has not been 'voluntarily' adopted since by many others, that it is not convenient to share such a perspective with others, nor even to say that it matters very much – most of the time. But whereas we feel it is perfectly natural that other people can and do place themselves in our ('universal') time perspective, we do not feel it is equally natural for us to place ourselves in others' ('local') time perspective – just every now and then. Nor are we aware that some Jews and Muslims live in an entirely different time perspective today (the latter make their time begin in 622 AD), as do many Hindus and Buddhists (the latter make their time begin in 544 BC), or that our year 1996 corresponded to 4694 in the Chinese lunar calendar (the Year of the Rat).

Thus 'objective' terminology about time and space hides subjective ideological connotations in many ways, as do many other seemingly objective categories employed universally. Let us take a closer look at just a few of the more basic terms used in everyday journalistic language.

Mental frames

Let us imagine a TV news item. It might say something like:

> The Middle East conflict has claimed another Western victim. An American citizen was kidnapped outside the Peace Hotel in East Jerusalem on Saturday, December 24. The incident occurred at 9 p.m. (7 p.m. GMT). He was subdued by four masked men and driven away in a van. The victim is James Johnson (33), a black preacher from Trenton, New Jersey. He had come for a tour of the Holy Places with the church choir. Israeli authorities say responsibility has been claimed by the armed March 13 group. They have said they want to exchange the hostage for a fundamentalist cleric, who was arrested during a retaliatory raid against a terrorist base in Southern Lebanon last week.

This is a small and rather average news item. It provides an answer to the basic questions: who, what, where, when, why? But these answers might in turn generate a hundred other questions, some of which can easily be answered, but some of which cannot. Many things are implied, can be read between the lines, can be interpreted by whoever knows the right cultural codes. Why was this event reported? Would it also have been noticed if something similar had happened in the outskirts of an African capital, on another date, if the inferred motive had been criminal rather than political, or if the victim had a different nationality? East Jerusalem: is that not the part which used to belong to Jordan, and isn't its Arab name Al Qudz?

Saturday: is that not the Jewish Sabbath, right between the Islamic and the Christian holy days?

Many more questions can be imagined. Holy Places: which holy places? Church: what church? Why 'authorities' on the one hand, and 'terrorist group' on the other? We do know what 'December 24' refers to, but what does 'March 13' refer to? What happened at that time? Why is the capture of one person labelled 'kidnapping', and that of the other an 'arrest'? Why is one action a 'terrorist' act, and the other a 'retaliatory' raid? Because we implicitly reject one act as illegitimate and accept the other as legitimate. Are there just Islamic 'fundamentalists', or are there also Jewish 'fundamentalists' and Christian 'fundamentalists'? If fundamentalists are a multi-faith phenomenon, why are they labelled differently? What does this imply?

We will return to many of these mechanisms later, such as the 'intuitive' use of legitimating and delegitimating language by journalists in international news reporting. Here we will just limit ourselves to a further reconnoitring of some even more elementary labels, which return in many such international reports. They simply seem to denote places and people and times in a most casual way, but they also connote them in ideological ways. Most of the time, they look at the world through a Eurocentric grid: from a Christian or Judaeo-Christian point of view, from a white point of view, from an Anglo-American point of view. This holds even for the key components of world NEWS: North, East, West and South.

EAST AND WEST 'East is East and West is West, and never the twain shall meet,' Kipling said, as if East and West were essential and fixed qualities. But the opposite is true. As we have seen, there is a North Pole and a South Pole, but there is no such thing as an East pole and a West pole (although – as one commentator reminded me – there is in the stories about Winnie the Pooh). Whereas the notions of North and South have fixed 'natural' reference points, the notions of East and West are floating categories. Everything is both to the East and to the West of everything else: such labels therefore have a high degree of arbitrariness. For this reason, they are even more prone to ideological overlays. Of course there is an Eastern hemisphere and a Western hemisphere, if we accept that convention. But the curious thing is that these notions are almost never used in a more or less objective way, but almost always as more or less 'subjective'.

Proclaiming London/Greenwich as the zero line puts part of England and all of America together in the category of 'the West', which is in itself an interesting cognitive operation. But it also puts most of Europe in the category of 'the East', whereas Europe is never considered the East. Instead 'the East' is grouped around Europe in various ways. The label 'Near East' was variously meant to include areas stretching from north-west Africa to West Asia. The label

'Middle East' was used to include areas stretching from the Mediterranean to the Gulf coast. The label 'Far East' was meant to include areas stretching from India to China.

Of course, ethnocentrism is not a uniquely West European or North American affliction. The name China, for instance, derives from the term 'land of the middle'. But the difference is that the Euro-American frame of reference was exported globally, including many of its implicit value judgements. In Eurocentric language, the geographic denotation of 'the East' often became overlaid with connotations such as overpopulated, apathetic, despotic, conservative, old, dark, sinister; whereas the geographic denotation of 'the West' often became overlaid with connotations such as wide open spaces, dynamic, democratic, progressive, new, enlightened, open-minded. 'Orient' and 'Occident' have become highly ideological notions. The notion of 'the far West' of North America as a rich and empty territory which was once supposedly up for grabs (for instance, in the very popular genre of the western) is of course an ideological conception.

NORTH AND SOUTH Even the terms North and South are often used in an ideological sense. When we think and speak of the countries and populations of the 'Northern hemisphere', we tend to forget that in fact it includes many of the countries and populations which we tend to place in the 'Southern hemisphere'. Mentally, we have moved the Equator – the Great Divide – up by thirty degrees or more. In recent years, Northern European policy-makers have introduced a new euphemism for immigrants from Islamic countries, calling them people from the 'southern shores' of the Mediterranean. This category is meant to include Turkey, which happens to be on exactly the same latitude as Greece, Italy, Spain and Portugal.

THIRD WORLD The blanket term 'Third World', which is widely used today, also implies assumptions about primacy, both historical and geographical. In this usage of the term, the 'First World' consisted of the highly developed 'capitalist' nations, primarily those of Western Europe and North America. The 'Second World' consisted of the semi-developed and underdeveloped 'communist' nations, primarily those of Eastern Europe and Central Asia. The 'Third World' consisted of the 'developing' nations, primarily those of the rest of Asia, Africa, Central and South America (which sometimes also adhered to a third or non-aligned political stance during the Cold War). In recent years, the term 'Fourth World' has been proposed to denote the emergence of a global ethnic underclass, either of semi-legal or illegal immigrants in the big urban centres of the First World, or of indigenous peoples in the rural periphery of the Third World, or both.

Although these terms have sometimes been adopted as proud nicknames by (the representatives of) the countries in question, they basically betray a Eurocentric perspective. They lump together countries which have little in common, except that they are 'not us'. They basically distinguish between 'the West' and 'the rest'.

In the course of modern history, continents and countries, cities and monuments have been given names celebrating this or that 'discoverer' or 'conqueror' or 'empire-builder'. The continued use of these labels seems to imply some kind of posthumous acceptance or even legitimation of their enterprise. After the demise of Nazism in Germany, the names of many towns and streets were changed, or changed back again. After the demise of Communism in Russia, the same thing happened; for instance Leningrad returned to Saint Petersburg again.

Most continents, by contrast, do still carry European labels dating back to Graeco-Roman times and subsequently 'imposed' upon them by European expansion. After becoming independent, many (leaders of) countries and peoples of the Third World rejected the colonial names attached to their states and cities, for instance, in Africa. The former Belgian colony of Congo changed its name to Zaïre (and then back to Congo again), Leopoldville became Kinshasa, Elisabethville became Lumumbashi, Stanleyville Kisangani, etc.

'Gold Coast' became Ghana, and 'Rhodesia' Zimbabwe. But many names of European royals and 'explorers' are still commonly attached to the landscape and used in the maps, even though the royals may never have been there (whereas the local nobility had), and the explorers 'discovered' mountains and waterways that native peoples had always known to be there. This is obvious in photographs and films of those days, but we seem to overlook it. The white man had himself been accompanied by scores of guides and translators and carriers who knew the terrain; but he was supposedly discovering something, they were not.

America was named after the explorer Amerigo Vespucci, its southern straits after the explorer Magellan, and Colombia after Christopher Columbus. El Salvador was named after the Christian Messiah, Santo Domingo was named after the patron saint of the Dominican order, that is to say, of the Inquisition. Other names skip the spiritual aspirations of the colonizers, and once again betray more immediate material preoccupations: Puerto Rico, Costa Rica, Argentina.

'New Spain' changed its name to Mexico, but few places kept indigenous names, and some supposedly indigenous names turn out not to be so indigenous after all. According to Shohat and Stam (1994: 142):

> Colonialism stripped 'peripheral' places and their inhabitants of their 'unpronounceable' indigenous names and outfitted them with names marking them as colonial property. Often the names themselves were

degrading, or the product of European misrecognitions. The Mexican province now called 'Yucatan' (Mayan for: 'We don't know what you are talking about') got its name when the Spanish confused the local people's expression of bewilderment with a place name.

All over Africa and Asia and Latin America, historic names continue to orient present-day claims. When the pro-Western Shah ruled Iran, there was little reticence in speaking of the Persian Gulf – although key parts of it were contested and in fact subject to armed conflict. After the anti-Western Ayatollah Khomeini took over, the prefix 'Persian' was often intuitively dropped in the Western media and only 'the Gulf' was left. When Iran and Iraq subsequently got into a full-scale war, and when Saddam Hussein was considered an objective ally, occasionally the label 'Arabian Gulf' emerged. When Saddam Hussein turned out to be a dangerous enemy, the embarrassed label 'the Gulf' returned.

Although geographical names can of course never legitimate political claims, they are often treated as if they can (witness disputes in the 'Sea of Japan', the 'China Sea', the 'Gulf of Vietnam', etc.). Therefore place-names are often not neutral or 'innocent', in the sense that they are coupled with very specific events and aspirations. The fact that a large part of the world is still described by European colonial names, which global mass media often use as if they were completely unproblematic, is in itself highly revealing.

Framing people

The apparently 'objective' vocabulary about 'ethnic minorities' is also highly subjective, and overlaid with all kinds of ideological twists and turns. Jews were the first large-scale 'ethnic minority' which was identified as such throughout Europe. For many centuries, they were considered 'Semites', not 'Caucasians'. They were perceived as easily identifiable strangers. They had no equal rights and were actively persecuted. After the Holocaust, however, there was a partial reversal. Many Christians began to speak of a common Judaeo-Christian religion. From then on, most considered them part of the same culture, part of the same 'race'. Some of the subjective differences had objectively disappeared.

This was less the case with other peoples, however. The Europeans themselves were the first 'illegal immigrants' on a global scale, tens of millions of them. They seized the territory and property of entire continents, imposing their trading conditions and their legal system by military means. At the time, the word 'native' gained a pejorative sense. 'Natives' were made to die in millions, were supplanted by slaves and 'coolies', who were in turn made to die. Then came independence, first in settler-dominated states, then in 'native'-dominated states.

Since many of the latter countries remained poor, non-Europeans in turn became migrants. As long as they were needed, they were (for instance, in a Dutch idiom) called 'guest workers'. But when they outstayed their welcome, they were soon relabelled immigrants or even 'illegal' immigrants – under nationality laws which had been introduced by others. Policy-makers in European countries have since wrestled with devising a new vocabulary to 'reframe' these groups. In the Netherlands, the preferred term has become *allochtoon*, which is basically just a more pompous word for 'non-native'. Whereas in colonial usage it was the word 'native' which acquired negative connotations, in post-colonial usage it thus became the word 'non-native' which acquired negative connotations.

Even most policy-makers and many statistics, however, do not use these words in an objective or literal sense, but rather in a subjective or figurative way. Most of the time, whenever scientists and media refer to non-natives and immigrants, they do not include upper- and middle-class 'white' people from 'developed' countries, but only lower-class 'non-white' people from 'underdeveloped' countries. Their elaborate research often does little more than observe that rich people have fewer problems than poor people, framing the observation in the language of race, ethnicity, nationality, migration, etc.

WHITE AND BLACK   Similar tricks of magic categorization are implied in the non-reflective use of the distinction between 'whites' and 'people of colour' or POCs. If white is not a colour, then neither is black. When Europeans went abroad, they labelled Asians as 'yellow', American Indians as 'red', Africans as 'black'. They preferred not to see themselves as pinkish, but rather as lily-white; they choose to see all others as coloured, as 'dark'. The continued use of these labels today is far from innocent. White is often associated with 'pure' and a wide variety of other positive connotations and expressions in most languages; dark is associated with 'dirty' and a variety of negative connotations and expressions. (Early white anthropologists even claimed that 'people of colour' could 'by definition' not blush, and therefore knew no shame.)

But the problem lies even deeper. The colour labels pretend to refer to skin colour, although of course they do not. There are no yellow, red, black or even white people: most people have a skin colour in various shades of beige and brown. But why should we persist in denoting people by their supposed skin colour, rather than the colour of their hair or eyes, or the colour of their shirts or shoes for that matter? Why is the supposed skin colour of people used as if it were one of the most fundamental aspects of their cultural and biological identity? Because it denotes race. The widespread use of colour labels in the media implies that race is treated as if it were an essential category.

Naive readers and listeners may think that race is a current 'scientific' concept, but it is not. It is an ideological concept, and scientists have long ago begun to abandon it as a collective term. Of course, certain groups which lived together during relatively prolonged periods in relatively isolated situations do share a certain number of common biological traits. But such genetic communities exist on many different levels, stretching from a single family to humankind as a whole. Furthermore, the differences within such genetic communities are much larger and more crucial than the differences between such genetic communities. The categorization of humankind into half a dozen different 'races' therefore a priori has no more scientific value than a categorization into two or into a hundred races.

The ideological nature of these widespread labels becomes even more apparent when we leave the field of theory and take a closer look at everyday practice. Within most white-dominated countries, and particularly in Anglo-Saxon settler states such as the United States, the label 'black' is not used at all in a genetic, scientific, objective sense. If something like that were the case, anyone who had three 'white' grandparents would be labelled white, and anyone who had three 'black' grandparents would be labelled black. In real life, however, both are usually labelled black. In fact, many people who are not considered 100 per cent white are often automatically considered 100 per cent black. Although a 'white' who has spent a day on the beach may be more 'coloured' than someone like the American general Colin Powell, the latter is still widely considered a 'black'. Of course, this labelling has often been internalized and/or proudly adopted. That is not the point here.

In recent years there has been quite a struggle over such labels. Terms such as 'nigger' and 'negro' (Spanish for 'black') were once employed by 'whites' in a most casual way; and it took quite a long time to have them replaced by the English word 'black', by 'Afro-American', or even African American. Each of these terms tends to highlight certain elements of physique, culture, history, politics, and to obliterate others. The word 'Hispanic' emphasizes a background in Spanish language and culture and therefore tends to exclude those with a background in Portuguese language and culture (i.e. people of Brazilian descent). In that sense, 'Latino' or even 'Iberian' would be more appropriate, although all these terms once again emphasize European (that is to say 'white') origins rather than a 'mixed' background. American 'Indians' have in turn been relabelled as 'Native' Americans (or American Americans).

The point is that there is no 'politically correct' label per se: the respectfulness or otherwise of a label depends on how it is experienced by the people concerned (in that time and place). Even a seemingly objective label may have acquired undesirable subjective connotations, and therefore had better be changed. Any label has a

CANADIAN WINS GOLD MEDAL   **JAMAICAN · CANADIAN ACCUSED OF STEROID USE**   **JAMAICAN STRIPPED OF GOLD MEDAL**

Figure 1.2   *Framing people. Cartoon by P. Edwards following another incident with drug-taking in athletic sports.*
Source: Jan Nederveen Pieterse (1992) White on Black: Images on Africa and Blacks in Western Popular Culture.

shifting network of connotations attached to it. Similarly, there is no simple and neutral way of speaking about countries and peoples. Therefore it is important to know who speaks about whom. There is simply no way of escaping from the problems of mediation and representation.

Similar problems concern the naming of specific groups. The best-known example is of course that of the Native Americans, who got stuck with the label Indian because Columbus thought he was in Asia. Something similar holds for specific 'Indian' peoples. The word Navajo seems to derive from the Spanish for 'thieves', and they are currently trying to get back their original name of 'Dineh' (people). The word 'Eskimo' is similarly an imposed label for 'those who eat raw meat'; they call themselves 'Inuit' (human beings). The word 'Lap' reportedly has negative connotations in some Scandinavian languages. The terms Bohemians and Gypsies refer to European travelling people claimed by some to originate from Central Europe or Egypt (and even the Balkans or India). Once again, they prefer to refer to themselves as 'Rom' (that is to say, 'people').

The major Western languages contain a large number of blanket derogatory terms, which refer to 'strangers' from specific foreign groups in earlier times: assassin (for 'hashishin' in Syria during the Crusades), barbarians (first Greek, then French for people from the opposite coast, the Berbers), pharisees (for hypocritical Jews in the Bible), philistines (for 'uncultivated' Palestinians in the Bible), vandals (for destructive German tribes), etc. Note that the implied value judgement is much more virulent than in similar expressions which European peoples have for each other.[2]

News and views

Why do we need this protracted demonstration that our spatial and time perspectives on world geography and history, on categorizations and language, are all tainted to some extent by an ethnocentric or Eurocentric frame? Because journalists, teachers and scientists are continually made to believe that they are 'free' to think and to say whatever they want, forgetting that this act is preceded and conditioned by innumerable social and psychological mechanisms. It is more than a mere coincidence that they (belonging to a certain civilization, language area, culture, nationality, class, gender, age group, etc.) work for a certain type of organization, do a certain type of job and are in a position to express themselves in the way they do. It is more than a mere coincidence that they (products of a certain upbringing, education, training, experience) think and say whatever they do think and say. They do necessarily bring with them a certain world-view, which in turn conditions their view of the world. It makes them see certain things and ignore others.

What is the most striking thing about our world-views? First: that we deny that we have any. Scientists, teachers, journalists often claim that they produce and reproduce a world of pure 'facts'. They forget that the word fact stems from the Latin word *facere* or making. In this sense, all observed and reported facts are artefacts: they are wo/man-made. There are no facts which speak for themselves. They are made to say certain things by certain people and certain 'instruments'. Observations about reality are determined by the way in which the observation is organized; reports about these observations are determined by the way in which these reports are organized. They inevitably imply pre-selection and pre-interpretation, for instance, in the choice of words, images, sequences, a 'logic', etc.

Second: our world-views are heavily mediated. In earlier ages we may have maintained that they stemmed from our direct experience of nature, of work, of society. Today, we primarily experience the world through the intermediate lenses of science, of education, of the media. Within the most developed countries, the average child goes to school for twelve years before 'really' entering society. It learns geography, history and similar subjects. It is thus heavily socialized in a particular world-view, before it begins to think of its own. This world-view is constantly nourished by the media during later life. (We will return to this subject in later chapters.)

Third: our most central political convictions are often based on information which is even more heavily refracted and mediated than our peripheral political convictions are. Whereas we may experience democracy and respect for human rights first-hand, for instance, the real horror stories about dictatorship and massive violations of human rights were often handed down from long ago and far away. Our most fundamental world-views are mainly painted in white and black, in dichotomies of good and bad. The mediation process implicitly uses our own way of life and our own values against which to measure the way of life and values of others. There are constant processes of 'patterning' and 'disorganization', of 'normalization' and 'alienation' at work.

The Burda model

Through all its stages and aspects, this mediation inevitably leads to a selective articulation of certain aspects of reality, to a certain emphasis and organization in our views of reality. It is a major misunderstanding that it is a question of truth versus falsehood. It is a question of one truth (or family of truths) versus many other truths (or families of truths). The problem with ethnocentrism in intercultural communication is not what the 'correct' way of seeing things is, but admitting that there are many legitimate ways of seeing things in the first place. This is much easier said than done. Everyone adheres to these noble goals in principle, but few can live up to them on an everyday basis. Journalism is no exception to this rule.

Certain 'facts' are constantly being observed and reported, others not. Certain 'relations' between facts (attributed motives, perceived causalities) are constantly being observed and reported, others not. There is a continuous process of what I call 'selective articulation', by which the media do literally 'make sense' out of the unordered chaos which surrounds us. This can be illustrated by what I have chosen to call the 'Burda model'. Burda is the name of a prominent German publishing family. It is also the name of a prominent German fashion magazine. It is one of those global fashion magazines which appear in various editions, and in maybe a dozen or more different languages.

The Burda magazine is primarily aimed at women who make clothes at home. Each issue provides a number of sewing patterns in a number of sizes: for shirts and trousers, skirts and dresses. All of these sewing patterns are printed onto one big folded piece of paper, which is usually attached in the centre. In theory, the different patterns can easily be distinguished, because they have different colours, stripes and dots in different sizes and combinations. In practice, however, it is rather difficult to grasp them at once. Particularly in the older editions, the page is filled with a bewildering criss-crossing of lines. One really has to take a felt-tipped pen to follow the various lines and mark the selected pattern before one can clearly see it standing out.

This is exactly how 'reality' presents itself to us in everyday life. Science, education and the media are like the felt-tipped pen which helps us to see certain patterns standing out and ignore others. The question is, of course: do they systematically favour certain patterns over others which may originally have been just as prominent and coherent? Do the Western media 'mediate' the world to us in a particular way, which is consonant with the presuppositions of both key media professionals and major media audiences? Do the collective ego and the collective narcissism of these groups play a role? Is the 'positive' role of the 'First' world emphasized out of proportion, and is its 'negative' role in past and present blotted out? What does this mean for the images which reach the 'Second' and the 'Third' world?

The social construction of 'knowledge'

Sociology (and its 'non-Western' branch, cultural anthropology) note that every type of society has always known privileged categories of professional people, engaged in the production of what is to be considered as 'true knowledge' about the 'real world'. They are 'liberated' from ordinary work, awarded a high degree of nominal autonomy, and engaged in the production and reproduction of the very 'core meanings' which hold that society together, which keep it from falling apart. They do this through a wide range of routinized activities which appear to be non-routine and unique. Within traditional religious societies, priests perform this function. Within modern secular societies, journalists, teachers and academics perform this function. They view their routines and activities, their status and roles, as self-evident.

Although this book discusses a wide variety of approaches to news, its prime affinity is with a family of approaches related to the German traditions of 'sociology of knowledge' (Marx, Weber, Scheler, Mannheim, Schutz, and others); the American traditions of ethnomethodology and symbolic interactionism (Garfinkel, Blumer, Goffman, and others); and the French traditions of structuralism, post-structuralism and discourse analysis (Barthes, Althusser, Foucault, and others). We will return to the latter traditions in the two chapters on linguistics and semiology. All traditions emphasize in one way or another that our notions of what is 'real' do not so much derive directly from reality itself, but are mediated by the ways in which we construct and 'test' notions of what is to be considered 'real'. One modern classic is an elegant little book by Peter Berger and Thomas Luckmann on *The Social Construction of Reality*.

As we have seen, within present-day (and largely secular) Western society, three professions are primarily charged with the production and transmission of knowledge: science, education and the media. The vast majority of professionals in these fields share similar ideals of empiricism, objectivity and neutrality. The problem is that these ideals as such are most certainly worth while, but they can never be fully attained. One might even say that the repeated and over-confident claims about their being easily attained every day does in certain respects do more harm than good, because they hide the contingent, socio-historically embedded nature of these truth-claims from critical scrutiny, and invite excessive confidence in their universal validity. They also hide the (sub)cultural ideologies contained in them, and therefore lead to unjustified feelings of superiority.

One field in which this process has gradually been demonstrated is that of the sociology of science. One early modern classic to confront absolute knowledge claims with (sub)cultural relativity was Thomas Kuhn's study of *The Structure of Scientific Revolutions*. He noted, among other things, that scholars tended to form 'paradigmatic communities' adhering to one particular view of their respective fields, which might or might not face a crisis if anomalies persisted in manifesting themselves. Some more recent studies have applied even more radical versions of these ideas to present-day 'hard' natural sciences such as biochemistry: Karin Knorr-Cetina's study of *The Manufacture of Knowledge*, for instance, or Bruno Latour and Steve Woolgar's *Laboratory Life*.

A modern classic applying similar ideas to media studies was Gaye Tuchman's *Making News: A Study in the Construction of Reality*. She spent over ten years doing 'participant observations' on and conducting interviews with journalists at various American 'news sites' (a television station, a major daily, the New York City Hall press room), and with reporters covering the women's movement. She noted how they tended to cover time and space, how they wove a 'web of facticity' and constructed 'news as frame'. She concluded that:

> The production of meaning is intricately embedded in the activities of men and women – in the institutions, organizations and professions associated with their activities and that they produce and reproduce, create and recreate. By implication, various kinds of knowledge, including that taught at universities, can be viewed as products of the knowledge industry, replete with objectification, reification and affirmation of the status quo. (1978: 216)

Around the same time, the German author Winfried Schulz published a similar study of 'the construction of reality in the news media', and the British author Philip Schlesinger published *Putting*

'Reality' Together: BBC News. Using similar techniques, he tried to answer questions such as:

> What sort of work processes have to be gone through before a news bulletin hits the air? And is such news really the product of accidents of space and time or is it rather the result of heavily routinized activity? What sort of effect does the journalistic obsession with being up-to-date have on the news, and what are its origins? Are the BBC's journalists producing news for an audience they actually know – or are they producing news according to their own 'professional' intuitions? How does a vast organization such as the BBC manage to control the way in which its newsmen produce stories? And are those newsmen really as free from control as they think? Is the BBC's news really 'impartial'? And can it realistically claim that it is, in view of its position in British society and its relationship to the state? (1987: 12)

Think, for instance, of Northern Ireland and of the Falklands.

In more than fifteen years that have passed since these books, dozens of other studies – large and small – have contributed to a further elaboration of this 'social construction' perspective on news. I will refer to a number of them throughout this book. The important thing to note is that they do not speak so much about how journalism is supposed to be functioning, but how it is actually functioning; they are not only about abstract theories but about concrete practices. There turns out to be a huge contrast between the two.

The approach of the book

This introductory chapter was meant as a preliminary encounter with the problem of 'news and views'. Is it possible to look well at anything at all, if one does not choose a vantage point and maybe use some aids, such as binoculars or glasses, a telescopic lens or a microscope? These refract the light, place some things in the centre of our field of vision, and temporarily exclude others from it. This book claims that it is not possible to maintain complete objectivity; only a certain degree of intersubjectivity is possible, but this intersubjectivity is always situated and shaped socio-historically. Of course it is possible to take successive looks from different perspectives, in order to gain a better understanding, and that is what we will try to do here.

This book tries to understand *the creation of the world in the news*. It approaches the news media as some kind of optical instrument or a camera. The camera may register a more or less adequate picture of the world, but the picture does not coincide with the world itself. Light is refracted through a system of lenses, which may make certain things seem closer, others more distant. The picture is two-dimensional, the world is three-dimensional. The picture has a limited frame, the world does not. We can see only the subject in front of the camera, not what is behind the subject, nor what is behind the camera. We can only see the image of the instant that the shutter was open, not what happened before or after that. We can see only the shades and colours which can be registered on the film and the print, and so on. It is the same with news.

Many books about international news look at only one of these various aspects: at the optics of the lenses, at the mechanics of the shutter, at the chemistry of the film, or at the composition of the picture, the style of the photographer. That is a legitimate enterprise, and I owe many of the observations in this book to such more specialized studies. But each taken separately is not sufficient to get a more or less comprehensive overview because by focusing on certain aspects, they often limit the understanding of just how arbitrary and contingent a particular photograph is – or even an entire piece of reportage or a complete collection of photo-reports about the world 'out there'.

This book therefore aims to look briefly at many different (though not all) aspects of this type of communication, one after the other, and also at their interrelationship. Classical rhetoric identified six questions which an effective speaker would have to answer before he or she got to work: *quis* (who), *quid* (what), *quo modo* (how), *quibus auxiliis* (with which means), *ad quem* (to whom), *quo effectu* (with what effect)? (Fauconnier, 1973: 51).

In a famous article, the American political scientist Harold Lasswell transposed this grid to communication studies, and proposed that we ask the following five questions about each 'act of communication' or each series of acts: 'Who? Says what? In which channel? To whom? With what effect?' Others have since proposed two additional questions: 'Under what circumstances?' and 'For what purpose?' Subsequent authors have criticized this whole 'atomistic' approach as being somewhat simplistic and misleading, as it incorrectly suggests that such acts of communication can be considered as unambiguous, singular, unilateral and isolated – and thereby distracts attention from the layered, complex and contradictory nature of 'meaning'. But it may nevertheless be useful to adopt this grid as a heuristic device.

In this book, therefore, I will seek the answer to seven questions about international news (although in a slightly different way and in a slightly different order) namely: what, which, who, where, when, how and with what effect? Since relevant studies have been done in a wide variety of disciplines, I will look at each question from the perspective of one particular discipline: philosophy, economics, sociology, political science, geography, history, linguistics, semiology and psychology.

Each chapter consists of at least half a dozen sections and identifies at least a dozen different mechanisms which tend to orient both press and broadcasting news in certain directions but not in others. There are mechanisms which exert a minor influence all of the time or a major influence some of the time. On the whole we might well claim that there are '101 mechanisms which each make a 1 per cent difference'. Each mechanism taken apart may have only a marginal impact, but taken together they make all the difference, and tend to contribute to the constant production and reproduction of an ethnocentric view of the world. This is not because foreign news reporters and editors are stupid or lazy: many are well-educated and hardworking. It is because they are inevitably caught in a myriad of social and psychological structures, which cannot be wished away.

This book focuses on various forms of bias, and in that sense it is one-sided. It should not be read as a series of reproaches, but as an attempt at deconstruction of very complex and subtle machinery: the transnational news industry. A better understanding of these recurring mechanisms may help present and future journalists improve the quality of the information they convey to citizens and politicians alike, and thereby contribute to better intercultural understanding and more adequate decision-making. It is not enough to promote our own values; it is also important to see why others adhere to different ones.

Both an individual's maps and a society's maps are views of the world which are determined by world-views; they are cultural representations. The same holds for our grids of place and time: the zero meridian, the metric system, or 'universal' time. The language and categories, the statistics and numbers in which we 'frame' foreign lands and peoples are inevitably ethnocentric too. Our education, science and media tend to 'selectively articulate' certain 'facts' and relations, and to ignore others, just as we choose certain sewing patterns out of the chaotic tangle printed on the centre-fold of a home sewing magazine. The 'social construction' approach to knowledge gathering and knowledge distribution emphasizes that we are always guided by mental representations resulting from cultural interaction.

Notes

1 In *Public Opinion* (1947), ch. 1, pp. 13–15.
2 Of course these mechanisms are not limited to the 'white' use of labels for supposedly 'non-white' groups. The Dutch term of abuse *kaffer*, which was imported through South Africa, stems from the Arabic word *kafir* (for 'infidel'). The Dutch words *Boer* (for 'farmer'), *Afrikaner* (for 'settler') and *Apartheid* (for 'segregation') gradually changed connotations abroad, during the years of the black struggle for emancipation.

Further reading

Global journalism in practice: Rosenblum. *Eurocentrism*: Nederveen Pieterse; Shohat and Stam. *Social construction of news*: Altheide; Schlesinger; Schulz; Tuchman.

2 WHAT IS NEWS, AND WHAT IS 'NOTHING NEW'?

THE PHILOSOPHY OF THE NOTABLE AND THE INCONSPICUOUS

....

> Obviously, passing events that are typical or representative don't make news just for that reason; only extraordinary ones do, and even these are subject to the editorial violence routinely employed by gentle writers. Our understanding of the world precedes these stories, determining which ones reporters will select and how the ones that are selected will be told . . .
>
> The design of these reported events is fully responsive to our demands – which are not for facts but for typifications. Their telling demonstrates the power of our conventional understandings to cope with the bizarre potentials of social life, the furthest reaches of experience. What appears, then, to be a threat to our making sense of the world turns out to be an ingeniously selected defense of it.
>
> Erving Goffman, *Frame analysis*[1].

Many journalism textbooks and communication studies ponder the key question: what is 'news'? But this way of putting things may in itself be considered slightly misleading. A better question might be: what is 'nothing new'? because it draws attention to the central dimension of our 'selective articulation' of what is noteworthy and what is inconspicuous in the world around us. Why are certain 'tragic deaths' reported emphatically and highly emotionally, for instance, and why are others consistently overlooked? What are the underlying news criteria and news values, how 'objective' or 'subjective' are they really? Is not news itself a somewhat arbitrary category, particularly in the intercultural communication field, because it is ultimately defined by hidden notions of what is expected and unexpected, ordinary and extraordinary, normal and abnormal?

If we ask someone the question 'what is news?', she or he might answer with something like 'the really important events'. Most laymen (as well as a considerable number of professional journalists, teachers and scientists) live in a 'common-sense' world which is taken for granted. To them, 'the facts' seem to speak for themselves. To question the meaning of such obvious words as 'real', 'important' and 'event' looks like sterile philosophical chicanery to them. As we will see again in this and in subsequent chapters, even such simple words upon closer inspection reveal very specific grids of selection and interpretation as to what is noteworthy and what is not.

The news media bring some features of 'reality' to our attention, placing them in the light, whereas most of the rest is kept in the dark. It is mostly the same features which are brought to our attention time and time again. But even then, the illumination is intermittent at best: it is rather like the beam of a lighthouse, the stroboscopic lights in a disco, or the flash of a camera lighting up the night every now and then. It permits us to develop only a very partial and slanted view of our environment. Walter Lippmann said: 'The press . . . is like the beam of a searchlight that moves restlessly about, bringing one episode and then another out of darkness into vision. Men cannot do the work of the world by this view alone. They cannot govern society by episodes, incidents, and eruptions' (1947: 364).

Some people and some tragedies are more important to the global media than others. Rosenblum (1993: 39) describes an illuminating scene which took place in the run-up to the Gulf War, when Western citizens previously said to be held as a 'human shield' were finally released by Saddam Hussein. Passengers on a flight from the Iraqi capital of Baghdad were eagerly awaited by journalists at the airport near the Jordanian capital of Amman.

> Entering the terminal, they were blinded suddenly by a thousand points of light and hammered with questions shouted in five languages. The surprise party from hell. Peering at dozens of Greeks, Egyptians and others trying to escape them, reporters yelled at one another: 'Was anyone on board? You see anyone?' They meant people who mattered, American or British or even French. When all else failed, they settled for Arab wives of white people. No one intended any ethnic slurs. They just knew what they were after and had no time to mess around with niceties.

One might add that the tens of thousands of 'foreign workers' who were forced to flee the Gulf states during these same months, many of whom often ended up camping on the desert border in utter destitution, received relatively little attention in the Western (and world) media. Is it true that 'the world news media' only get highly emotional on very specific occasions; that we are made to empathize with some victims, but not with others; that things like social 'victimhood' and political 'responsibility' are constructed in a very particular way? In this chapter, we will look at the hidden ideology behind news values, at the seemingly neutral grids which guide the 'creation of the world in the news'.

'Tragic death' in a global perspective

Let us take a closer look at one apparently obvious category in the news, that of 'tragic death'. The rule is: 10,000 deaths on another continent equal 1,000 deaths in another country equal 100 deaths in an outpost equal ten deaths in the centre of the capital equal one celebrity. Such statements are often presented as a cynical editor's joke, but they are an everyday media reality. Things are even more complicated: skin colour and nationality, wealth and profession count as well. Every day, the newspapers and television news may bring a few tragic deaths to our attention: ten, a hundred, a thousand on very rare occasions. But how many people die every day, and of what? Like most readers and viewers, I did not have the faintest idea, so I tried to find out. I learned that an average of two people per day are attacked by tigers in India; and that an average of one person per two days gets poisoned by the rare fugu fish delicacy in Japan, but it is only logical (or is it?) that such threats would get little exposure elsewhere.

The *Bulletin of the World Health Organization* (1994: 72 (3), pp. 447–80), carried one of the most detailed estimates to date: an article on 'Global and regional cause-of-death patterns in 1990' by C. J. L. Murray and A. D. Lopez. It gives annual rates, which I have translated into average daily rates for the purpose of this comparison. The total number of deaths every day is something like 136,907. Of course, there is no way in which the media could report on all of these, or even on a significant proportion; nor can they be expected to. Most of the time, only between 1 per cent and 1 per 1,000 (or even 1 per 10,000) hit the news. But on what criteria is the choice based? Some are 'objective' criteria, but some are highly subjective; some are logical, but some are highly arbitrary.

We should be aware of the fact that every single one of these deaths is a 'tragic death', and every single one of them could also be taken as an indicator of a larger medical or social or economic problem, which might well be considered newsworthy. We should also be aware of the fact that every single one of these deaths has a story to tell, and a million family members and friends, acquaintances and colleagues are ready to tell such a story to an interested journalist every day. But in 99.99 per cent of cases, no journalist ever turns up, let alone a representative of the major world media. As far as they are concerned, these people remain a statistic, and that is of course completely 'logical'.

At the same time the question remains: why are some 'tragic deaths' emphatically brought to our attention? Why are we made to sympathize with them, to feel sorry for them, to suffer with them, to feel that something must be done, here and now, on the spot and at once? On the other hand, we are made to feel that others are victims of fate, that nothing can be done about it, that things have always been like that and will always remain so. Take children. Of all these tragic deaths every day, 34,676 are under five years of age. Most die from preventable elementary diseases resulting from undernourishment and vitamin deficiencies, from lack of clean water and hygenic conditions.

Twice a week, then, a Hiroshima bomb strikes the toddlers of the Third World. Every month, more than a million of them die unnecessarily. This figure does not include older children, adolescents and adults. Half a billion children have probably died this way since the United Nations organization was founded fifty years ago and postwar international cooperation began. The major media do not paint this as an acute disaster which warrants immediate foregrounding. It is a chronic situation which remains in the background. The figures turn up in weekend features every now and then, and in late-night documentaries. But most of the time, no sense of urgency or emergency is really conveyed. Thus 'tragic death' is a highly 'social' construction: certain tragic deaths are systematically under-reported, others are systematically over-reported. This can be illustrated by other examples too.

Let us look at some other categories, for instance, at people dying from 'unintentional injuries': 7,656 every day. Close to one-third of these die in 'traffic accidents'. We will usually read and hear and see photographs of major public transport accidents with buses, trains, ferries, airplanes crashing, exploding, burning, sinking, because in such accidents, ten or a hundred or more people will die at a time. We will read and hear and see much less about car crashes, by contrast, because usually they do not kill more than ten people at the time. There are many of such events every day, but they remain mostly subliminal: they do not cross a minimal threshold of news-worthiness, particularly if they are far away. One result (among others) might be that people hear a lot about the 'lack of safety' of public transport, and many develop an 'irrational' fear of flying, for instance; whereas they continue to trust their own good luck in driving a car and may continue to overestimate it. Something similar can be observed about accidents at work.

Let us also look at people dying from 'intentional injuries': 3,924 every day. More than half (2,241) are 'self-inflicted', that is to say suicides. We will hear very little about them: often families and authorities concur in keeping them quiet. The opposite is true for 'homicide and violence': 801 people are murdered every day. We will only hear about some, but those we hear about will be enlarged out of proportion. They receive multiple coverage: we will hear about them on the occasion of the crime itself, its aftermath, the search, the arrest, the imprisonment, the trial, the appeal, the execution or release, etc. Media loathe murder, and so does the public. But then they are fascinated by it as well, and often cannot get enough of it.

Terrorism is an even clearer example. Of course the threat exists, but it is magnified beyond reasonable proportions – even within countries that are really prone to terrorism. As Goode and Ben-

Yehuda (1994) observe in the introduction of their book on *Moral Panics*: 'the number of individuals who have been killed in Israel and the [occupied] territories by political violence in the past six years is under a thousand souls, of whom perhaps 200 were Jews killed by Arab terrorists. The chance of dying in an automobile accident is far greater.' Thus, five years of highly publicized terrorism in Israel made fewer victims than one day of under-reported wars in the rest of the world.

An average of 882 people get killed in war every day. Most of the time, we will hear about only the handful where First World interests are at stake, not about the dozen or so raging on each of the continents of the Third World. There are also an estimated 100 million land-mines in place: they kill or maim 500 people (usually non-combatants) per week. According to conservative estimates by the Red Cross, 'in the so-called "post-war" period since 1945, at least 20 million people have died in over 100 conflicts. A further 60 million people have been wounded, imprisoned, separated from their families and forced to flee their homes or their countries.' Yet many of these conflicts and victims have been largely ignored in the news. Why?

What is news? An early American study

Over the last few decades, there has been a range of major research projects devoted to this key question. Rather than skimming the surface of a great number of them, we will limit ourselves to a more extensive discussion of a few major 'classical' studies, which have since inspired many copies and variations. Two examples stand out. One is a study of the major American news power, the United States; it focused mainly on national news, but also covered some international news – primarily about other major powers in the First, Second and Third Worlds. Another is a study of a minor peripheral European country, Norway; it focused mainly on international news – primarily on conflicts in minor countries of the Third World. Some other studies will be discussed in other chapters.

The first 'classic' to be discussed is Herbert J. Gans's *Deciding What's News* (1980). It is a study of the evening news on two major American television networks (CBS and NBC), and of two major American weekly news magazines (*Newsweek* and *Time*). For reasons of time and money, Gans had to omit a third medium in each category (ABC and *US News and World Report*). Between the late sixties and the late seventies, Gans combined 'participant observation' of the editorial staff of these major news media and 'content analyses' of their published output, trying to figure out what they considered news and why. First of all, he found that certain very specific actors and activities invariably dominate the news.

ACTORS IN THE NEWS   News turned out to be about individuals, rather than about groups or social processes. The individuals could be divided into 'knowns' and 'unknowns'. 'Knowns' took up between 70 and 85 per cent of all domestic news. They belonged primarily to five categories: incumbent presidents; presidential candidates; leading federal officials; state and local officials; and 'alleged or actual violators' of the laws and mores. Overexposing some people and underexposing others often had important implications, Gans showed.

There proved to be a marked emphasis on 'formal' political leaders, for instance, rather than on 'informal' ones (such as behind-the-scenes campaign contributors and/or power-brokers). Furthermore, there proved to be a marked emphasis on political leaders, rather than on (equally important) economic or military ones. Thus the media put some people in the spotlight, but kept others out of it. 'Unknowns' in the news proved to be mostly 'convention-breakers', also belonging to five categories: protesters, 'rioters' and 'strikers'; victims (of social and natural disorders); once again 'alleged and actual violators' of the laws and mores; participants in unusual activities (such as fads); and finally voters, survey respondents and other aggregates. Many of these people were not identified as individuals at all.

ACTIVITIES IN THE NEWS   Gans also concluded that eight types of activities dominated the domestic news in the US at the time: (1) government conflicts and disagreements; (2) government decisions, proposals and ceremonies; (3) government personnel changes; (4) protests, violent and non-violent; (5) crimes, scandals and investigations; (6) disasters, actual and averted; (7) innovation and tradition; and (8) national ceremonies. Much of it therefore centred on government, law and order; minor breakdowns of these fields, and their subsequent restoration. He also noted that this resulted in a very particular construction of nation and society, their divisions and their unity.

DIVISIONS IN NATION AND SOCIETY   Conflicts were in general constructed around certain demographic categories, such as age (the 'generation conflict') and gender (the 'feminist movement'). These groups were not construed as pursuing different interests, though; the reasons for their protests remained obscure most of the time. Race occurred in a very specific way: 'Generally speaking . . . the national news features middle- and upper middle-class blacks who have overcome racial, economic, and especially political obstacles, with less affluent blacks more often newsworthy as protesters, criminals, and victims.'

Class occurred in a very specific way too: 'The news pays attention to racial differences, but it does not often deal with income differences among people, or even with people as earners of income.' Class, class groupings and class differences were rarely reported, he said, and even then only in the context of features on (mostly 'upper middle-class') lifestyles and fashions. Ideology occurred in a very specific way as well: enemy nations were thought to be ideological, but 'most American political groups are thought not to be ideological'; rather, they are 'perceived as shades of opinion'.

THE UNITY OF NATION AND SOCIETY   Many news stories emphasized the basic unity and harmony of the American nation and society. To give one example: 'The coverage of the July 4, 1976, Bicentennial ceremonies moved the normally objective anchorpersons to express their feelings of pride in the nation on the air, while the otherwise anonymous editors of the two news magazines contributed signed articles along the same line.' At the same time, the nation was also constructed as a unit *vis-à-vis* other units, often in anthropomorphic terms. One US overseas action was described as 'a daring show of nerve and steel by a nation whose will, after Vietnam, had come under question around the globe'. Such habitual constructions also affected other images of the outside world.

DOMESTIC THEMES IN FOREIGN NEWS   International news was often presented from a purely national perspective, Gans said. He also concluded that the American news media 'tend to follow American foreign policy, even if not slavishly, but they hew closer to the State Department line on foreign news than to the White House line on domestic news. Foreign news adheres less strictly to objectivity than domestic news.' This proved primarily related to the values reporters shared with the rest of the citizens and leaders, their selection of sources and other factors (Gans, 1980: 8–38).

News value: an early Scandinavian study

Another classic study concerned the 'news value' of items as judged by foreign editors. This study of 'The structure of foreign news' (1965: 64–91) was done by Johan Galtung and Mari Holmboe Ruge, of the Peace Research Institute in Oslo. They were particularly interested in how major crises (of the Third World periphery) were reported in their own small country (of the First World periphery). In order to find out, they made a content analysis of how the Congo (Zaïre), Cuba and Cyprus crises of the early sixties had been reported in four (radical/liberal and morning/afternoon) newspapers in the Norwegian capital.

One of their first findings was that the vast majority of 'spot news' items originated from a very limited number of international news agencies. They also identified a dozen factors that seemed to mark an event as newsworthy. The first factor is 'the *time-span* needed for an event to unfold itself and acquire meaning'. This has to be relatively short, and to fall within the publication frequency of the news medium – usually one day. An event taking weeks or months or years to emerge in no uncertain terms may not be noted as news at all. The second factor is the *scale* and intensity of an event (in both absolute and relative terms): 'there is a threshold the event will have to pass before it will be recorded at all'.

The third factor is the *clarity* of an event: 'the less ambiguity, the more the event will be noticed.' The category in which it fits must be clear: otherwise it may not find its place. The fourth factor, *meaningfulness*, has two aspects. One is cultural proximity: 'the event-scanner will pay particular attention to the familiar, to the culturally similar, and the culturally distant will be passed by more easily and not be noticed.' The other aspect is relevance: 'the culturally remote country may be brought in via a pattern of conflict with one's own group.' The fifth factor is *consonance*: someone has either predicted the event will happen, or wants it to happen. 'In the sense mentioned here "news" are actually "olds", because they correspond to what one expects to happen – and if they are too far away from the expectation they will not be registered.'

The sixth factor, by contrast, emphasizes *unexpectedness*. Within the set of the meaningful and the consonant, 'the more unexpected have the highest chances of being included as news.' Unpredictability and scarcity both play a role. The seventh factor is *continuity*: 'once something has hit the headlines and been defined as news, then it will continue to be defined as news for some time even if the amplitude is drastically reduced.' The eighth factor is *composition* of the available news, and the balance between various categories. For instance, 'if there are already many foreign news items the threshold value for a new item will be increased.'

The ninth and tenth factors are references to well-known, rich and/ or powerful *élite nations* and *élite persons*, since they are seen 'at least usually and in short-term perspective' as 'more consequential than others'. While 'ordinary people are not even given the chance of representing themselves', others (authorities, experts) often speak in their place. The eleventh factor is *personification*. There is a definite preference for telling news stories about individuals or even groups of persons, presumably because they are more concrete and favour empathy or disapproval. The twelfth and final factor is *negativity*, rather than positivity: 'bad news is good news' for the media.

How 'news values' affect the values in the news

Apart from identifying these various factors and subfactors, Galtung and Ruge (1965) also formulated hypotheses concerning their inter-relations, such as:

1. The more events satisfy the criteria mentioned, the more likely that they will be registered as news (*selection*); 2. Once a news item has been selected what makes it newsworthy according to the factors will be accentuated (*distortion*); 3. Both the process of selection and the process of distortion will take place at all steps in the chain from event to reader (*replication*).

They also felt that these mechanisms led to grave unbalance in foreign news reporting, and that media should 'try to counteract all twelve factors'.

Galtung and Ruge pointed out that their news values and factors were not only strongly interrelated to form a coherent frame, but also that this coherent frame has profound ideological implications which usually remain hidden from sight. Let us limit ourselves to taking a closer look at only the last two of the twelve factors: how the tendencies towards personification and negativity affect the ideological shape of the news.

PERSONIFICATION AND SOCIAL FORCES   It is easy to see how the tendency to personification fits into the general news framework. Persons can be pictured and described in concrete ways, they act in a short time-span and provide an object for identification by the reader, listener and viewer – who can sympathize or disapprove of them. At the same time, they say, personification corresponds to a (rich country, middle-class) idea 'according to which man is the master of his own destiny and events can be seen as the outcome of an act of free will'. One might just as well look at the news from another (poor country, lower-class) perspective. 'The alternative would be to present events as the outcome of "social forces", as structural more than idiosyncratic outcomes of the society which produced them.' The consistent favouring of the former perspective over the latter does of course have profound ideological implications.

There is also a distinct tendency in the news to identify the actions of social movements, political parties or national governments with the actions of their leaders. The point is that they represent the aspirations of much larger groups, which may have contradictory interests and views and which may therefore clash. There is a definite tendency in international news reporting to ignore this and to construct a black and white world, in which the good guys clash with the bad guys. This hampers mutual understanding, negotiation and compromise.

NEGATIVITY AND POSITIVE TENDENCIES   It is also easy to see how negativity fits into the general news framework. Negative events usually take less time, are more unexpected and unambiguous: 'compare the amount of time needed to bring up and socialize an adult person and the amount of time needed to kill him in an accident; the amount of time needed to build a house and to destroy it in a fire; to make an aeroplane and to crash it, and so on.' It may take decades to build a dam or an irrigation system; it takes only hours for it to break and flood the valley.

This principle of negativity applies even more to culturally distant nations than to culturally close ones. The result is, many poorer nations claim, that there is very little 'development journalism' and attention to the real achievements of these countries under extremely difficult circumstances, very little attention to the patient work of local groups, the everyday courage and energy, inventiveness and solidarity of billions of people. And there is just a one-sided emphasis on 'coups and earthquakes', on everything that goes wrong, which makes large parts of the Second and Third Worlds look like eternal problem areas, incapable of achieving anything on their own, and continually stretching out their hands for alms.

World news as submerged world-views

We might even go one step further than the original studies by Gans, Galtung and Ruge, and others. We might consider the provocative view proposed by some authors that for all its factual posturing, news is inherently ideological – by its very nature. News is what seems to stand out, what is unusual. We all know the famous formula: 'When a dog bites a man, that is not news; but when a man bites a dog, that is news.' But this presupposes heaps of cultural knowledge: for instance, that we live in a society of 'animal lovers' keeping dogs as pets, but also in a society of 'meat-eaters' consuming beef as food. There are Asian societies where the opposite holds true: some that eat dogs, and others that venerate cows. Therefore even this seemingly obvious formula presupposes a particular world-view.

News is something which is (perceived as) 'new' within a specific society, and not something which is (perceived as) 'nothing new'. It is something which is (perceived as) unexpected, extraordinary, abnormal, not something which is (perceived as) expected, ordinary, normal. The definition of both series of notions is of course highly questionable (see, for example, Leblanc, 1987; but also Fiske and Hartley's (1992) notion of 'claw-back', to which we will return in Chapter 9). True: we have already seen that in the notions of the unexpected, the extraordinary and the abnormal, notions of the expected, the ordinary and the normal form the background of these news judgements. But the former are often made largely explicit, the latter remain largely implicit. The former are often foregrounded, the latter are left in the background. The 'facts' are emphasized, but the underlying ideology remains disguised. It is like the proverbial iceberg: a brilliant and impressive 10 per cent of its mass is visible above the water-line, a dark and treacherous 90 per cent remains invisible under water. Those who let themselves be attracted and dazzled by the former, may be shipwrecked and sunk by the latter.

Here again, however, the central question is: whose ideas about what is new and 'nothing new', about what is unexpected/extraordinary/abnormal rather than expected/ordinary/normal dominate global news? The central answer is the major news-gathering organizations and the major news media of the major Western countries. Whose ideology is the major hidden key to the preselection and pre-interpretation of global news? The quasi-consensual ideology of the major Western countries, which does not recognize itself as such, but sees itself just as 'natural' common sense. In this perspective, news production and news consumption can also be seen as a twenty-four-hour ideological repair shop for our world order and our world-views. Possible anomalies are identified, checked and 'normalized', so that the ideological machine keeps running smoothly.

To use yet another metaphor: daily TV evening news can be seen as a form of collective therapy. Possible threats to our world order and our world-views are evoked, identified, labelled, categorized, dealt with and dispatched again. For this purpose, anchor men or women summon a daily parade of authorities and experts. They put our minds at rest, so that we can go to bed reassured. But it is the concerns and values of the First World which remain central, those of the Second and Third Worlds remain marginal.

Deviant behaviour and moral panic, in Paris and Singapore

Just as it is with 'tragic death', so it is also with 'amoral behaviour': some of it is arbitrarily made to stand out in the news, some of it not. Between behaviours which were and are widely considered acceptable in most times and places (for example, eating bread in public), and behaviours which were and are widely considered punishable in all times and places (for example patricide) lies a huge grey zone. On the one hand, there is also a large category of behaviours which are considered reprehensible within some cultures, but which are not illegal. On the other hand, there is a huge category of behaviours which are considered illegal, but still remain culturally defined. What is considered 'obscene' or 'offensive', for instance, differs between times and places and groups – even within one society.

Rule-makers and rule-breakers are often not the same groups. Criminologists have pointed out time and time again that in all times and places 'white-collar' crime (in Western society: white upper-class crime) has been dealt with much more leniently than 'blue-collar' crime (in Western society: 'non-white' underclass crime). It is true that the latter may often be more violent than the former (at least more directly and openly violent), but there is more to it than that alone.

Since the former groups have more possibilities for illicit enrichment, for instance, they have fewer incentives to use violence. Many liberal professions (doctors, lawyers, journalists) are to a certain extent thought to 'police' themselves, whereas many other trades are policed by others. Stuart Hall and others (1978) have published a study about reports of 'mugging' in England along these lines; Kees and Chrisje Brants (1991) have noted, by contrast, that 'fraud' in the Netherlands came to stand out in similar ways.

Something similar is the case with deviance: it is a matter of definition. Erving Goffman was one of the first to write a study of the relation between *stigma* and the process of stigmatization. Richard Ericson noted in turn:

Today we no longer parade deviants in the town square or expose them to the carnival atmosphere of Tyburn, but it is interesting to note that the 'reform' which brought about this change in penal policy coincided almost precisely with the development of newspapers as media of public information . . . [N]ewspapers (and now radio and television) offer their readers the same kind of entertainment once supplied by public hangings or the use of stocks and pillories. An enormous amount of modern 'news' is devoted to reports about deviant behavior and its punishment: indeed the largest circulation newspaper in the United States prints very little else . . . [These reports] constitute our main source of information about the normative contours of society. In a figurative sense, at least, morality and immorality meet at the public scaffold, and it is during this meeting that the community declares where the line between them should be drawn. (quoted by Goffman, 1986: 7–8)

The 'construction of deviance' is a social process, which may gradually amplify itself. That is to say, some individuals or groups may define (certain actions of) others as 'deviant'. They may start to make a fuss about it, attracting the attention of like-minded people and media to it. This may make the deviant acts stand out even more, which further fuels the fuss. In the end there will be a widespread call to do something about it (see also Trowler, 1991: 56). Processes like sensitization, amplification and convergence feed the scare. This phenomenon is extremely widespread, both in media coverage and opinion formation (Figure 2.1). Similar phenomena had previously been studied in the fields of mass or crowd psychology and the sociology of collective behaviour (see Van Ginneken, 1992, 1993b).

The analysis of this subject was particularly well developed by Stanley Cohen, in his book *Folk Devils and Moral Panics: The Creation of the Mods and Rockers* (1993). A South African exile in Great Britain in the sixties, he noted a peculiar sequence of reactions to a few weekend skirmishes in a seaside resort, which involved adolescents.

A condition, episode, person or group of persons emerges to become defined as a threat to societal values and interests; its nature is presented in a stylized and stereotypical fashion by the mass media; the moral barricades are manned by editors, bishops, politicians and other right-

initial deviant activity

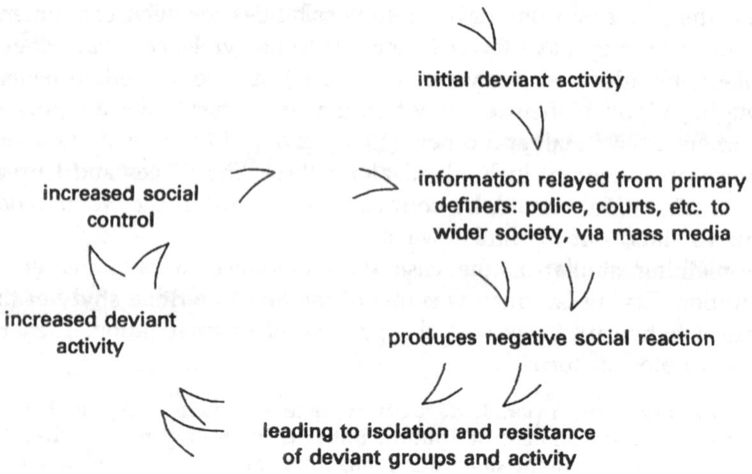

information relayed from primary
definers: police, courts, etc. to
wider society, via mass media

increased social
control

increased deviant
activity

produces negative social reaction

leading to isolation and resistance
of deviant groups and activity

Figure 2.1 *Amplification of deviance. (Reproduced by
permission of Methuen & Co. from O'Sullivan et al.,* Key
Concepts in Communication, *1988.)*

thinking people; socially accredited experts pronounce their diagnoses and
solutions; ways of coping are evolved. (p. 9)

Over subsequent decades, a wide range of new studies confirmed
the nature and workings of the phenomenon. Erich Goode and
Nachman Ben-Yehuda have recently provided a major overview in
their study *Moral Panics: The Social Construction of Deviance* (1994).
They propose several criteria: concern; hostility; consensus; dispropor-
tionality; and volatility. They elaborate well-known ancient examples,
such as the medieval European witch-hunts. But they also elaborate
lesser-known modern-day examples, surrounding issues such as sexuality, drugs and crime. Although they do not get around to discussing
intercultural coverage by the mass media, this is precisely a domain
which stands out as particularly prone to moral panics. Let us look at
a few very recent examples of the 'otherizing' (or alienation) of certain
cultural practices.

IMMIGRANTS AND DECENCY   'Native' grumbling about the 'outlandish'
features of relative 'newcomers' has been something familiar in all
times and places. Ritual slaughter, cooking habits, body odours are
periodically identified as irritants. During the 1993/4 school year, a
major moral panic filled the mass media in France, and indeed in
many other European countries. A (very) limited number of traditional Muslim parents made their daughters wear scarves in public
and to school, since they felt the girls' uncovered hair was indecent

and provocative. This sounds weird to present-day Europeans, but not necessarily so to conservative Arab and Turkish families from predominantly rural backgrounds. Until then, it had largely been considered a prerogative of the parents to decide how their children should be dressed.

A (very) limited number of schools refused admission to the girls, saying that they infringed the 'republican principle' of separation between religion and state, and also the century-old rule that no 'ostentatious religious signs' should be worn in secular state schools. This rule had not often been enforced against Jewish boys wearing a yarmulka (or skullcap), nor against Catholic girls wearing a golden cross. But suddenly there was widespread insistence that the rule should be enforced against young Islamic girls wearing scarves, and also to protect them against the tyranny of elders and males within their own groups.

No one seemed to recall that as little as a few decades before, the very strictest of similar dress codes had been enforced against all girls. Wearing long trousers or short skirts was forbidden, receding necklines and armholes were closely watched. Scarves or hats were imperative in all Christian churches, and regular church visits were enforced in Catholic schools.[2] Thus the French 'outrage' over Islamic scarves can be seen as a moral panic, fulfilling all five conditions identified by Goode and Ben-Yehuda.

EXPATS AND CRUELTY The reverse happens as well. European and American expatriates working overseas have to live by the law of the land. The Western news media often consider it silly that drinking alcohol in public should be forbidden anywhere, or close dancing, or extramarital affairs. In colonial times, the British introduced a law in 'Malaya' which made certain acts of vandalism punishable by caning. This law was never abolished in Singapore, and hundreds of 'non-whites' were caned without the Western media ever taking the slightest notice of this. Then came the day when an American boy was convicted of vandalism and was to receive a few strokes with a cane.

There was widespread outrage in the Western media, which lasted for weeks and months on end. One of my own favourite newspapers, the very thin and serious *International Herald Tribune*, suddenly devoted an incredible number of items and an incredible amount of its (very limited) space to the issue. True: it is primarily an American expatriate newspaper with many readers in Singapore and similar places. Yet it seemed like a typical 'moral panic', once again fulfilling all five conditions set by Goode and Ben-Yehuda. Similarly, thousands of death penalties are carried out every year, without anyone taking great notice of them. But when a white person is convicted in a non-white country, coverage suddenly surges out of all proportion.

Table 2.1   *Example of a moral panic*

Note: In the spring of 1994, a Singapore court condemned an 18-year-old American boy to a few strokes with a cane for vandalism. The very compact 'global' newspaper the *International Herald Tribune* devoted an extraordinary amount of its very limited space to the case over the next two months.

News items: date (number of columns), heading

- 29–03 (4):   Father challenges motive of caning
- 30–03 (3):   Of crime and punishment: Singaporeans unleash debate
                    Court to consider appeal for US teenager
- 01–04 (3):   Court rejects appeal of caning sentence
- 02/03–04 (1):   Mother sets crusade to halt caning in Singapore
- 06–04 (1):   US bishop backs flogging in Singapore
- 13–04 (1):   Singapore's Lee supports caning
- 14–04 (2):   Will Singapore show any mercy?
- 16/17–04 (4):   Bush, in Singapore visit, calls caning 'brutal'
- 18–04 (3+1):   In caning case, doubts about confession
- 20–04 (3):   American 'ready' for caning – Father says teenager has 'no
                    hope at all'
- 21–04 (5):   In caning case, questions about police brutality
- 22–04 (4):   On crime and punishment:
                    US-Asian gap deepens
- 22–04 (2):   Teenager's case divides Americans
- 22–04 (2):   Another Singapore caning – Hong Kong youth sentenced for
                    vandalism
- 23/24–04 (5):   Teen's mother petitions Singapore over caning
- 25–04 (2):   Caning 'must be done', Singapore official says
- 26–04 (4):   US teen prays for Singapore clemency
- 27–04 (2):   Singapore ready to say 'no' to teen's petition
- 30–04 (4):   Singapore daily's mail runs against teenager
- 02–05 (2):   Singapore responds to critics of caning
- 03–05 (2):   Singapore's Lee says caning is a duty
- 04–05 (4):   Suicide risk in caning, US doctor warns
- 05–05 (3):   Responding to Clinton's plea, Singapore cuts 6 lashes to 4
- 06–05 (2+1):   Singapore carries out caning of US teenager
                    He receives 4 lashes for vandalism; Clinton calls sentence a
                    'mistake'
- 07/08–05 (5):   Mother denounces caning as torture
                    Teenager shows his wounds to a US consular official
- 09–05 (2):   Singapore says teenager was able to smile and walk after
                    caning
- 11–05 (1):   US [trade representative] opposes trade talks in Singapore
- 12–05 (2):   Singapore relieved Kantor isn't backed
- 18–05 (3):   Singapore spares 2nd US teenager

Editorial comments: date (number of columns) title, author, affiliation

- 21–03 (4):   Troubling signs of a sense of cultural superiority (Jim Hoagland,
                    Washington Post)
- 04–04 (2):   For clemency in Singapore (*New York Times*)
- 06–04 (2):   This caning in Singapore won't make America safer (Richard
                    Cohen, WP)
- 07–04 (3):   They mind other people's business (Philip Bowring,
                    International Herald Tribune)

Table 2.1 *(cont.)*

• 08–04 (3):	Singapore's assertion of a right to torture is intolerable (William Safire, *NYT*)
• 11–04 (2):	No to torture in Singapore (from *NYT*)
• 12–04 (2):	'Justice' in Singapore (WP)
• 16/17–04 (1):	What about the fate of Asians? (A.M. Rosenthal, *NYT*)
• 20–04 (5):	In Singapore, unusual law doesn't bring about unusual order (Philip Bowring, *IHT*)
• 03–05 (1):	Singapore isn't tidied by caning (Stan Sesser, *NYT*)
• 09–05 (2):	Shame on Singapore (from WP)
• 13–05 (1):	Singapore behind the times (Jeane Kirkpatrick)

It is also interesting to look at implicit notions of 'cruel weapons' used in armed conflict between the West and its pro-Western allies, and non- or anti-Western parties and their allies. It has been observed that putting pointed bamboo spikes in a trap-hole in the ground and covering it with leaves during a guerrilla war, for instance, was long presented and defined as a 'cruel way' to fight. Launching fragmentation bombs or napalm or agent orange, by contrast, was not (initially) considered a cruel way to fight.

Even today, the guerrilla fighter who kills an opponent with his bare hands is often presented and considered as a primitive brute, while the bomber pilot who flies ten kilometres high and pushes the button for 'carpet bombing' is presented and considered as a 'skilled professional'. Yet others (for instance in a 'macho' culture of 'courage and honour') might see the former as a 'brave hero' and the latter as a 'cynical coward'. Hidden cultural definitions therefore guide media coverage and opinion formation to a considerable extent.

An intercultural example: Drugs

Let us look more closely at one series of related issues: the production, trade, promotion and use of drugs – often linked to the activities of 'strangers', either within the West itself or beyond.

Many popular Western soft drinks once contained (or still do contain) some kind of drug, even if in minute quantities: Coke, Tonic, etc. Traditional Western drugs such as alcohol and tobacco, produced and promoted by major Western companies, are defined as 'legal' drugs in the West: their negative effects have until recently received little and belated attention in the Western media. Traditional non-Western drugs, produced and promoted by others, are often defined as illegal drugs in the West: their negative effects have received large-scale attention in the Western media. At some times (for instance, when the British Empire imposed opium imports on China), the danger of these substances was belittled. At other times, it was enlarged.

In some American states and European countries, the growing and smoking of marijuana and hashish at home are tolerated as relatively innocuous, in other American states and European countries they are heavily criminalized and punished severely. Media portrayals differ accordingly. Dutch media will hardly mention a police interception of a small amount of these drugs; French media may bring it in as 'big news'. At the same time, there is also relatively little media attention given to the extremely widespread use of cocaine, amphetamines and similar substances by celebrities and hundreds of thousands of others within the 'creative' professions, but there is very great media attention to the use of heroin and similar substances by a few thousand urban marginals within major cities. The stereotypical image is that of the out-of-control addict, the prostitute and thief, the socially mal-adapted. Yet this group is only a very small proportion of regular drug users, maybe one or a few per cent. It is true that they seem to cause more problems to others, but there is more to it than that. The disproportionate attention to chaotic 'drug scenes' in certain city centres (Zürich, for instance) also frames the issue in a particular way, making further criminalization seem the only possibility, and controlled decriminalization out of the question.

Jock Young (in Cohen and Young, 1973: 313–16) describes the process:

> The mass media carries a mythology of the average man and the deviant – within which Mr. Average is seen to prosper and be content in his universe of hard work and industrious consumption and the deviant is portrayed as being beset by forces which lead to ineluctable misfortune . . . For if a person lives by a code of conduct which forbids certain pleasures, which involves the deferring of gratification in certain areas, it is hardly surprising that he will react strongly against those whom he sees to be taking short cuts. This is a partial explanation of the vigorous repression against what Edwin Schur calls 'crimes without victims': homosexuality, prostitution, abortion and drug taking.

In their book on *Moral Panics* (1994), Goode and Ben-Yehuda note that drug use and acceptance in the US went up during the seventies and early eighties, and down again in the course of the eighties. Yet there was relatively little and rather benevolent media attention during the former decades, and much more of a moral panic during the latter one. It is true that problems with certain types of drugs, such as crack, increased during this period. But some related scares were completely artificial, such as the one around supposed 'crack babies', he says. The fact that the drug issue was taken up by conservative politicians, such as Ronald Reagan and George Bush, made its visibility increase exponentially. Whereas the *Reader's Guide to Periodical Literature* for 1979/80 mentioned only 15 articles about various drug-related subjects, this number sky-rocketed to no fewer than 280 in 1986. Whereas the issue was hardly mentioned as one of the most important problems facing the country in Gallup polls between 1979 and 1984, it rose to 64 per cent in the September 1989 *New York Times*/CBS News poll. All kinds of new legislation and harsher punishments were introduced, although they did little or nothing to stem the tide.

Goode's co-author Ben-Yehuda noted a similar moral panic in Israel. Various studies of the seventies and early eighties had indicated 'that only between 3 and 5 percent of Israeli adolescents between the ages of 14 and 18 had used at least one illegal psychoactive drug (usually hashish) one or more times during their lifetimes'. After one investigation had been derailed in the mid-eighties, however, some police authorities and the head of a parliamentary commission claimed (on the basis of an incomplete report) that no less than 50 per cent did. The claim was echoed in many major mass media and in public opinion. 'In 1993, in an unpublished internal police report based on a nationally representative survey of hundreds of Israeli citizens, the number one police problem in Israel was seen to be – not terrorism, not crime, not car accidents, not the threat of war, but – drug abuse' (1994: 133–4, 185–223).

Very often the authorities, the media and the public of the drugs-consuming countries do not blame themselves, their authorities and their policies for their failure to curb the habit. At the same time, they tend to shift the blame to the authorities, the peasants and the smugglers from the drug-producing countries abroad. P. Bell did a study on 'Drugs as news'. He found that narrative and social roles were typically filled by the social types that embody the same ideological values as they do in fiction. The 'villains (or drug runners/dealers) were typically not Anglo-Saxon or, if they were, they had their Asian or Latin connections stressed. Social or racial deviance is the sign and embodiment of evil in news as in fiction' (Fiske, 1993: 295). The various drug 'cartels' of Colombia and the drug 'lords' of Burma provoke a steady stream of exotic stories. Yet there is a very simple truth which is most often overlooked.

As Goode and Ben-Yehuda (1994) explain:

> According to the Surgeon General of the United States, in the US the use of tobacco cigarettes is responsible for well over 400,000 premature deaths each year, while alcohol use causes some 150,000 deaths; a crude extrapolation from hospital and medical examiners' data yields premature acute deaths for illegal drugs (or the illegal use of prescription drugs) in the 20,000 or so territory. Again, discrepancies such as these should cause us to speculate that, perhaps, currently or recently, concern over illegal drug use might provide an example of a moral panic. (p. 44)

Similar observations had already led Jock Young to formulate the following 'Law of Information on Drugs' in even more provocative terms: 'The greater the public health risk (measured in number of mortalities) of a psychotropic substance, the less the amount of infor-mation (including advertising) critical of its effects' (Cohen and Young, 1973: 314). We will return to the subject of reporting on the health risks of smoking in the next chapter.

News is usually said to concern the 'really important events'. This answer seems satifying until one comes to realize that it is not at all obvious what is 'real', what is 'important', or what is an 'event'. The tragic death of some is, for instance, but the tragic death of many others is not. Public transport accidents are, but private car accidents to a much lesser extent. Murder is, suicide less so. Terrorism is, civil strife in distant places much less so, etc. One early study identified actors and activities which are routinely over- or under-reported in the news, and the ways in which the unity or divisions of society are conventionally represented. Another early study identified a dozen different criteria which are usually applied by journalists, but most often unreflectively. A closer analysis reveals that these criteria all con-tribute to the 'selective articulation' of certain facts and relations, and the overlooking of others. This is particularly true of even minor examples of cultural deviance, which often receive media attention beyond all reasonable proportion.

Notes

1 *Frame Analysis: An Essay on the Organization of Experience* (1986), pp. 14–15.

2 Only after the Dutch edition of this book had already been published did I learn that there are at least thirty to forty Protestant schools in the Netherlands which still oblige girls to wear skirts, and send home those presenting themselves in trousers. Of course, this had never been considered 'news' until then.

Further reading

News criteria: Gans; Galtung and Ruge (in Tunstall, ed.). *News ideology:* Hartley; Manoff and Schudson. *Moral panic:* S. Cohen; Goode and Ben-Yehuda.

3 WHICH ARE THE WORLD'S MOST INFLUENTIAL MEDIA?

THE ECONOMICS OF RICH AND POOR MEDIA MARKETS

The economies of scale operate in many manufacturing fields, and especially in fields where the research and development costs are high – such as new drugs, aircraft production or computers. In these three fields the United States has achieved supremacy. But the economies of scale work in an even more extreme way in some media fields.

In order to achieve extra overseas sales you have physically to manufacture and sell additional aircraft, or computers or pills – and a similar situation obtains with books and records. But in other media fields the additional cost of extra 'copies' is negligible. Only one copy is needed to show on a national television network. Only a smallish number of copies of feature films are required for one country.

Jeremy Tunstall, 'Media imperialism?'[1]

On a world scale, only a few dozen media and media organizations play a key role in the 'selective articulation' of life experiences, media messages and news definitions across all continents. Why do the US and the UK dominate, along with a handful of other major Western countries? Is that just related to their professionalism or also to their power? How concentrated or how diverse are they really? What are the sources of income of those media organizations? Is it true that any type of medium can exist, just as long as its public is sufficiently large? Or do audience orientation and purchasing power also play a role? Is it true that advertising revenues have no influence on format definition and editorial content? What are the implications of all this for the values promoted and the facts reported by the global media?

If we look at the media landscape on a global scale, it is obvious that some organizations and publications carry more weight than others. Some are only of local or regional or national significance, while some are of international or even intercontinental significance. Although these latter groups and outlets usually have a strong home base, they also have real clout in various overseas markets. Their formats may set the tone, their views shape the news. The question is, of course, why it is that one country or a few countries have come to dominate the world's media industry and the world news industry?

During the seventies, there was a major public debate among communication experts about whether there was such a thing as a global US 'media imperialism'. The American author Herbert Schiller was among those who argued that there was, in the sense that he perceived a deliberate policy on the part of major corporations, government agencies and the military establishment to promote the penetration of Third World and other foreign markets and to promote the introduction of American media models and values there. French authors such as Armand Mattelart and Yves Eudes also subscribed to this view.

The British author Jeremy Tunstall argued, by contrast, that the emerging global US media hegemony was largely the product of 'blind' historical mechanisms – primarily economies of scale. In this chapter we will take a closer look at some of the economic mechanisms which favour the dominance of certain countries, organizations and formats within the global media landscape. Why are the US and to a lesser extent the UK, to a still smaller extent France and a few other major Western countries the major media powers and 'news definers' in the world? And does it make a difference?

The economics of objectivity

In the empiricist view of the world, the problem does not exist: the observer simply mirrors what is out there, so it does not matter where she or he comes from. Whereas this view may take one a long way (though not all of it) in natural science, it may take one (not even) half the way in social science, in education and in the media, particularly in the fields of historical or cultural differences. The problem is that subject and object get mixed up in these cases: we apply our seemingly obvious categories ('in here') to the world, and then apparently see the validity of these same categories confirmed by the world ('out there').

Naïve empiricism thus often becomes a way of recycling ideologies into 'hard facts'. This is exactly what might happen when an 'objective' anthropologist or an 'objective' reporter looks at another society from the outside. It is not a problem of being somewhat more alert to possible prejudice. There is simply no way around a considerable amount of prejudice. Herbert Gans (1980: 182) quotes an article by Peter Schrag in this regard: 'Every reporter operates with certain assumptions about what constitutes normative behavior, if not good society, and the more "objective" he tries to be, the more likely those assumptions will remain concealed.'

But let us take a closer look at what objectivity or subjectivity really mean in a philosophical, or even an epistemological, sense. An observation report is said to be 'objective' if it is governed by the characteristics of the object, that which is being perceived; an observation report is said to be 'subjective' if it is governed by the characteristics of the subject who is perceiving. Complete objectivity or subjectivity are only extremes on a scale; they are never reached, because most observation reports are governed by varying degrees of inter-subjectivity, that is to say, by varying degrees of agreement between subjects about the characteristics of the object. These various degrees of agreement are also the result of more or less successful 'claim-making' tactics and strategies. Some (for instance, 'laboratory experiments') are widely considered as leading to 'objective' results. Others (for instance, 'storytelling') are widely considered as leading to 'subjective' results. The result of neither is absolute; it is always relative.

The notions of 'objectivity' and 'subjectivity' are fairly recent ones, in science as well as in education and the media. In fact they are nothing but a more or less pragmatic device to make a distinction between those limited aspects of an observation report that one feels the most relevant groups of subjects can easily agree upon, and those other aspects of an observation report that they might not be able to agree upon. One chooses to focus on consolidating the former and setting the latter aside for later debate. That is what objectivity and subjectivity really mean in this context.

In his book *Discovering the News* (1978), Michael Schudson has demonstrated how the ideal of news media objectivity gradually emerged in the US over the last century and a half; similar processes took place in the United Kingdom and other countries. The reasons were not idealistic but material. News agencies such as the Associated Press and newspapers such as the *New York Times* emerged and prospered by catering to several different groups of clients at once. In order to be able to do so, they had to focus their news reports on those aspects of perceived reality that all relevant audiences would be able to agree upon, and to set aside those aspects that relevant audiences might differ about. In that context, objectivity is purely an economic device.

In the context of my own book, it is very important to retain this fundamental claim: the notion of objectivity (or even inter-subjectivity) is always implicitly related to the notion of (an agreement between) relevant audiences. Therefore, what might appear as 'objectivity' to Western audiences (all relevant groups agreeing about that point of view), may appear as pure 'subjectivity' to non-Western audiences. The same holds for upper and lower classes, men and women, etc. This is in fact one of the key problems we will be talking about.

The same problems are linked to related notions of neutrality and impartiality: they imply an identification of relevant parties. What might be perceived as neutral (because bipartisan) in mainstream US or UK politics, for instance, may not be perceived as neutral (because not tripartisan) by sympathizers of third parties, let alone by overseas enemies (say in Panama or Argentina, on the occasion of recent armed conflicts). Similar questions recur with other notions: detachment from what; balance between whom; freedom from values: whose values, whose freedom? Journalists are confronted with eternally recurring dilemmas and paradoxes: to what extent can or should one try to remain aloof?

The ideal of neutrality is certainly sympathetic, but it implies that one is really willing and able to put oneself in the shoes of all others. Very often, this is simply not feasible. Western media organizations active on a global scale will first of all cater to Western media audiences and their values. Rich clients such as the Japanese may be taken into account on occasion, but poorer clients from the Second and Third Worlds are obviously of marginal concern, particularly if their sensibilities clash head-on with those of clients from the First World. In these cases, their concerns will often be all but ignored. As the age-old saying goes: 'Who pays the piper calls the tune.'

The global news agencies

This relationship can easily be demonstrated in news-gathering, for instance, by the international agencies. They have three major types of client and are reluctant to alienate them. Their first and foremost client was and is the business world in the developed countries. This is illustrated by the origins of the major European agencies. The forerunner of the French national agency AFP was founded by Charles Havas in 1835. The forerunner of the German national agency DPA was founded by Bernard Wolff in 1849. The forerunner of the British national agency was founded by Julius Reuter in 1851. They came from, and primarily catered for, the financial world. It was only later that they linked up with newspapers as well.

The second and most visible group of clients are the media in developed countries. This is illustrated by the history of the major American agencies. The forerunner of the Associated Press or AP agency was founded by half a dozen New York dailies in 1848, gradually extending its membership to most other American newspapers (and later including Canadian ones as well). The forerunner of the United Press International or UPI agency was founded in 1907 by the newspaper tycoon Edward Willis Scripps, who was later joined by another newspaper tycoon, William Randolph Hearst. Eventually, the three major European agencies also came to collaborate closely with national press associations and/or newspaper chains. In the case of Reuter's (now spelled Reuters), this role was extended to newspaper groups from white-dominated settler states such as Australia,

New Zealand, South Africa, as well as to some other parts of the British Empire.

The third group and the least visible clients are the national administrations of certain developed countries. They have an obvious interest in the rapid collection and distribution of news around the globe. The three major European agencies explicitly divided the world among themselves in 1859 and served the politics of their respective empires on numerous occasions. Government institutions often reciprocated by ordering large numbers of valuable subscriptions. In the run-up to the First World War, however, and then again in the run-up to the Second World War, the US openly came to resent the supposed 'manipulation' of world news by the European agencies.

Kent Cooper, for more than twenty-five years the general manager of AP, complained, for instance:

> International attitudes [about the US] have developed from impressions and prejudices aroused by what the [European] news agencies reported. The mighty foreign propaganda carried out through these channels in the last 100 years has been one of the causes of wars. [Of America], these agencies told the world about Indians on the warpath in the West, lynching in the South, and bizarre crimes in the North. For decades, nothing credible to America was ever sent.[2]

The British sarcastically responded through the establishment magazine *The Economist*: 'Like most business executives, [Cooper] experiences a peculiar moral glow in finding that his idea of freedom coincides with his commercial advantage' (Frederick, 1993: 160, 180). The arguments sound surprisingly similar to those later used in the UNESCO debate about the necessity of a New World Information and Communication Order (we will return to that subject in Chapter 7). But by that time the Americans had already united with the Europeans; and it was the Africans, Asians and Latin Americans who challenged their global monopoly of definition.

Today, only three agencies retain a truly global role – but they still reflect the three predominant types of client. The British (former British Empire) agency Reuters is primarily a private company, now deriving most of its considerable wealth, income and profits from its financial services. The American agency AP also runs a strong financial service (together with the Dow Jones company which also owns the *Wall Street Journal*), but it primarily remains a media cooperative. The French agency AFP thrived for a long time on generous government subscriptions, but increasingly it is trying to shift its emphasis to media clients. It is currently boosting its English-language services, in order to stay in the race. The American UPI agency went bankrupt; its remains were put up for sale, and were finally bought by an Arab media group. After the demise of the Soviet Empire, the Russian Tass agency was downgraded to an ordinary medium-sized national agency with limited overseas influence – just like the German, Spanish or Japanese agencies.

Although there have been recurrent attempts to compare the remaining three global agencies in size, this makes only limited sense with the available statistics. Figures relating to the number of words processed per day or the number of client countries are mere artefacts. The same holds for the number of clients (how much do they pay?), the number of employees (at home or abroad, journalists or other personnel, full-time or free-lance?), the turnover (what kind of services does this include?). There are some indications, none the less: Reuters claims 1,312 journalists of a total 1991 number of 10,810 employees, with 30,000 subscribers worldwide, a 1993 turnover of 1.87 billion and a profit of 0.44 billion pounds (some 2.8 and 0.65 billion dollars respectively) – in large part deriving from its financial services. Associated Press claims 3,157 employees; 1,800 newspaper and 7,000 broadcasting clients in the US, and over 15,000 media clients abroad; a 1994 budget of 383 million dollars. Agence France Presse claims more than 1,000 full-time journalists and 2,000 part-timers or free-lancers; 7,000 newspaper clients, 2,500 radio, 400 TV and 2,000 others; a 1993 income of 1,067 million and a loss of 17 million francs (some 180 million and 3 million dollars respectively) (Frémy and Frémy, 1995: 1262).

A crucial development of recent decades was the gradual emergence of global news-film agencies. Reuters took a major stake in the Visnews agency, alongside the British public-service broadcaster, the BBC. UPI lined up with the Independent Television News (ITN, on the commercial ITV network) to form UPITN, the forerunner of the present WTN. Reuters/Visnews and WTN are also lining up with the major American commercial broadcasters NBC and ABC respectively. The third major US commercial general interest network CBS sells its own news-film abroad. Most of the 'exotic' news-film shown on the TV evening news in lesser countries comes from these three sources. In recent years, however, thematic channels with their own news film-gathering organizations such as CNN, have decisively entered the game as well.

This emerging Anglo-American monopoly was lamented by Hervé Bourges, a former president of the French public-service channels, and a central figure in audiovisual policy-making. He contributed an article to Le Monde newspaper after the Gulf war, regretting that France had been so dependent on foreign images and foreign image-making. He also suggested that some allied misinformation had contributed to spoiling the traditionally good relations with some Arab countries on this occasion (3 April 1991). If key mainstream players in such major Western countries also express concerns about the unbalanced flow of international information, then there really must be a problem.

Media markets, rich and poor

There is a simple economic rule of thumb: the strongest media groups have their home base in those media markets which are not only the largest in their category, but also the richest. This holds on the local or regional, on the national and on the international or language area level. Let us briefly consider media markets at various levels in the world.

If we look at the largest urban agglomerations, for instance, we see that the majority are located in the so-called developing countries. They include Mexico City, São Paulo, Shanghai, Peking, Rio, Bombay, Calcutta, Seoul, Buenos Aires, Jakarta, Cairo, Bogotà. But if we multiply their numbers of inhabitants by the country's Gross Domestic Product per capita, we get an entirely different picture. This (admittedly rough) estimate of the agglomeration's economic power produces a much more reliable indication of where the major local or regional media markets in the world are. The top ten richest agglomerations are: New York, Tokyo, Los Angeles, Osaka-Kobe, Paris, Chicago, the Rhine–Ruhr area, Mexico City, London and São Paulo. Out of the first nine urban agglomeration markets in the world, eight are thus located in the five major developed countries of the world. Three are in the US, two in Japan, and one each in the UK, France and Germany.

If we look at the most populous countries in the world, we get a similar picture. The list is topped by China and India, with Indonesia, Brazil, Pakistan, Bangladesh and Nigeria also in the top ten. None of these is a major global media power. If we look at GDP, however, the list is topped by the US, which holds almost twice as much economic power as Japan, followed by Germany, France, Italy and the UK. These are indeed the half-dozen or so major media powers in the world, although not necessarily in that order.

Finally, if we look at the largest transnational language areas of the world, the same things apply. Mandarin Chinese tops the list, with Hindi, Russian, Arabic, Bengali, Malay in the top ten. If we try to make an estimate of the combined GDP of the core countries (or parts of multilingual countries) sharing a certain language, the results are clear and unequivocal. I estimated the combined GDP of the US and (part of) Canada, of the UK and Ireland, of Australia and New Zealand to be more than 8,417 billion dollars. The combined GDP of Germany, Austria and (part of) Switzerland was considerably less: 2,065 billion. The combined GDP of France, plus a proportion of Canadians, Swiss and Belgians was 1,562 billion. The combined GDP of Spain and the Spanish-speaking countries of Latin America was something like 1,275 billion. The combined GDP of China, Taiwan, Hong Kong, Singapore was 874 billion. Portugal and Brazil added up to 494 billion, and the Arab-speaking world to some 421 billion. This seems to be a perfect illustration of the potential relative strength of

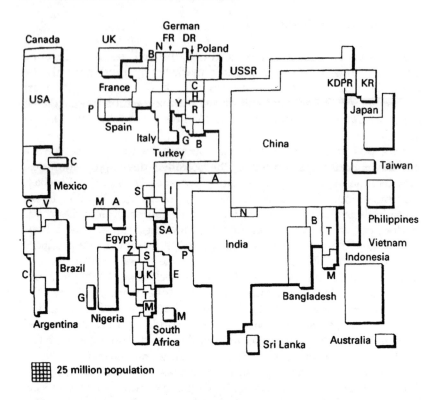

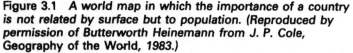

Figure 3.1 *A world map in which the importance of a country is not related by surface but to population. (Reproduced by permission of Butterworth Heinemann from J. P. Cole, Geography of the World, 1983.)*

media markets in various languages. (Figures refer to 1992/3, and were published in 1994 in handbooks for 1995.)

At the same time one has to acknowledge that the relative advantage for the very strongest may even be much greater than is apparent here. On the one hand, I have limited myself to first-language speakers, whereas we might also look at second-language and third-language speakers. The political, economic, cultural prestige of the strongest languages is such that they radiate far beyond the core countries considered here. On the other hand, Anglo-American, German or Francophone media companies can make considerable investments in better products, write them off in their home base, make a profit and still have money left to be set aside for translations, voice-overs, subtitles in other languages. Smaller players simply do not have that kind of power, therefore the trend is for the big to become bigger still.

In conclusion, we may say that a limited number of large G-7 media companies control most of the transcontinental flows of media

material. G-7 is shorthand for the Group of Seven of major industrialized nations: the US, Canada, the UK, France, Germany, Italy and
Japan. In some cases, the number is even smaller; in other cases, it is
slightly larger. Whatever the case, the group of 'free-market' industrialized nations allied within the Organization for Economic
Cooperation and Development, OECD, dominates the entire spectrum.
Whereas the G-7 nations have less than 10 per cent of the world's
population, they probably dominate as much as 90 per cent of transcontinental flows of media material. Some feel this is a good thing,
since they have accumulated long experience with media professionalism. Others feel it is a bad thing, since a minority of the world's
population tends to shape the news and views of a majority about
other parts of the globe, particularly since it seems an ever decreasing
group of ever larger conglomerates is dominating key parts of the
entire media spectrum.

Media ownership and concentration

Within the US and other G-7 nations themselves, the degree of media
decentralization or concentration has long been a major issue of
public concern. Everyone agrees that some degree of pluralism is
essential to the functioning of democracy, and indeed of a highly
developed society as such. But whereas some claim that a wide
variety of media voices can be heard, others maintain that the actual
range is relatively narrow and is narrowing even further. On the one
hand, this is a question of definition: how does one delineate markets
and identify competitors? On the other hand, it is a question of
evalution: when does one speak of oligopolies or semi-monopolies?

At the outset, there is the matter of basic media technologies and
how 'affordable' they are for individuals and groups. There are two
contradictory tendencies. The first is towards decentralization. Average citizens of OECD nations do indeed have access to a wide variety
of technological means, and can often communicate their news and
views to others. Personal computers, word processing, graphic design
and page-making programs, electronic printers, photocopying
machines and photo-offset machines make it relatively easy to produce and multiply printed matter in a more or less professional way.
Fax machines make it possible to distribute messages instantaneously.
Digital tapes and recorders have brought small-scale audio and video
productions within easy reach. The camcorder revolution is clearly a
boon to counter-culture. Furthermore, there is undeniably an explosion of small-scale broadcasters on the air and on cable. The Internet
is an even more eloquent illustration.

At the same time, the second and opposing tendency reflects
concentration. Ever larger conglomerates control the major means of

information, communication, distribution. Major data banks, electronic news processing and modern printing plants for newspapers require large initial investments. It takes many millions more to launch a new daily paper and take major initial losses, before possibly establishing it in a profitable market niche. It takes billions to set up a satellite or cable infrastructure, and wholesale access to them is not always within reach of lesser players. The production of a major television spot alone may cost a million dollars today, the production of a major mini-series may cost 10 million, the production of a major Hollywood blockbuster movie may cost up to 100 million. So, whereas some maintain that the glass of access for all is half-full, others claim it is half-empty.

The debate about media decentralization and concentration in the 'developed' countries peaked in the US in the early eighties, and resurfaced in the EC in the early nineties. One of the first really comprehensive overviews in the US was the book *Who Owns the Media? Concentration of Ownership in the Mass Communications Industry* (1979). It was edited by Benjamin M. Compaine, executive director of media studies in the Program on Information Resources Policy at Harvard University. It covered some 35,000 to 40,000 American media outlets, but observed that the various markets were dominated by a much more limited number of large conglomerates: 'Of these, 11 are dominant in newspapers, 16 in broadcasting, 16 in magazines, 14 in book publishing, 9 in cable and 10 in motion picture distribution.'

Since there was some overlap between them, the total number at the time amounted to no more than 58, he said (p. 319). He noted three different types of combinations: vertical integration (for example, a publisher owning a distributor, a printer and a paper manufacturer); horizontal integration (for example, a newspaper chain having an interest in a broadcasting company) and conglomerate mergers (for example, a non-media firm having a major stake in a media firm). These patterns were not unlike those found in other sectors of the economy, he claimed, and there was no particular cause for alarm, particularly since a few years later new technologies were blurring the boundaries of traditional media formats and content and thus were further encouraging competition.

In contrast to this relatively 'optimistic' view, another book presented a much more pessimistic view of the same system. It was titled *The Media Monopoly* (1983), and subtitled *A Startling Report on the 50 Corporations that Control what America Sees, Hears and Reads*. It was written by Ben H. Bagdikian, later to become dean of the Graduate School of Journalism of the University of California at Berkeley. He said that the larger part of the US media spectrum was controlled by a rapidly decreasing number of huge corporations. And a rapidly increasing proportion of these was on the well-known list of the 500 largest corporations, compiled annually by the business magazine

Fortune. They included electronics companies, weapons producers, nuclear-power firms and raw-material traders with considerable stakes in national policy-making and public opinion. According to him, they all had interlocking directorates and shared considerable financial interests.

The book related cases of corporate interference with editorial policies. On the one hand, unwelcome publications had been blocked on occasion. On the other hand, advertisers shaped entire media formats. The general tendency, he suggested, was to deflect serious critical attention from the corporate world and focus it on various forms of government 'interference'. Even if this was not the explicit goal, it was the implicit by-product of commercial media management procedures.

Bagdikian prolonged this same line of argument in a later article:

> Typical assertions of the vitality of the media marketplace have, I believe, two basic flaws. One is the equating of the quantity of media outlets, the volume of their output, and their impressive revenues with diversity and richness of content. This is done, I think, because that equation is quantifiable and, in our national reverence for numbers, is accepted as unassailable proof . . . The other common flaw is to ignore one of the two basic processes by which the mass media relate to their society.

On the one hand there was 'an extraordinary volume of media output in print, broadcasting, and recordings', he conceded. But on the other, only a very limited group had easy access, and 'the US media are becoming more homogenized in content and structure' (*Journal of Communication*, 1985: 81–109). By this time the number of companies that controlled the larger part of media distribution had shrunk to twenty-nine. Others predicted that this would soon dwindle further to twenty or even ten. At the time of writing (1996/7), another round of mega-mergers seems to be accelerating the shake-out.

The debate continued in the United States throughout the 1980s, but basically along similar lines. It also resurfaced in the Europe of the early nineties, due to a number of circumstances: a rising number of cross-border alliances between national media companies, the rapid internationalization and commercialization of broadcasting, a few conspicuous cases of alleged power abuse by media tycoons. Two new overviews were *Die Medienmultis* (1989) by Peter Muzik (a Viennese economic journalist) and *Media Moguls* (1991), mostly written by the communication professors Jeremy Tunstall (of the City University of London) and Michael Palmer (of the Sorbonne Nouvelle in Paris).

Both books pointed to the fact that in each of the four major EC countries, maybe half of the most influential media (sometimes slightly more, sometimes slightly less) were owned by only a handful of tycoons. This held for the press (magazines and newspapers, national and regional, élite and popular), as well as for the audio-visual industry (commercial radio, television and film production). In the United Kingdom they included Rupert Murdoch (formerly based in Australia, now in the US), Roy Thomson and Conrad Black (both Canadian), and of course the now notorious Robert Maxwell.

In France they included fathers and sons: Bouygues, Hersant, Lagardère (of Matra-Hachette) and the Seydoux brothers. In Germany, they included the Bauer, Burda, Kirch, Mohn (Bertelsmann) and Springer families. In Italy, they included the Agnelli (Fiat), Benedetti (Olivetti), Berlusconi (Standa, AC Milan and many others) and Gardini families (Feruzzi). Some of these tycoons and families were more or less apolitical, but a few used their power to promote definite political goals. Berlusconi became the most visible example as a subsequent party leader and prime minister. Some have left the scene since; others have emerged. Some were heavily in debt, but others were able to generate considerable surpluses, which in turn enabled them to profit from temporary but crucial market opportunities (particularly in the commercialization and internationalization of European television).

Japan has similar tendencies, with a limited number of giant hardware producers, but few media software producers making a major trans-cultural impact, except in a few fields (animation, video games, etc.). There is little doubt that the vast majority of the hundred largest media companies in the world have their home bases in the US, the G-7 nations and the OECD as a whole. It is their perspective which prevails in most media material distributed across continents. There are only very few major non-Western media software producers, which might provide a different perspective on the world. A Eurocentric perspective prevails, even if it is extended to settler states dominated by groups of European origin.

Sources of media income: to be or not to be

So far we have shown that the world media landscape is dominated by a limited number of commercial companies from major Western countries, but we have not yet discussed the financing of media organizations and formats themselves, and whether these may affect the content. The usual cliché is that a medium can exist if there is an audience for it. That is, of course, a gross simplification. There are many audiences in the world which do not have a medium to express themselves in, or who are not even being addressed as such by others. Various economic forces favour the emergence or survival of particular types of media format. Basically, media have several potential sources of income: subsidies from governments and/or major social institutions, subscriptions from and sales to audiences and, last but not least, advertising. The balance differs from country to country and from sector to sector.

SUBSIDIES There are various ways in which governments and major social institutions can favour media financially. They may work directly by integrating them into their organizational frameworks and budgets. This used to be the case in most totalitarian states, whether of the right-wing fascist, or of the left-wing communist variety. Or institutions may work indirectly by creating various kinds of favourable economic conditions for the functioning of the media (covering some of their costs, helping them to find subscribers). This used to be the case in various Western European countries, where political parties, trade unions, religious organizations and similar institutions favoured their own media. Gradually, however, most major Western media have given up such openly ideological alliances, and are transforming themselves into purely market-driven media.

There has long been one notable exception where media were more or less directly on the government budget – even in free-market countries. These were the media of cultural diplomacy (in the broadest sense) whereby countries propagated their way of life and view of the world: through cultural centres, exhibitions, magazines, films and broadcasting. In the news field, high-frequency (short-wave, long-distance) radio was and for some still is a medium of major importance. It was the first mass medium to reach across borders and continents without being obstructed.

When this technology emerged in the inter-war period, major countries were quick to adopt it as a key information tool in times of peace and war. Various bodies were formed, nominally public-service broadcasters. For obvious reasons, the major colonial powers were the very first to take an interest. Great Britain has its BBC World Service, France has its Radio France International or RFI, and the Netherlands has its Radio Nederland Wereldomroep.

During the Second World War, and then again during the Cold War, short-wave radio became a major instrument of cultural diplomacy and of ideological confrontation as well. The American State Department and its US Information Agency sponsored the Voice of America, for instance. The communist countries had Radio Moscow, Radio Peking and Radio Havana. In recent years, the US has tried to undermine the Castro regime by beaming television into Cuba through 'Radio Marti'. It is true that the collapse of the Soviet Empire was greatly facilitated by the Eastern European reception of Western European television, both of the public-service and the commercial type.

SUBSCRIPTIONS AND SALES Most normal media have subscriptions and sales' as their most visible revenue. But some audiences are more interesting as potential sources of revenue than others. On the one hand, this depends on their disposable income. On the other hand, it depends on the relevance 'good' information has for them. Most studies distinguish between prestige (quality, élite) news media and popular (quantity, mass) media. But just like the old socio-economic distinction between upper and lower classes, this distinction is too crude. It was gradually replaced by a distinction between upper, middle and lower classes; or even upper, upper-middle, lower-middle and lower ones. Although class distinctions and media audiences do not entirely run parallel, it may be useful to distinguish four types of media audiences: business, élite, general and popular. Whereas the first is aimed at maybe 1 or 2 per cent of the general audience, the second is aimed at 10 or 20 per cent, the third at 30 or 40 per cent and the fourth at all.

One core audience of the media (and particularly of the news media) is the financial and business world, which is often not explicitly mentioned as such in the literature, but carries a disproportionate weight. For obvious reasons, investors and traders have a high interest in speedy and trustworthy information. Some of the best-informed media organizations in the world are therefore primarily business media organizations. This holds for the lucrative on-line financial services of major news agencies (discussed above) and for specialized financial news agencies such as Bloomberg. It also holds for a wide variety of insider newsletters. No less than one-quarter of all American correspondents abroad, for instance, work for business news organizations rather than general ones.

The financial and business media occupy central positions in the entire spectrum. Think of dailies such as the American *Wall Street Journal* (which sells close to 2 million copies per day in the US and is now also branching out into Europe and Asia), the British *Financial Times*, the French *Les Échos*, or news magazines such as the American *Business Week*, the British *Economist*, the Hong Kong *Far Eastern Economic Review* (the major English-language news magazine of the Pacific rim), as well as magazines such as the American *Forbes* and *Fortune*, the German *Capital*, the French *L'Expansion*. Similar media exist in Germany, Switzerland, Japan and other major economic powers.

The second type of media audience is formed by the élite in the widest sense. The élite media often call themselves quality media or prestige media. They aim at a portion of the population which is actively interested and involved in public life. They include some of the better known élite news dailies and weeklies. In radio and television, some talk shows or news magazines belong to this group. The third type includes less sophisticated but relatively 'decent' press organs and broadcasting programmes aimed at a general public.

The fourth type consists of typically 'vulgar' media, which openly privilege sensationalist material over correct information. Hypocritical sex and violence reports, chauvinism and xenophobia often form the main ingredients. The British *Sun* and the German *Bild Zeitung* are well-known examples. They are both major cash cows and rabble-rousers. They may play a role in helping to define the national mood – particularly in crisis situations, but their direct impact abroad is usually limited.

Advertising and the *Umfeld* effect

It is often thought and said that sales and subscriptions are the prime source of income of the major world news media. This is a widespread misunderstanding, because it is simply not the case. Most media income comes from a another source: advertising. Of course, the share of advertising income varies with the medium. For many daily newspapers and news weeklies, it is 50 to 60 per cent. For many illustrated magazines, it is 70 to 80 per cent. In American broadcasting, it used to be 90 to a 100 per cent for a long time. In European broadcasting, there is a general shift from public to commercial broadcasting too.

The major advertising agency Saatchi estimated worldwide advertising expenditure for 1995 at 261 billion dollars. The largest advertisers in the world are Procter & Gamble (US) and Unilever (UK and the Netherlands), who each spend many billions of dollars a year. Some expect that global advertising expenditure will grow sevenfold over the next quarter-century, most of all in East Asia. The 'senior vice-president of forecasting' of the major advertising agency McCann predicted that by the year 2020, North Americans would probably spend as much as 2,300 dollars per capita on advertising, Western Europeans 1,100 and Eastern Europeans 600 dollars. Even the latter sum will probably still exceed the annual income of large parts of the world's population by that time. Most of that sum will be spent through the media, boosting the budget of certain types of media and shunning others. It will be a huge factor in deciding which media are 'to be or not to be'.

The next question is whether this preponderance of advertising revenue affects the media landscape in any way. The usual answer is no. Advertisers are interested in reaching the widest possible audiences. But that is again too simple. There are various sorts of advertising: classified advertising, local retail advertising and major national product campaigns, for instance. The first two have a limited influence, the latter may have a more significant one on occasion. We have seen that there are also various sorts of media: daily newspapers and weeklies, illustrated magazines, commercial television. The former are only marginally affected by advertiser preferences, but the latter are often affected in more significant ways.

Advertisers primarily use four criteria when choosing media outlets for campaigns. The first criterion is the size of the audience reached.

This has a tendency of favouring the lowest common denominator of media and formats. The second criterion is the purchasing power of the audience reached. This has a tendency to favour up-market media and formats. The third criterion is the specificity of the audience reached, favouring special-interest audiences. The fourth criterion is the *Umfeld* (German for – editorial – environment) in which the audience is reached, which has a tendency to favour consumption-oriented media and formats, giving them a premium.

At first sight, these four tendencies seem to be contradictory and to cancel each other out. But upon closer inspection, they do in fact promote the over-representation of certain media and formats within the global media landscape, and the under-representation of others. The lowest common denominator media and formats tend to shy away from real political debate, for instance. Emphasis on up-market media and formats disadvantages the representation of lower classes and ethnic minorities within the media landscape. The special interest audiences are mostly catered for as consumer groups, not as simple demographic categories. Elderly people were long neglected by the media, for instance, because they were thought to spend too little money (but this has changed in recent years). Finally, the *Umfeld* or co-optation effect leads to the vigorous adoption of purely hedonistic media and formats, which also tend to blot out social problems.

The combined effect of these mechanisms is obvious in the average news-stand (particularly in the common orientation of most glossy magazines) and in commercial television (particularly in the common orientation of prime-time programming). In these media and formats real political debate and social problems are mostly overshadowed, critics say, by 'mindless' entertainment and daydreaming. If these co-optation mechanisms affect the media landscapes of the Western countries themselves only in limited ways, they may have consider-able effects on the shape of emerging Third World media landscapes. Once major multinational corporations entered Third World markets, they tended to bring their own advertising agencies with them, which in turn tended to co-opt and create their own congenial media environments. As Hamid Mowlana (1986: 83) says: 'It has been said that transnational corporations can change the "cultural ecology" in a country through increased media ownership and penetration of foreign advertising.'

Many of the newer (for example, audiovisual) media in developing countries therefore seem to promote the values of developed coun-tries, that is to say, individual adherence to the consumer society and the goals of upward social mobility. Often, critics add, this is not only detrimental to the national development process but it promotes further international migration as well: on the one hand of educated professionals (the brain drain), and on the other of unskilled workers

Table 3.1   *Major media markets*

Largest city	Population (millions)	Territory	Population (millions)	GDP (billion $)
TRANSCONTINENTAL LANGUAGE AREAS				
ENGLISH				
New York	7.3	USA	261	6,379
London*	6.8	Great Britain	58	1,039
Toronto	3.9	Canada (E: 61%)	28	595
Sydney	3.7	Australia	18	309
Dublin	0.5	Ireland	3	48
Auckland	0.9	New Zealand	4	47
		Core regions, total		8,417
FRENCH				
Paris*	10.6	France	58	1,287
Bruxelles*	1.0	Belgium (F: 42%)	10	212
Geneva*	0.4	Switzerland (F: 18%)	7	241
Montréal	3.1	Canada (F: 24%)	28	595
		Core regions, total		1,562
SPANISH				
Madrid	3.0	Spain	39	535
Mexico C.	8.2	Mexico	92	295
Buenos Aires*	8.0	Argentina	34	200
Caracas	4.0	Venezuela	21	61
Bogotà	4.8	Colombia	35	48
		Other Latin American (13)	97	136
		Core regions, total		1,275
PORTUGESE				
São Paulo*	15.2	Brazil	159	416
Lisbon*	2.1	Portugal	10	78
		Core regions, total		494
CONTINENTAL LANGUAGE AREAS				
GERMAN				
Berlin	3.4	Germany	81	1,726
Vienna	1.5	Austria	8	182
Zurich*	0.8	Switzerland (G: 65%)	7	241
		Core regions, total		2,065
CHINESE				
Shanghai	7.8	China	1,222	517
Taipei	2.7	Taiwan	21	218
Hong Kong	5.7	Hong Kong	6	89
Singapore	3.1	Singapore	3	50
		Core regions, total		874

continued overleaf

Table 3.1   *(cont.)*

Largest city	Population (millions)	Territory	Population (millions)	GDP (billion $)
ARABIC				
Jeddah	1.8	Saudi Arabia	17	113
Cairo*	9.8	Egypt	58	44
		Other Arab (14)	133	264
		Core regions, total		421
PRIMARILY NATIONAL LANGUAGE AREAS				
Tokyo	7.9	Japan	125	3,870
Rome	2.7	Italy	58	1,147
Moscow	8.8	Russia	150	374
Bombay	12.6	India	914	272
Karachi	8.0	Pakistan	131	50
Dacca	6.1	Bangladesh	125	25

* = agglomeration

Note: Tables compiled from two recent overviews of official statistics: *L'état du monde, 1995* (Paris: La Découverte, 1994) (national populations, GDP); and Dominique and Michèle Frémy, *Quid 1995* (Paris, 1994) (other figures). Most figures refer to 1992/3.

which then come to form a Southern ethnic underclass within the major Northern agglomerations ('the Fourth World').

An example of the *Umfeld* effect: advertising and smoking

Glossy magazine formats and commercial television programmes are increasingly being developed in such a way that they do not hurt the sensibilities of (potential) advertisers but instead provide a flattering environment for their products. Critics say that this has largely contributed to shaping (and distorting) images of health and the hazards of cars, alcohol, drugs, smoking, food, etc. in both fiction and 'factual' reporting.

It is interesting to take a closer look at the slow evolution of media coverage of smoking, for instance. By 1954, the American Cancer Society had released the results of a study of 187,000 men, which definitely concluded that smokers had a death rate from all diseases which was 75 per cent higher than non-smokers, and a death rate from lung cancer which was even 1,500 per cent higher. Smoking killed six times more people annually than accidents did. Over more than three subsequent decades (during which several million Americans died from the effects of smoking), the press and broadcasting media reported on the link only very reluctantly. Shocking pictures were extremely rare if not totally absent, whereas the tobacco companies spent over 10 billion dollars in glamour advertising – a budget unequalled for any other product in previous history.

Broadcasters explicitly ordered their script-writers always to associate smoking with heroes and pleasure, never with victims and illness. When tobacco advertising was nevertheless banned from television in 1970, huge budgets shifted to the printed media. Only the *Reader's Digest* and the *New Yorker* refused tobacco advertisements. R. C. Smith in the *Columbia Journalism Review* (1978) looked at the next seven years and concluded: 'In magazines that accept cigarette advertising I was unable to find a single article, in several years of publication, that would have given readers any clear notion of the nature and extent of the medical and social havoc wreaked by the cigarette-smoking habit.'

Elisabeth Whelan used to contribute to women's magazines on health topics, and said she had been 'told repeatedly by editors to stay away from the subject of tobacco'. When she later approached the ten leading magazines to run articles on the subject, they all refused: *Cosmopolitan, Harper's Bazaar, Ladies' Home Journal, Mademoiselle, Ms., McCall's, Redbook, Seventeen, Vogue* and *Working Woman*. When the magazine *Mother Jones* did write on the subject, tobacco companies cancelled their ads. Even the big news weeklies *Time* and *Newsweek* proved extremely reticent. Ben Bagdikian (1983: 171–5), whom I quote here, adds that the newspapers did not do very much better. In 1980, 'there were still more stories in the daily press about the causes of influenza, polio and tuberculosis than about the cause of one of every seven deaths in the United States.'

The result of these editorial policies was

> that surveys in 1980 by Gallup, Roper and Chilton found that 30 percent of the public is unaware of the relationship between smoking and heart disease, 50 percent of women do not know that smoking during pregnancy increases the risk of stillbirth and miscarriage, 40 percent of men and women had no idea that smoking causes 80 percent of the 98,000 lung cancer deaths per year, and 50 percent of teenagers do not know that smoking may be addictive.

The journalist Peter Taylor, in *The Smoke Ring* (1984), gives similar examples for Britain. He also reported on the fate of a documentary he made for Thames Television. *Death in the West – the Marlboro Story* visited and interviewed six real-life American cowboys, who were all at one time heavy smokers and were in various stages of dying from cancer or emphysema. The broadcast made a considerable impact, but the Philip Morris company, which uses the Marlboro cowboy as its major promotion image, took out an injunction in the High Court in London, preventing the producers from selling the film or ever showing it again – while at the same time continuing their own campaign. The issue was revived only five full years later, when an anti-smoking activist in California received a copy of the videotape in a brown envelope, and got a local channel to show it. Only then was it gradually taken up by other broadcasters at home and abroad.

Now that the climate of opinion in most Western countries has (finally) changed, American and British tobacco companies have launched a huge advertising, marketing and promotion offensive through the newly commercialized media of the Second and Third Worlds, particularly in the emerging markets of Asia. If current trends continue, official estimates of the World Health Organization say, tobacco deaths worldwide will therefore rise to 10 million per year over the next quarter-century. Only the skin colour will change: in future, only 30 per cent of the victims will still be white; 70 per cent will be 'non-whites'.

Economics and values

The final question is whether the global export of the Western media model, of Western media organizations, formats and news, is a value-free or a value-laden phenomenon, or, put differently, whether Western values are universally applicable to all, or whether they are specifically related to Western history and the emergence of a Western-dominated world system.

As Wallerstein and others have demonstrated, the last five (or ten, or more) centuries have seen the gradual emergence of an economic world system consisting of various layers of centres and peripheries. This economic world system, furthermore, became intertwined with a new political system of nation-states. The states drew borders, organized an administration and laws, and defined citizenship. In essence, it defined who was to be a 'have' and who was to be a 'have not' for centuries to come.

According to some authors, the centres and sub-centres advanced through their considerable talent and energy, but the peripheries and sub-peripheries will automatically follow. According to other authors, the former and the latter are partially locked into a system of unequal exchange, which enriches some and impoverishes others both materially and culturally. In their view, it will not be so easy for some major countries of the Third and Second Worlds to really catch up with the major countries of the First World under the current rules – in spite of impressions to the contrary.

Everyone agrees, however, that over the last one or two centuries at least, the two major world powers were the UK and the US. Both occupy a very specific position within the moderate climate zone on both sides of the Atlantic. As an island group and as a near-continent, both stood somewhat apart from the rest of the world and from the shifting alliances on the Eurasian mainland. No foreign invasion violated their national integrity and interrupted their integration or growth. Instead, they became major seafaring powers, dominating world trade. Great Britain built the largest formal empire in world history, and after the balance had shifted, the United States built the largest informal empire.

The centre of worldwide capital accumulation gradually shifted from the City of London to New York's lower Manhattan and Wall Street. The privileged economic position of the Anglo-Americans, world system theorists say, also resulted in a low degree of social conflict and a high degree of political stability. Neither country has experienced any major violent uprisings or a radical regime change in over a hundred years. Thus the UK and the US share more than just the English language. They share a very specific set of cultural values: the values of world hegemony.

At first, these interests and values were not shared by the rest of the Western world. But gradually, the alliance grew to include others – for instance, other Anglo-Saxon colonies turned into settler states and smaller countries on the European mainland. Larger countries on the European mainland, such as France, Germany and Italy, mounted successive military challenges, which they lost, before integrating into the world system as well. So did Japan and, more recently, some other countries on the Pacific Rim. But what were the core values of the UK and the US, which were gradually embraced by all G-7 and OECD states? What were the core values, which also came to dominate their media system and their news reporting? To what extent do these core values apply to others, to those outside the golden circle?

ECONOMIC VALUES: FREE ENTERPRISE AND A FREE MARKET Some argue that these values caused economic hegemony, while others argue that they (also) reflect economic hegemony. Many Western nations were protectionist when they built their own economies and became free traders only once they were ready to face serious competition. Most non-Western nations are criticized in the media whenever they are (or appear) protectionist or overly regulatory. They are told that the rapid introduction of unfettered free trade will solve all their problems at once. However, such First World assurances have often failed to materialize, most recently, for instance, in Russia and other former Second World countries, and in Mexico and other Third World countries.

SOCIAL VALUES: INDIVIDUALISM AND SOCIAL MOBILITY Some argue that these values caused middle-class merits to emerge, while others argue that they reflect a middle-class meritocratic outlook. The 'American dream', for instance, was successful in a very peculiar set of economic circumstances with unlimited access to supposedly 'free' land and 'free' resources. Something similar applied to settlers in colonial countries. The idea that the enterprising individual can conquer all odds and become upwardly mobile by a simple act of will is also rather misleading. It is true that the advanced nations have always attracted (and admitted) valuable people and profitable capital from less advanced nations. But it is silly (and even counter-productive) to claim that such mobility can entirely solve the problems of the urban and rural lower classes around the world.

POLITICAL VALUES: PRAGMATISM AND 'MODERATION'   Some argue that these values caused political stability, others argue that they reflect political (social, economic) superiority. The democratic regimes of the UK and the US did not only emerge from but even coincided with long episodes of massive exploitation, repression and genocide. The same holds for many of the other Western democratic nations. Now that their hegemony is firmly entrenched, they admonish others to seek only peaceful change. These are worthwhile ideals, but also slightly hypocritical. One should not be surprised that other national or social groups have a different sense of entitlement, of the urgency of change, or of the justification of challenges to the new world order.

LIFESTYLE VALUES: MATERIALISM AND AUTONOMY   Some argue that these values led to a better way of life, while others argue that they are simply the reflection of the consumer society. Material goals are at the heart of our lives, but spiritual goals are increasingly marginal. Consumption patterns define social identity. The collective, the nation, the ethnic group, the social class, the neighbourhood have no claims over the individual. The extended family shrank to the nuclear family which shrank to the one-parent family. Marriages and divorces are not arranged, but serial monogamy is based on romantic decisions. Sexuality is pleasure-oriented, not procreation-oriented. All that is fine: the problem is that this often becomes the yardstick against which to measure the mores of other cultures and to dismiss them.

IDEOLOGICAL VALUES: WE HAVE NO IDEOLOGY   Most citizens of major Western nations – and that includes most journalists – are deeply convinced that their society not only represents the very apex of civilization, but is also willing to do all it can to help others reach this stage as soon as possible. The idea that the Western alliance as a whole may be held partly responsible by some for introducing current inequities into the world system, and also for maintaining these same inequities in a variety of ways, seems totally absurd to them. Yet quite a few prominent Third World citizens and journalists do hold this view. Latin American authors such as Eduardo Galeano and Gabriel Garcia Marquez have repeatedly undertaken to document it as well.

Many people think that the political mainstream of the West has no ideological views but only scientific ones, that only right-wing and left-wing 'extremists' in the First World have ideologies, as well as all those extremists in the Second and Third Worlds. This is the very hallmark of an effective ideology: that it is not recognized as an ideology at all, but is naturalized as common sense. It is impossible not to have an ideology: without it one could never find one's place in the nation and society. (We will return to this problem in Chapter 8.)

Michael Schudson (1978: 184) quotes Jack Newfield in this regard. He summed it up quite well:

> So the men and women who control the technological giants of the mass media are not neutral, unbiased computers. They have a mind-set. They have definite life-styles and political values, which are concealed under the rhetoric of objectivity. But those values are organically institutionalized by the *Times*, by AP, by CBS . . . into their corporate bureaucracies. Among these unspoken, but organic, values are belief in welfare capitalism, God, the West, Puritanism, the Law, the family, property, the two party system, and perhaps most crucially, in the notion that violence is only defensible when employed by the [our] State. I can't think of any White House correspondent, or network television analyst, who doesn't share these values. And at the same time, who doesn't insist he is totally objective?

Objectivity is primarily an economic notion, then. It focuses on those aspects of observations that relevant audience groups may easily agree upon. Other aspects they might differ about, by contrast, are set aside for further debate. But the notion of 'relevant audience groups' is the key here, because most global media organizations are primarily geared to the interests and views of audiences in the G-7, the largest Western nations. What they consider objective and true may very well seem rather subjective and questionable to audiences in many non-Western nations. The news and views which are selectively articulated by commercial media on a world scale are also shaped by other mechanisms. The primordial role of advertising, for instance, has profound implications. According to some critics, it leads to an undue glamorization of the consumer society and consumer products, with all that implies. One example is the belated attention given to the detrimental effects of smoking.

Notes

1 In *The Media are American – Anglo-American Media in the World* (1994), p. 42.

2 Quoted from Kent Cooper, *Barriers Down* (New York: Farrar and Rinehart, 1942), p. 36; and Herbert Brucker, *Freedom of Information* (New York: Macmillan, 1951), p. 214. One might add that the managing director of Reuters between 1916 and 1941, Sir Roderick Jones, had indeed at the same time been the British Director of Propaganda at the end of the First World War, and was later discovered to have received 64,000 pounds for propaganda purposes at the beginning of the Second World War (Tunstall and Palmer, 1991: 48).

Further reading

Objectivity: Schudson. *American domination*: Schiller; Tunstall. *News agencies*: Boyd-Barrett. *Concentration, North America*: Bagdikian; Compaine. *Concentration, Western Europe*: Muzik; Tunstall and Palmer. *Advertising*: Barnouw, O'Barr. *Smoking*: P. Taylor.

4 WHO ARE JOURNALISTS AND HOW DO THEY WORK?

THE SOCIOLOGY OF PROFESSIONALS AND LAYMEN

Culture is 'this theory to which a native actor refers in interpreting the unfamiliar or the ambiguous, in interacting with strangers (or supernaturals), and in other settings peripheral to the familiarity of mundane everyday life space; and with which he creates the stage on which the games of life are played . . .

But note that the actor's "theory" of his culture, like his theory of his language may be in large measure unconscious. Actors follow rules of which they are not consciously aware, and assume a world to be "out there" that they have in fact created with culturally shaped and shaded patterns of mind.'

R. Keesing, 'Theories of culture'[1]

Most people live in a common-sense world, in which the meaning of things, of facts and relations, is taken for granted and self-evident. Journalists are no exception. But could it be that the way they see things is also affected by the threefold prior processes of socialization? Primary socialization leads into a specific culture and subculture (nationality, ethnic group, class, gender, etc.). Secondary socialization leads into a professional subculture, with all its dos and don'ts. Tertiary socialization leads into a specific organization, with its own goals and rules. Could it be that his or her work is also embedded in larger patterns, over which he or she has only limited control, such as vertical hierarchies of people and horizontal processing of messages? And that their conformity is furthermore subtly regulated by occupational values and peer groups?

Journalists, intellectuals and artists are 'cultural' in a dual way: they belong to a specific culture and to specific professional subcultures. Yet many prefer to think of themselves as supra-cultural, as a *freischwebende Intelligenz*, as a free-floating or socially unattached intelligentsia, a sort of interstitial social stratum relatively free of interests or *parti pris*. Whereas other social groups may indeed have a specific social background, a specific social position and specific social aspirations affecting their views of the world, so the reasoning goes, the intelligentsia spiritually transcends such limitations of culture and class, time and space. It is therefore also considered to be relatively unproblematic for journalists to report on other cultures; it is supposed to take only a combination of some extra measure of energy and honesty. Instead, it is a daily struggle for any honest journalist to continue to doubt and question his or her own innermost and hidden frames of mind, because we have internalized and are often prisoners of a particular world-view. The sociologists Peter Berger and Thomas Luckmann (1996: 150) describe the process:

> The ontogenetic process by which this is brought about is socialization, which may thus be defined as the comprehensive and consistent induction of an individual into the objective world of a society or a sector of it. Primary socialization is the first socialization an individual undergoes in childhood, through which he becomes a member of society. Secondary socialization is any subsequent process that inducts an already socialized individual into new sectors of the objective world of his society.

(In this case, 'objective' means independent of his or her 'subjective' volition.)

One illustration is the attitude of Western media people toward other religions. A study of ten 'élite' national media organizations with their headquarters in the north-eastern United States found that 20 per cent of the journalists said they were Protestants, 13 per cent Catholics and 14 per cent Jewish. Although close to 50 per cent declared a religious affiliation, 86 per cent reported that they 'seldom or never attend religious services' (Lichter and others, quoted in Shoemaker and Reese, 1991: 69). Most people working for élite media organizations in Europe, too, may have a religious background but hardly ever go to church. The vast majority considers itself vaguely humanist.

Yet in their portrayals of other cultures, they often implicitly use Judaeo-Christian religion as a yardstick of civilization, and implicitly look down upon other religions as 'primitive'. Shohat and Stam (1994: 202–3) provide a detailed analysis of how and why African (and South American) 'voodoo' religions are invariably depicted as they are. One might add that these stereotypes move from feature films to documentaries and news film. Similarly, portraits of South Asian Hinduism often emphasize 'fanaticism'; portraits of South-east Asian Buddhism often emphasize 'superstition', and only certain more abstract strands of Hinduism and Buddhism are generally treated with respect or even sympathy.

Journalists, then, have on the one hand internalized the civilization, language, nation, ethnic group, social class, age cohort and gender they belong to – with all this implies; and, on the other hand, their status as 'knowledge-producers' and 'news-gatherers'. They may well go against the tide: a little bit all the time, or a lot some of the time. But they cannot easily shed their entire social identity just as they would change clothes. It would be rather like changing skins: a painful process, which may be accomplished in part, but is almost impossible to complete in full

A French example: the event that did not happen

Let us take a look at one particular case, this time from France again. In Chapter 2 we discussed examples of moral panics: the disproportionate amount of attention given by media and audiences to relatively minor occurrences. Here we will look at the opposite: a disproportionate lack of attention to rather grave events, right under their own eyes. One reason is an excessive trust in official sources, to which we will return in Chapter 5. Another is an uncritical acceptance of 'enemy images', to which we will return in the last chapter. But these are only two ways, in which journalists identify with their own cultures and not with strange ones.

Around 17 October 1991, the French journalist Jean-Luc Einaudi published a book to commemorate the thirtieth anniversary of *La Bataille de Paris*. This had become the code name for a massive massacre right in the heart of the French capital, the true extent of which had been ignored by all major media for some twenty years – and continues to be ignored by many memoirs and history books today. It is an amazing story.

The French colony of Algeria had been in insurrection for many years. Tens of thousands of Frenchmen had died, and many hundreds of thousands of Algerians. The French army and police in Algeria were increasingly restive, and finally General Charles de Gaulle had been brought back to power in Paris to find a solution. There were 400,000 Algerian immigrants in France, who were the main fund-raisers for the independence movement (the National Liberation Front). The FLN in Paris staged attacks against opponents and also against police stations – until an order was given to end these by early October 1961.

Yet the government decided to go ahead with the imposition of a curfew – just for Algerians in France. Immigrant organizations called a protest demonstration for the evening of 17 October, in the centre of Paris. It was forbidden, but 30,000 to 40,000 people turned up anyway: men, women and children. Police charged, the crowd dispersed, there were skirmishes all around. The official version the next day was that one Frenchman and two Algerians had been killed, that thirteen policemen and fifty-one civilians had been wounded. Some 10,000 Algerians had been arrested, and were kept for weeks in the Palais des Sports (which was then evacuated for a Ray Charles performance), in the Olympic Coubertin Stadium and in Vincennes.

It was claimed that demonstrators had shot at the troops and had initiated the violence, but there was never any proof of that. Yet most newspapers blamed the Algerians and excused the French police. Here are some of the major headlines. *L'Aurore*: 20,000 MUSLIMS, ORGANIZED BY FLN LEADERS, HAVE DEMONSTRATED WITH VIOLENCE. *Le Figaro*: VIOLENT DEMONSTRATIONS OF ALGERIAN MUSLIMS IN PARIS. *Le Parisien Libéré*: VIOLENT NORTH AFRICAN DEMONSTRATIONS YESTERDAY EVENING IN PARIS. The article in *Paris Presse* said: 'at movie time, they attacked on the boulevards.' The article in *Combat* said: 'heavily organized Algerian Muslims have demonstrated violently.' The illustrated weekly *Paris Match* had a cover on A NIGHT OF DISORDER IN PARIS and mentioned a 'wave of menacing faces'. The TV evening news had two minutes which focused on a sequence of material destruction and orderly intervention. The three film news-reels of that week all devoted 20 to 72 seconds to the subject, with the same emphasis.

A few papers such as *Le Monde* blamed the demonstrators but still noted a few police excesses. During the first few days, however, only very few mainstream newspapers noted the widespread police violence: just *France Soir, Libération* and the communist *L'Humanité*. A few British and American correspondents were also rather critical. The climate shifted somewhat when persistent eyewitness reports continued to claim that the number of casualties must have been higher, that police had systematically beaten up prisoners, and that they continued to do so days afterwards.

A few dailies and weeklies began to publish appalling eyewitness reports. Some journalists ventured that the number of casualties had not been two or three but rather twenty to thirty. Only a few intellectuals, peace groups and pro-Algerian groups maintained that the figure was even higher. These protests found few echoes in public opinion. Higher figures and interviews appeared in marginal journals such as *Verité – Liberté, Les Temps Modernes* and *Esprit*. But they were all seized and the information was not systematically relayed by the mainstream media. One film-maker shot a documentary with eyewitnesses: but it was immediately seized. Belgian television shot a report with eyewitnesses, but it was not broadcast. Basically, the truth never reached the general public.

After *Libération* had been the first to commemorate the massacre a year earlier, *Le Monde* and other media only did so on the twentieth anniversary of the event in 1981. On that occasion, the TV evening news even devoted four and a half minutes to it. In subsequent years, the truth gradually came out in magazine articles and books. Jean-Luc Einaudi went to verify suspicious deaths in the relevant registers at the cemetery. His conclusion was that 197 deaths from those days were suspicious. Algerians had been drowned in the River Seine by the dozen, shot or beaten to death in the improvised camps until many days after the events themselves: right in the heart of Paris, under the nose of the French and international media. He was even able to identify most names. He was also able to trace the secret archives of the FLN of those days, which claimed that 327 people had been killed or had disappeared.

These figures of 200 to 300 deaths (or a hundred times higher than the original Paris newspaper estimates) are widely accepted by serious researchers today. Yet the official history books, the memoirs of President de Gaulle, his prime minister, his information minister, the minister of the interior, the police chief and others either ignore the event or stick to the official version of a 'few victims'. Politicians of the right and the left have maintained that the police archives will remain closed for several decades to come. For most Frenchmen and Westerners, therefore, the massacre never happened. Just like dozens of similar massacres of 'colonial subjects' during the latter days of the French (Belgian, Dutch, British, Portuguese, etc.) empires.

Less than three months after the original event, on 8 February 1962, police charged another group of demonstrators at the Métro station of Cambronne in Paris. There were nine victims: all French. There was a huge outcry, and the burial was followed by half a million people.[2]

Primary socialization: culture

Journalists have just as much of an ideological and cultural framework as other people, and this inevitably conditions their reports on 'Others' and their interaction with sources. Culture guides all of our interaction and communication. That is why *Communicating with Strangers* (or even about them) is so difficult, as anthropologists William B. Gudykunst and Young Yun Kim explain in a 1992 book with that title, because we are guided by other presuppositions about the nature of truth and reality.

There is no way around it. We always have to recognize that: (1) communication is symbolic activity; (2) it is a process involving the encoding and decoding of messages; (3) it is transactional; (4) it takes place at varying levels of awareness; (5) communicators make predictions about the outcomes of their communication behaviour; (6) intention is not a necessary condition; (7) every communication message has a content dimension and a relationship dimension; and (8) communicators impose structure on their interactions (pp. 6–10). Journalists therefore cannot function outside a cultural grid, and nor can anyone else.

Transnational corporations have learned this over recent decades – often the hard way. The American computer maker IBM was one of the first to introduce company surveys around the world. The Dutch social scientist Geert Hofstede took some of the early results and analysed them statistically. He found culturally accepted behaviour varied along four major dimensions, which he labelled: individual-ism–collectivism, masculinity–femininity, power distance and uncer-tainty avoidance. Related research with Michael Bond in an East Asian context turned up a fifth dimension: short-term versus long-term thinking. In interaction and communication between people from different countries, let alone from different continents, this proved to lead to recurrent misunderstandings, to problems with the fine-tuning of everyday social behaviour.

This may be obvious for language: words – even translated – never mean the same thing to people from different cultures or epochs, because they fit into a network of different denotations, connotations and associations. This is easy to see. But it is harder to recognize that language is also preceded, accompanied and followed by a range of non-verbal cues, which also modify its meanings to various partici-pants in an intercultural exchange. The experience of social space is different: interpersonal distance, touch, sensory involvement. The experience of social time is different: being on time, spending time together, being business-like or informal, living for the moment or investing in the future relationship. The experience of gestures and facial expressions is different; and also of what is clean and pure, of what is natural and supernatural. The constant violation of implicit expectations may easily provoke negative emotions, even when both parties are well-disposed towards each other.

Edward Hall was one of the first to make a systematic exploration of these contrasts, in a series of monographs on the 'hidden dimensions' of culture. He also distinguished 'low-context' and 'high-context' communication. A low-context message is explicit: all the information you need seems to be in the words and images themselves. A high-context message, by contrast, is implicit: most of the keys to its decoding are (supposed to be) in the psyche of the other, in the social or the physical situation. Here again, misinterpretations and misattributions (of motives and intentions) may easily occur. Many diplomats get at least some training in intercultural communication, but many foreign correspondents and international reporters do not. Very few journalism schools devote much attention to these problems.

This lack has a dual result. On the one hand, foreign travellers – whether professionals or laymen – unknowingly tend to depart with a repertory of stereotypes, tend to interpret an ambiguous confron-tation with strange cultures in these terms, and tend to return with their preconceptions reconfirmed. In his book on *Culture and the Ad* (1994), William O'Barr included an interesting exercise of scrutinizing our own exotic holiday pictures for their unwitting reproduction of travel agency stereotypes (Chapter 5).

On the other hand, when encountering intercultural friction, we fall back on quick categorizations. This typically occurs when First World journalists arrive in a Second or Third World country for a quick piece of reportage, and have to deal with the local administration. They will soon feel it is bureaucratic (slow, paper-based, etc.) and authoritarian (hierarchical). Their counterparts, by contrast, may feel they are arrogant and disrespectful (asking for special treatment and immediate access). Both reactions are rooted in the normal way of doing things within each organizational culture, which is logical and legitimate from its own point of view, but not from the other's.

Recruitment of media people and the 'glass ceiling'

In the previous chapter we have seen that most media material circulating across continents is produced by Euro-American media organizations. They primarily employ Western media people to cater to Western media audiences. Non-Western media people and non-Western media audiences play only secondary roles. This is particularly true for news. Not only do most major definers come from the US and other Anglophone settler states, from Great Britain and France, but even within these societies certain social groups are over-represented within key segments of the intelligentsia and of journalism.

The French sociologist Pierre Bourdieu has published a long series of studies on the question of how societal élites tend to reproduce themselves and consolidate their positions. He says this does not only depend on their economic capital, but also on their cultural capital. Early on in life, middle-class children acquire a middle-class habitus, for instance, a habitual way of thinking, feeling and acting. They may also find it easier to deal with school and other cultural institutions, which are organized according to middle-class norms and values. Therefore, they will be over-represented within higher-level professional schools and universities. Even within a purely meritocratic system, they will therefore find it easier to acquire the knowledge and skills necessary to occupy higher, and more central, positions within the social pyramid. The net effect is, that this naturalizes and consolidates the advantage they had over others from the start. This mechanism applies to the journalistic profession, as well as to the intelligentsia in general.

Most journalists are middle-class in social background, social position and social aspirations (even if there are considerable variations between upper and lower, old and new middle class). This holds particularly for the international affairs field, which requires certain language skills and social networks. Worldwide, the vast majority of influential journalists have English or another major Western language as a mother tongue, and the nationality of an Anglo-Saxon or other major Western country. Most consider themselves to hold liberal or centre-left leanings, and believe this offsets possible conservative or centre-right tendencies within the social organizations they depend upon (that is, among media owners). Needless to say, these 'moderate' political labels apply to the Western political spectrum, and to that alone; within a non-Western political context they might well be labelled 'extreme'. Traditionalists, for instance, might consider them decadent on lifestyle issues, or social reformers might consider them wishy-washy on radical change. But even these terms are misleading, as they suggest that the West occupies the ideological middle ground. The reverse is true: such notions were introduced from a Western perspective in the first place.

Let us once again take a closer look at the most influential media country, the United States of America. Some ten years ago, a survey by Weaver and Wilhoit (1986) concluded that 'the "typical" US journalist is a white protestant male who has a bachelor's degree, is married and has children, is middle-of-the-road politically, is thirty-two years old, and earns about $19,000 a year.' Shoemaker and Reese (1991: 55–9) add that the relatively low age and income result from the fact that journalism is primarily 'a young person's career': many people start out as journalists, but move on to other better-paid communication professions in mid-career, by becoming information officers, public relations consultants and the like.

In the context of intercultural reporting, it is particularly revealing that most managers are white. On the very day that I was writing the first version of these lines, the *New York Times* carried an editorial on a major investigation which a bipartisan commission had carried out on behalf of the US Secretary of Labour. Its eloquent title was 'The glass [ceiling] is really there'. Its conclusion was:

> Despite 30 years of affirmative action, 95 per cent of senior management positions are still held by white men, who constitute only 43 per cent of the work force . . . White women hold close to 40 per cent of the jobs in middle management, but black women hold only 5 per cent and black men even less. Something is blocking their further advance up the ladder, and it is not just a lack of qualified candidates moving through the pipeline. (*International Herald Tribune*, 17 March; see also 18–19 March, 1995)

All this confirmed what earlier studies had reported over the previous dozen years in the field of the media too.

If the employment of minorities in North America is skewed, there is no reason to believe that it is any better in Western Europe. Although film studios and broadcasting channels, magazines and newspapers have, over the last dozen years or so, promoted some minority representatives to positions of high visibility, they are still far from anything even distantly resembling proportionality. In a sense, the situation is even worse. On the one hand, there are not even good and reliable statistics, because of the variety of minorities and nations involved. On the other hand, there are few strong minority pressure groups within the European Union (certainly not across borders), which could push for improvement.

Secondary socialization: professionalism

Journalists belong not only to a culture and a subculture, they also belong to a profession. Professional groups (although sometimes large and extremely varied) share certain ways of doing and seeing things; they share an additional subculture of professionalism. Around the mid-eighties, the US Bureau of Labour Statistics counted close to a million people in media occupations: reporters and correspondents; writers and editors; photographers and camera operators; radio and TV announcers and newscasters; actors, directors and producers; marketing, advertising and public relations managers and specialists. A few years earlier, the total news workforce had already been estimated at well over one 100,000 people (Shoemaker and Reese, 1991: 53). Of course, their contribution to 'the creation of the world' is quite unequal. Only a small proportion working for key media can be considered real opinion-makers; most of the others follow their leads. But certain views are shared widely throughout the profession.

To what extent can journalism be considered a true profession, with its own ideology (for instance, the ideology of objectivity)? Free or independent professions 'inherit, preserve and pass on a tradition . . . they engender modes of life, habits of thought and standards of judgment which render them centres of resistance to crude forces which threaten steady and peaceful evolution' (Carr-Saunders and Wilson, quoted by Johnson, 1993: 14). The sociology of professions and professionalism has evolved considerably over the last few decades. It started out with a 'trait theory' of professions, based on classical but peculiar cases such as lawyers and doctors. Then followed functionalist and structural approaches, monopoly control and cultural theories.

The last two approaches are particularly relevant here. Andrew Abbott (1988: 2, 225) acknowledges that 'an effective historical sociology of professions must begin with case studies of jurisdictions and jurisdiction disputes.' It is true that 'the news jurisdiction has steadily grown in size and importance through this century, and the incumbent profession of journalism has come to extraordinary power.' But at the same time 'journalism remains a very permeable occupation; mobility between journalism and public relations is quite common, as is mobility between journalism and other forms of writing.' Only a broad, 'action sociological' definition is appropriate here, it seems:

> Professionalization is the striving of an occupational group to get the societal significance of its occupation accepted in accordance with its own conception of it; in order to accomplish this one does not only attempt to extend and shape professional activities, but also to legitimate them.
> (Schütte and Mok, quoted by Van der Krogt, 1981: 93)

This is reflected in various elements.

The first element is the existence (and gradual expansion) of professional education, in which students acquire the necessary skills, knowledge, but also professional ideology – through curricula indirectly supervised by the state in some countries. In the US, more than 340 universities give bachelors' degrees in journalism and mass communication today. By the mid-eighties, these institutions were already awarding more than 20,000 bachelors' degrees annually – more than six times the number just twenty years earlier (Shoemaker and Reese, 1991: 59–60). In the Netherlands, several universities have introduced a post-graduate degree in journalism in recent years, to compete with (and eventually outdo) a limited number of professional journalism schools. Today, almost three-quarters of newly employed journalists have a degree from a university or a professional school.

A second element is the existence of some kind of licensing or registration system, in this case the system of press cards issued by appropriate bodies (or a press visa). The profession gives certain privileges, such as greater access to authorities, institutions and events. This has to be balanced by obligations to prove that one is a bona fide, full-time (or most of the time) representative of the profession and/or that one is assigned by a legitimate media organization. Of course, certain well-known journalists working for well-known media can often do without such a press card, but for an anonymous free-lancer it is much better to have one.

The third element is the existence of more or less representative professional organizations including a large part of the profession. They usually restrict their membership, act strategically and tactically to try and protect the interests and the image of the profession as a whole, and often go out of their way to condemn 'quackery and charlatanism'. The US, for instance, has its Society of Professional Journalists; Holland has its Nederlandse Vereniging voor Journalisten. Such national associations often belong to international federations as well. They have their annual conferences, publications, and the like.

In his book on *Professions and Power* (1993), Terence Johnson observes:

> a developed network of communication and a high level of interaction through branches, discussion groups, journals, 'social occasions', etc., all help to maintain the subculture and mores of the occupation ... Ritualistic elements are significant; legends, symbols and stereotypes operate in the public sphere to formulate public attitudes to the profession ... A highly developed community language or jargon performs the double function of maintaining internal homogeneity and increasing autonomy from

outsiders, both competing specialists and laymen . . . Prestige within the occupation is dependent upon colleague evaluation . . . In all service-related matters the occupational community is believed to be wiser than the layman . . . Professionalism creates occupations with a high degree of self-consciousness, and 'complete identity'. (pp. 55–7)

The fourth element is the proclamation of a 'code of ethics' by the professional organization, and even the introduction of some kind of limited jurisdiction to guard against breaking the rules: an ombuds-man, or a special commission or council. Such bodies may not be able to impose real sanctions, other than occasionally reclaiming a press card or forfeiting someone's membership of the professional organiza-tion. But its public condemnation of certain practices, journalists, media, may affect their stature and effectiveness – particularly if it happens repeatedly. This professional jurisdiction is meant to supple-ment state jurisdiction, but also acts to ward off outside intervention.

The fifth element is that the profession has usually succeeded to some degree in having its view (that it performs a public service in the general interest) accepted by most of society – or at least its élites. Its relative autonomy is condoned because this intermediary level is 'seen as a positive force in social development, standing against the excesses of both laissez-faire individualism and state collectivism' (Johnson, 1993: 12). In the case of journalism and the media, there have been many complaints about abuses over the years, but the general feeling in most Western countries is that freedom of expression must prevail. Yet this cannot change the fact that some ideas are more freely expressed than others.

Vertical hierarchy: tertiary socialization and co-optation

Although most journalists think of themselves as free and auto-nomous, almost all work in (or are dependent upon) hierarchical organizations with goals of their own. Today, most Western media and news-gathering organizations are primarily run as businesses. That is to say, the owners expect a return on their investment. They want income up and costs down. They want advertisers pleased, major sources available, no libel suits from powerful individuals or institutions, no dysfunctional controversies. Apart from that, they rarely impose their views directly (although this happens on occasion, particularly with tycoons).

The owners hire editors to develop a particular format at a well-defined price for a well-defined audience. These editors in their turn hire journalists and other staff to carry out the work within these guidelines. They assign jobs and scan the resulting stories. New-comers are co-opted from the top, not elected from the bottom. At the same time, the rules of this game are hardly ever made explicit. Early in a career, the journalist watches anxiously what editors and senior colleagues seem to do and want, whereas editors and others watch closely how junior colleagues perform. Small hints may speak volumes.

Organizational socialization is a particular type of tertiary social-ization, with the recruit growing into one actual organization. Frederic Jablin (in Roloff and Berger, 1982: chapter 8) has outlined 'an assimilation approach' to 'the process by which organizational members become a part of, or are absorbed into, the culture of an organization' (that is, a daily newspaper or a broadcasting network). He distinguishes three stages. The initial or 'pre-arrival' stage includes 'forming expectations about jobs', that is to say about the profession, the organization and one's role in it. The subsequent or 'encounter' stage 'involves a pattern of day-to-day experiences in which the individual is subjected to the reinforcement policies and practices of the organization and its members'. The final or 'metamorphosis' stage includes developing a new self-image, new relationships, new values and new behaviours – including the vital distinction between pivotal, relevant and peripheral behaviours. This is done on the basis of both formal and informal communication, explicit and implicit messages, from superiors as well as colleagues (see also Shoemaker, 1991: 59–60).

The professional and organizational socialization of journalists and similar groups, and their actual internalization of the values involved, is extremely important. The sociologist Gaye Tuchman (1978) noted that:

> Since most of the reportorial work of gathering information takes place either outside the newsroom or over the telephone, editors cannot supervise this process. Direct supervision of the work process (rather than the product) would require an expensive organizational investment in more editorial personnel. News organizations maintain flexibility and save money . . . by encouraging professionalism among reporters . . . [that is] knowing how to get a story that meets organizational needs and standards. (pp. 65–6)

Is this borne out by the study of how actual newspeople work? Another sociologist, Warren Breed, was the author of an early disser-tation on *The Newspaperman, News and Society*. He conducted extensive interviews with 120 newsmen from small and middle-sized papers. A resulting article (Breed, 1960) dealt with the question of how 'social control in the newsroom' is maintained. There seemed to be a paradox, he noted.

> Top leaders in formal organizations are makers of policy, but they must also secure and maintain conformity to that policy at lower levels. The situation of the newspaper publisher is a case in point. As owner or representative of ownership, he has the nominal right to set the paper's policy and see that staff activities are coordinated so that the policy is

enforced. In actuality the problem of control is less simple, as the literature of 'human relations' and informal group studies and of the professions suggest.

Identification with the organization and morale seemed to be the keys, since rules were largely internalized.

There were several reasons for staffers' conformity, Breed concluded. Of course there were (1) institutional authority and sanctions, but also: (2) feelings of obligation and esteem for superiors; (3) mobility aspirations; (4) absence of conflicting group allegiance; (5) the pleasant nature of the activity (namely the in-group in the news-room, the interesting nature of the required operations and the non-financial perquisites). Point number 6, he said, was that news tended to become internalized as a value in itself. Under certain conditions, however, reporters could indeed succeed in bypassing policy, for instance, when the policy was not entirely clear in the area, when executives were ignorant of key facts, when reporters had star status, etc.

One might add that it is easier to be tolerated as a dissident within a major news organization if one starts out as a conformist, and climbs through the ranks before turning into a nonconformist, rather than starting out as a nonconformist and never acquiring the necessary leeway to make an impact. In the latter case, one is condemned to strike out on one's own, without organizational backing.

Horizontal processing: gatekeeping and shaping

Individual journalists are not only embedded in a vertical organization, but also in a horizontal organization of work. Very often, they receive news material, edit it and dispatch it to the next person in the assembly line. The editing process involves a number of acts: selection of elements, reviewing the sequence, reviewing the words or images, etc. It is obvious that the news editor has a key role in the production process. Selection is inevitable. Walter Lippmann (1947: 338) already noted that: 'All the reporters in the world working all the hours of the day could not witness all the happenings in the world.' And even if they could, someone would still have to sift through their reports: a so-called gatekeeper.

A recent monograph on *Gatekeeping* by Pamela Shoemaker (1991) traced the origins of the concept to the German-American social psychologist Kurt Lewin. He first mentioned the idea of channels being controlled by gatekeepers applying certain rules in a study on food chains, and added that it might also be used 'for the travelling of a news item through certain communication channels in a group' (p. 9). Kurt Lewin was one of the founders of the field of group dynamics, and few communication scientists seem to be aware of the fact that a number of early experiments actually investigated this process. Subjects were put in a series of boxes which were literally connected by channels, through which notes could be received and passed on again.

David Manning White learned about the concept of gatekeeping when he was a research assistant at the University of Iowa. He persuaded a 45-year-old wire editor on a small-city newspaper to keep all wire copy he received from three news agencies (AP, UPI and INS) during one full week and to provide brief explanations on why he 'as a representative of his culture' had kept or rejected each individual item. Interestingly enough, the editor proved inclined to reproduce spontaneously both the emphasis of the news agencies and the proportion devoted to various subjects. Another researcher repeated the study with the same 'Mr Gates' seventeen years later and found that little had changed. We discussed research on the news criteria themselves in Chapter 2.

It is important to retain two things at this point: on the one hand the amount of selection, and on the other hand the repetition of selection. An AP veteran said that only 20 per cent of the scores of thousands of words which cross AP and UPI foreign desks each day are relayed to subscribers. A Dutch study reported that smaller national news agencies relayed only 50 per cent of the international news they received. The original 'Mr Gates' in turn used only 10 per cent of the wire copy he received for his newspaper (Rosenblum, 1981: 113; Servaes and Tonnaer, 1992: 62; Shoemaker, 1991: 10). This suggests that often only 1 per cent of the news material available at the international agencies hits the pages of ordinary newspapers.

Along the way, there is repeated selection. Certain news items are successively processed by one or more eyewitnesses, one or more official sources, a stringer or free-lancer, a foreign correspondent or a regional desk, one or more editors at the headquarters of the inter-national news agency, a national news agency, a newspaper or a broadcasting station. McQuail (1983: 115) concedes that such sequential gatekeeping may indeed lead to repeated filtering:

> The evidence is insufficient to be certain about this, except perhaps in cases of news flow, but the probability is that much the same criteria are applied at each stage, thus in the process reinforcing any bias or tendency of content or form and diminishing the chances of variety, uniqueness and unpredictability. Here bias may mean no more than an accentuation of content characteristics which, (1) lend themselves to easy processing and (2) are believed to meet the market criteria (audience demand).

But there is another point which is noteworthy here. The gate-keeping metaphor tends to draw attention to the 'inevitable' selection processes, and away from the concurrent reinterpretation processes going on (reorganization, shifting emphasis, rephrasing, injection of new elements, etc.). As a matter of fact, the same tradition of social psychology and group dynamics has produced laboratory experiments on the serial distortion often occurring under such circumstances. Everyone knows the classroom game whereby an ambiguous message is whispered to one pupil, who will have to whisper it on to the next, and so on. It turns out that such messages are often remoulded, remodelled and reshaped along the way – and brought more into line with the preoccupations and presuppositions of the participants.

The rumour researchers Allport and Postman (1947) identified three processes in this regard: levelling (of dissonant elements), sharpening (of consonant elements) and assimilation (into existing views). They basically add up to a further alienation of others, and a further recognition of familiar people and events. As we will see, there is every reason to believe that such processes are also at work in high-pressure news-gathering and news-distribution, particularly if the news comes from a distant culture, and has to be presented to one's own.

Peer groups: conformity and *esprit de corps*

Even more important than the vertical and horizontal organization of news-gathering, however, are peer groups both inside and outside one's own media organization. Most reporters cover a limited domain. That is to say, they return to the same type of institutions and the same type of events on a regular basis, for instance, a ministerial press briefing or an environmental disaster. They will therefore continually meet the same colleagues on both scheduled and unscheduled occasions. They may even visit the same places when they are off-duty, such as journalists' cafés or press clubs. And they will try to reduce their own uncertainties by intensively exchanging definitions of the situation with their peers.

Timothy Crouse showed this in a famous study on election reporting, entitled *The Boys on the Bus: Riding with the Campaign Press Corps* (1973). He said working and living in such stable groups every day created

> womblike conditions that gave rise to the notorious phenomenon called 'Pack journalism' (also known as 'herd journalism' and 'fuselage journalism'). A group of reporters were assigned to follow a single candidate for weeks or months at a time, like a pack of hounds sicked on a fox. Trapped on the bus or plane, they ate, drank, gambled, and compared notes with the same bunch of colleagues week after week. Actually, this group was as hierarchical as a chess set. The pack was divided into cliques – the national political reporters . . .

and also the campaign reporters, the wire-service men, the network correspondents and other configurations (p. 7).

Similar types of interaction occur between journalists covering the same institution or region, a state visit abroad or a major crisis. Transient peer groups emerge in all such situations; they are usually loose and informal, and subject to opposing forces. On the one hand, they are competitors: they will all try to find that little extra information, that slightly different angle, which makes their report stand out from the rest. On the other hand, they are accomplices: they may swap basic facts and elementary leads, they may concur at 'grilling' a source, they may converge in framing an issue in a certain way.

There is no clear border between the in-group and the out-group; it is a series of concentric circles instead. The inner in-group is defined by cronyism, the outer out-group is defined by ostracism. Someone who broke the implicit rules, for instance, may be silently excluded from the exchange – without this ever being said aloud. Furthermore, there is an implicit pecking order with the more prestigious journalists of the most prestigious media at the top and the least prestigious at the bottom.

The important thing to note is that journalists function as each other's prime reference group. They may say that they do this or that because 'the audience wants it.' But their actual contact with the audience is extremely limited (usually to a few family members and occasional neighbours). By contrast, they are in almost daily touch with peers. Recognition by those same peers is usually much more central and important. Janis (1972) noted that 'groupthink' was promoted by high pressures in international policy-making and crisis management. Shoemaker (1991: 27–9) has proposed to apply the concept to journalism as well. It refers to 'a deterioration of mental efficiency, reality testing, and moral judgment that results from ingroup pressures'. The concept has been criticized for several shortcomings (see 't Hart, 1990). Yet it may well apply to phenomena such as 'media lynchings' and 'pack journalism' (to which we will return in Chapter 7).

One might add that media themselves also function as each other's prime reference group in many other ways. Ideas for items on the TV evening news (or TV talk shows) often come straight from the papers, while the lead items in the morning papers often derive from the TV evening news. If a few media hype an issue, others will often feel forced to follow. Here again, the most prestigious media are obviously more influential. In each country, most journalists tend to follow only a few of the same dailies, weeklies and TV programmes. They are the news-makers, the trend-setters. If they define something as important, it is important, and will often become more important still.

Finally, in spite of all competition, the journalistic profession shares with others (physicians, lawyers) a strong *esprit de corps*. Journalists who differ on many scores will often be unanimous in defending each other's prerogatives (keeping sources confidential, dismissing libel charges) and in fighting off outside criticism.

Occupational values and rituals

Just like some other occupations, journalism has an occupational ideology. O'Sullivan and others (1988: 161–2) sum it up thus:

> Occupational ideologies are informal codes, though they may be backed by institutional bodies with quite extensive powers (for example, the British Medical Association). Once initiated, a practitioner of the occupation will be expected to conform to this code in a spontaneous and routine way – it is not so much a rule book as a role model. Occupational ideologies are characterized by esoteric, specialist or jargon language, which is in fact a discourse that both marks and regulates the job . . . Clearly occupational ideologies will also include the historically amassed knowledges, myths and anecdotes which serve the internal solidarity, working practices and general social/political interests of the group in question.

Typical myths of the journalistic profession range from the Tintin comic strip to the film *All the President's Men* with Robert Redford and Dustin Hoffman in the heroic roles of the *Washington Post* 'investigative reporters' Bob Woodward and Carl Bernstein uncovering the Watergate scandal – leading to the impeachment of President Richard Nixon.

More specifically, however, occupational ideologies also bring certain frames of mind: 'patterns of cognition, interpretation and presentation, of selection, emphasis, and exclusion'. Gitlin (1980: 7) noted that 'Frames enable journalists to process large amounts of information quickly and routinely: to recognize it as information, to assign it to cognitive categories, and to package it for efficient relay to audiences. Thus, for organizational reasons alone, frames are unavoidable, and journalism is organized to regulate their production' (see also Shoemaker, 1991: 49).

Occupational ideologies and frames translate into specific techniques of news-gathering. Tuchman (1978: 160) says that 'By stressing methods – gathering supplementary evidence, presenting conflicting truth-claims, imputing facts through familiarity with police procedures, and using quotation marks, to name some techniques . . . newsworkers produced a full-blown version of the web of facticity.' We will return to these procedures and their hidden implications later. Tuchman also mentions 'strategic rituals of objectivity' in this regard. The claim that there is no ideology (or that it does not play a major role) seems to be the key element in the professional ideology.

Sigal (in Manoff and Schudson, 1987: 15–16) puts it this way:

Objectivity in journalism denotes a set of rhetorical devices and procedures used in composing a news story. Objectivity, in this sense, has no bearing whatsoever on the truthfulness or validity of a story. Nor does it mean that the story is free of interpretation or bias. No procedure can assure truth or validity or avoid interpretation and bias. Objective reporting means avoiding as much as possible the overt intrusion of the reporter's personal values into a news story and minimizing explicit interpretation in writing up the story. Reporters do this by eschewing value-laden vocabulary and by writing in the third-person impersonal, not the first-person personal. Above all, they try to attribute the story, and especially any interpretation of what it means, to sources.

Some of the rhetorical devices which are routinely deployed to emphasize the objectivity and 'factuality' of a news item are related to excessive 'precision' in identifying times (twelve minutes past four in the morning), places (120 yards from the main entrance), objects (a two-pound bomb exploded) and people (said Jan de Vries, a 26-year-old car salesman from Amstelveen, the Netherlands). Several elements stand out in this rhetorical emphasis on 'factuality'.

One such element, which Van Dijk has identified in various news items, is a 'numbers game'. 'News discourse abounds with numerical indications of many kinds: numbers of participants, their age, date and time of events, location descriptions, numerical descriptions of instruments and props (weight, size), and so on', he says.

Again, it is not so much the precision of the numbers that is relevant but rather the fact that numbers are given at all. They may be highly variable among news media, even when using the same news sources, and if incorrect they are seldom corrected in following news items. They are predominantly meant as signals of precision and hence of truthful news. (1988a: 87–8; cf. 1988b: 114)

Others, such as John Allen Paulos (*A Mathematician Reads the Newspaper*, 1993) have challenged the ways in which numbers are often (mis)used and (mis)interpreted.

The objectivity and factuality of news items is artificially staged and emphasized in other ways too. A well-known maxim has it that 'facts are sacred, comment is free', for instance, that the three categories of news, background and opinion should be kept completely separated. This is a worthwhile ideal, but not a realistic proposition. On many occasions, the claim itself may provoke more misunderstandings than it prevents. Nevertheless, the contrast between news, background and comment is emphasized and even dramatized in media presentation conventions.

In many newspapers, news items are not signed by identifiable people, for instance. They may have an anonymous byline saying 'from our staff', 'compiled from agency dispatches', or these agencies may even be identified as institutions: AP, Reuters, AFP, etc. In this way, everything is done to distract attention from the contingent nature of the report. Opinion columns, by contrast, usually display the name of the author prominently, and are often accompanied by a picture of the writer. They are printed in a separate space, often in italics. Their conventions allow for a much more open use of rhetoric and polemics. Although these various categories of text differ only gradually, and might well be placed on a sliding scale, their differences are thus enlarged artificially and reified in presentation.

The same thing happens with television reports, in even more extreme ways. We are almost never told who filmed the international items which we see in the evening news. This keeps us from even trying to guess why they selected and framed these images in this particular way. It artificially reinforces their claim simply to mirror the world as it is. There may be a whirlwind of new and old material, of 'real' and staged events. Theory has it that this should be indicated in superimposed titles, but in practice this rarely happens.

Fully-fledged documentaries, by contrast, usually do show a handful of credits at the end. Here it is suddenly acknowledged that it does make a difference who the producer, the researcher, the journalist, the cameraman, the sound engineer and the editor are. When we move to docudrama or to recognized fiction, this ritual of credits even takes on rather Byzantine and somewhat ridiculous forms. Dozens of assistants and assistant assistants are named in full and the broadcaster is often held by contract to show this entire roll, although the vast majority of these names do not mean a thing to the audience – and never will.

Here again, we see the strategic ritual of the differential staging of objectivity and subjectivity, of anonymity and authorship, to reinforce the illusion of a fundamental difference between news and views.

The example of the event that did not happen demonstrates that journalists are guided by all kinds of social patterns and mental frames in their recognition and reporting of 'the facts'. This is inevitable, and it is better to recognize and accept it than to deny and ignore it. One series of guiding elements can be found in the sociology of professions. They usually tend to play a role in education and degrees, licensing and registration, organization and communication, ethics and sanctions, as well as the public-service image they project of themselves. Often these processes are very subtle indeed. Occupational values and peer groups promote conformity, but there is little overt control, and most representatives of the profession consider themselves free to act as they please.

Notes

1 *Annual Review of Anthropology*, 3 (1981), pp. 73–97. Quoted in W. B. Gudykunst and Y. Y. Kim, *Communicating with Strangers* (1992), pp. 12–13. See also Roger M. Keesing, *Cultural Anthropology* (1981), ch. 4.

2 Jean-Luc Einaudi, *La bataille de Paris* (Paris: Seuil, 1991). See also Anne Tristan, *Le silence du fleuve* (Paris: Syros, 1991). After much hesitation, a first (Anglo-Australian) documentary on the events was only broadcast on 2 March, 1993 (see also *Le Monde,* 26–27 February 1993).

Further reading

Global journalism in practice: Rosenblum. *Culture*: Gudykunst and Kim; Hofstede; Keesing. *Professions*: Abbott; Freidson; Johnson. *Gatekeeping*: Shoemaker. *Groupthink*: Janis; 't Hart. *Journalist peer groups*: Crouse.

5 WHO GETS TO SPEAK IN THE WORLD NEWS?

THE POLITICS OF LOUD AND WHISPERING VOICES

....

News is not what happens, but what someone says has happened or will happen. Reporters are seldom in a position to witness events firsthand. They have to rely on the accounts of others . . .

Readers, whether they are attentive citizens or interested officials, tend to lose sight of the fact that news is not reality, but a sampling of sources' portrayals of reality, mediated by news organizations. To coordinate the activities of their staffs with a modicum of efficiency, newspapers can do little more than establish some standard operating procedures for sampling potential sources. Whatever procedure they adopt unavoidably biases their selection of content.

Leon V. Sigal, 'Sources make the news'.[1]

Journalists play a key role in formulating global media messages, but so do their sources. To what extent do reporters base themselves on neutral observers and eyewitnesses of events and developments? And to what extent do they consistently rely on interested parties, or – worse – on only one of the various interested parties? Do the imperatives of rapid news-gathering drive them to rely on the same 'official' institutional sources again and again? How do these sources play the game? What does all this imply for the 'social construction' of the words and images we read and see about the current state of the world? To what extent do interviews with political experts and ordinary people balance these views? And what about interviews themselves: do quotations really make us hear the unmediated voice of others?

News is based on a selective articulation of certain voices about supposed events: not only the voices of journalists themselves, but also their sources. A few voices can be heard loudly and clearly all the time, but many more voices are drowned out by the noise, and their vague murmur can only be heard intermittently in the background.

Few people are aware of the fact that most major news items are not directly based on eyewitness accounts. This is particularly the case for breaking news, for front-page news. Leon Sigal is the author of a classical study on *Reporters and Officials: The Organization and Politics of Newsmaking* (1973). He analysed a representative sample of 2,850 domestic and foreign news stories that appeared prominently in two major American quality papers over a period of twenty-five years. He found at the time that

> as a consequence of reporters' social location, newsgathering routines, and journalistic conventions, nearly half of the sources for all national and foreign news stories on page one of the *New York Times* and the *Washington Post* were officials of the United States government. Most transmitted information through routine newsgathering channels – press releases, press conferences and official proceedings.

Note that other sources were officials of other governments, major corporations and other established institutions. A total of more than three-quarters of all identifiable sources were official ones (Sigal, 1973: 121). Nearly a quarter-century later, a similar study of six daily newspapers, and another one on television news, confirmed that proportions were still about the same.[2] Michael Schudson concluded: 'This reality – that news gathering is normally a matter of the representatives of one bureaucracy picking up prefabricated news items from representatives of another bureaucracy – is at odds with all of the romantic self-conceptions of American journalism' (Manoff and Schudson, 1987: 25, 81–2).

British studies come to similar conclusions:

> The routine activity of news production is heavily dependent upon and directed towards these official and accredited sources and their representatives. As a consequence, a good deal of news coverage tends to reproduce and translate the interpretative frameworks and definitions generated by primary definers, and in such a way the media usually operate as secondary definers. (O'Sullivan et al., 1988: 181)

The American *Project Censored* claimed, for instance, that certain issues have a radically diminished chance of making major news, among other things because of this heavy reliance on 'official' spokesmen. Its 'top ten' of ignored stories for one particular year included repeated incidents with nuclear plants, preparations for biological warfare and the extensive use of radioactive material in spacecraft (Shoemaker and Reese, 1991: 95).

Entire segments of reality are framed by the way in which information officers and PR officials routinely (mis)represent certain subjects to the press. In the case of bank robberies, the financial institution will often not reveal the real amount of money missing but a much lower estimate, in order not to encourage repetition. In the case of a train stoppage, the railway service will often not say that someone committed suicide and that this happens quite often, because it might affect the image of public transport and its passenger potential. There are always good reasons, but the question is whether the media should pass on information which they may suspect to be imprecise or incomplete.

Agenda-setting: an alternative approach

Some classical authors in communication studies (such as Walter Lippmann) had already hinted at the process of agenda-setting and mental map-making, but the first postwar author to devote considerable attention to it was the American political scientist Bernard Cohen, in a study on *The Press and Foreign Policy* (1963). He noted:

> The press is significantly more than a purveyor of information and opinion. It may not be successful in telling its readers what to think, but it is stunningly successful in telling its readers what to think about. And it follows from this that the world looks different to different people, depending not only on their personal interests, but also on the map that is drawn for them by the writers, editors and publishers of the papers they read. Perhaps the notion of a map is too confining, for it does not suggest the full range of the political phenomena that are conveyed by the press. It is, more properly, an atlas of places, personages, situations, and events; and to the extent that the press even discusses the ideas that men have for coping with the day's ration of problems, it is an atlas of possibilities, alternatives, choices. (p. 13)

The interesting thing is that Cohen was very interested in how the press affected the agenda of the public on foreign-policy issues. He devoted much less attention to how – even before that stage – the foreign-policy élite affected the agenda of the press and how, in doing so, it also affected the agenda of the public. An agenda is a list of things one has to think about and/or act upon. An individual has an agenda, a committee meeting has an agenda, an organization has an agenda. If one has the power to set other people's agendas, one does to a certain extent have the power to influence what they will think and talk about, to draw attention to certain elements and divert it away from others. A major information-provider may therefore be a major agenda-setter for others. Accordingly, certain sources have the power to set some of the media's agenda, and certain media have the power to set some of the public's agenda. The two processes are inextricably linked.

A first major research project on the mechanism was related to election research. McCombs and Shaw (1972) noted an almost perfect correlation between the agenda of five dailies, two weeklies and two TV networks on the one hand, and the personal agenda of some hundred 'undecided voters' on the other. Crime and terrorism – which are often enlarged out of proportion in normal news coverage – are good examples. The same holds true for public diplomacy and international affairs. If a government has the power to put certain issues on the agenda of the world media, it may also exert considerable influence on world opinion.

The United States government has this power, more than any other institution in the world. But the British, French and some other governments also have some of this power. Quite regularly (every other month or so), for instance, the US government claims satellite observations show that this or that hostile government is importing sensitive technology, is building unconventional weapons plants, is redeploying army units along its frontiers in a 'threatening way'. Most of the time, the world media devote ample room to such accusations. The question whether these other governments have a right to do so (or are bound by international treaties to refrain from doing so) is often completely bypassed on such occasions.

The opposite hardly ever occurs, that is to say, the same sources and media drawing attention to the fact that the US itself is also constantly developing new non-conventional weapons systems and deploying them in ways which their opposite numbers might perceive as threatening. The net effect is that both sources and media constantly put the 'threat' posed by one side on the public agenda, but not the 'threat' posed by the other side. This has a tendency to rig the issue.

Classic examples were the dramatization of the discovery of the presence of Soviet missile sites in Cuba (whereas the previous existence of equivalent American missile sites in Turkey was completely passed over in silence), the 'discovery' of a Soviet army unit near Havana on the eve of the summit of non-aligned countries in that country (whereas the previous presence of American army units in similar countries – and indeed of a huge US military base on Cuba itself – was ignored), the discovery of crates with 'possible' parts of Mig-21 fighters in Nicaragua (whereas the massive military build-up in neighbouring Honduras was treated almost casually). But in fact hardly a month passes without major drummed-up news items in this category.

On such occasions, and in fact on all occasions where some 'threat' to the West is identified, the US government turns out to have a formidable power of setting the agenda of the world's media and even of various UN organs. The question is of course whether this is the result of conscious bias on the part of the reporting journalists, or whether it is the result of further 'blind' professional mechanisms.

Three criteria for news sources

When asked about their choice of sources, most journalists mention two criteria, namely authority and credibility.[3] Communication studies add a third and major one: availability. Let us take a look at how these criteria function in everyday news-gathering routines.

AUTHORITY   A first criterion is said to be the authority of the source, although there is some reason to call it a hierarchical position instead.

It applies to various levels. Within institutional hierarchies, the preferred source is the one who is supposed to be in the know. In general, higher levels are preferred over lower ones, and authorized spokesmen or women are favoured over unauthorized ones, except in the specific case of leaks.

Within looser social movements or opinion currents, the preferred source is one who is supposed to be an informal leader or a typical representative. In his book *The Whole World is Watching* (1980), about the coverage of the American New Left and student movement of the sixties, Todd Gitlin demonstrated that the media tend to co-opt and 'impose' highly vocal and/or colourful people under such circumstances (which may affect the direction and cohesion of such loose alliances). A final possibility is that individual people become celebrities in their own right. In such cases, they may become a potential source of information and comments as well.

CREDIBILITY The second criterion is said to be the credibility of the source, although there is reason to call it suspended doubt instead. Journalists are ready to believe, and have the public believe, some sources and not others. There have been many occasions on which the president or premier or minister of a major Western state was almost certainly known to be lying, yet his or her statements were reported as if they were pure facts. There have been many occasions on which the leader of an anti-Western government, institution or group was almost certainly known to be speaking the truth, yet his or her statements were reported as unconfirmed rumours or allegations. Thus, scepticism is often applied in quite unequal doses.

AVAILABILITY The third and certainly not the least important criterion is the ready availability of sources: during office hours, or – in an emergency – at any time of the day or night. On the one hand, this means their institutional availability. Someone who has an office, a spokesperson, a secretary (or even more than one), obviously has easier access to the media, and can be more readily accessed by the media, than someone who – for one reason or another – has not. On the other hand, this also refers to physical availability. Someone who has an assistant available for talks, for calls or even for fax exchanges, has easier access to the media, and can be more readily accessed by the media, than someone who is not. Since having a permanent office is so decisive, it is not surprising that official information prevails in spot news.

The crucial thing to note here, though, is that the routine application of these three criteria in international news provokes a heavy slant. Since authority, credibility and availability are judged primarily in relation to Western situations, Western audiences and

Are Fleeing North

Bush Insists U.S. Forces Won't Aid Iraqi Rebels

destroy earlier, President Hussein first quelled protest in southern cities, then turned his forces north to crush Kurdish revolt and remove the rebels from all major towns in the north.

Kurds are a non-Arab M people spread through Turk Iran, Iraq and Syria. They have many campaigns for autonom and are treated with hostility by of their host governments.

As reported, the exodus under way far exceeds the proj of the last major flight of ds from Iraqi attack in late But it nonetheless resuscit memories of that period, when 00 Kurds trudged into Turke telling of Baghdad's use of ical weapons against them.

A Turkish jou, just re-turned from nort Iraq, said Iraqi helicopters using phosphorous bombs st fugitives.

Although a rdish rebel spokesman in D cus said that the fighting had ned in the oil town of Kirkuk United States said that Iraq s occupied all major cities he same time, Washington acknowledged signs of unre ural areas. The official Iran press agency, IRNA, some fighting continuing in the southern port Basra, Iraq's second city.

In Dama a leading Iraqi Shiite cleric, stollah Moham-med Taqi M ni, said: "Planes and helicop bombing roads, leading to S Turkey and Iran, which are d with hundreds of thousands of s fleeing on foot from the sav ty of the regime.

Tehran d tens of thou-sands of K in 25,000 vehicles were waiti cross into Iran. Turkish offi accused Iraq of trying to d 220,000 Kurds across the rn border into Turkey.

After the e on Kurdish dissent in 19 President Hussein ordered a b icized campaign to destroy K rdsh villages and mov ts either to the cities th ow abandoned or into south q.

Bush Allowed CIA Aid to Iraq Rebels

The Associated Press
WASHINGTON — President

The findings were approved at about the same time the president

---

The Associated Press

JUPITER, Florida — President George Bush said Wednesday he had no intention of permitting U.S. forces to get involved in Iraq's internal struggles, saying "we've done the heavy lifting" and it was now time for the Iraqi people to resolve matters for themselves.

Mr. Bush, speaking with reporters after he finished a round of golf as he ended a four-day vacation, also said that he was willing to take "a new look" at restoring normal diplomatic ties with Iraq should a new government replace President Saddam Hussein.

They were Mr. Bush's first full comments on the situation in Iraq since he began his vacation on Sunday.

Asked about suggestions by the Senate Democratic leader, George J. Mitchell of Maine, and others that U.S. troops in Iraq be permitted to shoot down Iraqi combat helicopters, Mr. Bush said:

"We are not there to intervene. It is not our purpose. It never was our purpose."

"I do not want to see us get sucked into the internal struggle in Iraq," he said.

Mr. Bush said he had no intention "to commit our men and our women to further combat."

"We've done the heavy lifting," he said.

The president spoke to reporters in a rainstorm on the 18th hole b' the Jupiter Hills Golf Club. He was also to visit his ailing mother, Dorothy Walker Bush, 89, in nearby Hobe Sound before returning to Washington on Wednesday night.

He was to participate on his ar rival at Andrews Air Force Base near Washington in a live television salute to returning U.S. troops.

Mr. Bush declined to comment on the subject of a secret mission last week by his national security adviser, Brent Scowcroft, to Saudi Arabia and possibly other Middle Eastern countries. Asked if Mr. Scowcroft had been to Lebanon and Iran, the president said, "There are certain things that are better to keep quiet."

The president was asked if he would consider restoring normal relations with Iraq if Saddam Hussein was forced from office by the military. "I would be willing to take a new look if the army took matters into its own hands," he said.

He also renewed his prediction that Mr. Hussein would not remain in power much longer. "I'm still confident he won't be," Mr. Bush said. "I don't think he can survive. I don't think he will survive."

ROCKET: *U.S. 'Star Wars' Plan*

(Continued from page 1)

punch than conventional ones, whose engines are energized by chemical reactions that often involve the explosive burning of oxygen and hydrogen.

The reactor in the proposed rocket would heat liquid hydrogen to very high temperatures and blast it out the engine's nozzle in a gaseous vortex, creating a stupendous roar of thrust.

The standard measure of rocket performance is known as specific impulse, the length of time a pound of a given propellant produces a pound of thrust. The higher the specific impulse, the more dazzling the engine. The space shuttle's main engines — the most efficient rocket engines in the world, fueled by liquid hydrogen and liquid oxygen — have a specific impulse of 455 seconds.

The planned engines would have a specific impulse of more than 900 seconds.

Part of the reactor's secret is its high temperature, which is more than 3,000 degrees Fahrenheit (1,652 degrees centigrade), Mr. Al-terpool said. Conventional nuclear reactors usually operate at around 600 degrees Fahrenheit (314 degrees centigrade). The planned reactor would use tiny particles of

---

Figure 5.1   *Selective credulity. The US president is the most frequently cited and 'most' authoritative source for the Western media. News agencies and newspapers are reluctant to openly challenge his credibility in matters of national security. They would rather place an entirely separate (and slightly less prominent) item carefully attributed to another 'authoritative source' in Washington. (From the International Herald Tribune, 4 April 1991 and reproduced by permission of Associated Press.)*

Western editors, they also have a heavy tendency to favour Western official sources. The limits of acceptable discourse are judged by Western majority standards, thereby marginalizing other voices. Hearing other sides and checking information are done only within this overall framework, not outside it. Once some person or group is defined as weird or hostile, he or she is easily dismissed as a potential source of information or even checks – sometimes without justification.

IOU AND THE DANCE   There is still another way to put this. Mutual access between sources and journalists (particularly those in regular contact) is mostly regulated by proximity, both physical and social proximity. In Chapter 7 (on worldwide news flow), we will see again that news from the world periphery is often defined and refracted by 'authorities and experts' in the world centres. But even within the world periphery itself, journalistic representatives of the world centres are often close to the economic, social and political representatives of the world centres. They have gone to the same schools and universities, have mutual friends and acquaintances, move in the same circles, share more or less the same general world-views.

Within both the world centres and the world periphery, Western journalists and Western sources also belong to the same token economy, regulated by an invisible currency of IOUs (I owe yous). They are implicitly aware of the fact that they need each other, that they may contribute to each other's functioning, success and status. Although they know that their interests do not coincide, they will try to maintain a reasonably good everyday working relationship, by sharing snippets of information off the record, for instance, or by concealing the source of such a leak. If one party grossly upsets the balance of these implicit rules, he or she knows this will have negative consequences for their further relationship – or may even end it altogether.

The larger part of the world news is the product of such mechanisms of mutual access: the easy access of élite sources to élite media, and the easy access of élite media to élite sources. In the study *Deciding What's News* (1980), Gans has likened this to a dance, and added: 'Although it takes two to tango, either sources or journalists can lead, but more often than not, sources do the leading. Staff and time being in short supply, journalists actively pursue only a small number of regular sources who have been available and suitable in the past, and are passive toward other possible news sources' (p. 116).

Whereas contacts between establishment news sources and journalists in the world centres are almost continuous, contacts between alternative news sources and journalists in the world periphery are quite exceptional. Spokesmen for slum neighbourhood committees, rural labour unions, indigenous people's organizations and outlawed guerrilla movements or even 'average' poor people, are quoted only when there is a major crisis at hand – and even then in very specific ways.

Sound bites, photo opportunities and spin control

Powerful people and their PR consultants have become increasingly adept at image control. They are aware that they can often dictate the terms of a news item, if only they work with certain technical rules, such as the following ones. Deny direct access whenever it does not suit your purpose. Plan a news event and/or news release in relation to news deadlines. See to it that the speech or statement contains one highly condensed and colourful phrase, the ideal quote or sound-bite. See to it that the subject is in one particular place, and that all cameras are kept in another, so that the angle and backdrop can be controlled to provide the ideal image or photo opportunity. This backdrop may include a flag or some other well-chosen authoritative and/or patriotic symbol.

The insider Hedrick Smith explored such strategies in his book *The Power Game: How Washington Works* (1988). The White House communications director, David Gergen, proved quite open:

> We had a rule in the Nixon operation, that before any public event was put on his schedule, you had to know what the headline out of that event was going to be, what the picture was going to be, and what the lead paragraph would be . . . One of Nixon's rules about television was that it was very important that the White House determine what the line coming out from the president was and not let the networks determine that, not let New York edit you. You had to learn how to do the editing yourself.

Gergen later made a practice of calling network correspondents at the last minute from the White House, knowing that they would be obliged to include – or at least acknowledge – it in their comments (Shoemaker and Reese, 1991: 109–10).

Whereas Nixon failed to control his own media image in the end, Reagan was extremely successful. His aide Michael Deaver went even further with a two-pronged strategy. Since his boss was notoriously ill-informed and forgetful, he reduced the number of regular press conferences to a minimum. Whenever the president left for Camp David, he would see to it that the helicopter would be waiting with its engines already running. That provided a nice picture, but no possibility of shouting questions – although a network correspondent, Sam Donaldson, gained notoriety by trying stubbornly. At the same time the president was a consummate movie actor, who could produce prescripted lines in a most natural way, as if they were improvised on the spot. The other part of the strategy, therefore, was to try and bypass journalists altogether and have him address the public directly.

He also introduced the novelty of looking straight into the TV cameras much more often, and thus establishing a direct rapport with the viewers during the whole of a speech. For this purpose a special device was developed. Its basis was a teleprompter: a monitor on which a text is slowly rolled by, so that the speaker can actually read it aloud without seeming to, and without looking down at papers all the time. Reagan's teleprompter was concealed on the floor and its image reflected on a diagonal glass plate between the speaker and the camera. The reflection could only be seen from the standpoint of the speaker. From the standpoint of the camera (and the public) there was only a transparent and therefore invisible glass plate. This contraption enabled the aging president to play directly to the public throughout a long and complicated speech which would have been impossible to memorize. It added intensity and conviction to doctored speeches.

The world's prime news-makers

Over the last few decades, the power of all major Western governments to set the media's agenda has increased accordingly. Paradoxically, the last stage of the expansion process began with the sixties' critique of government secrecy, and the subsequent adoption of openness laws such as the Freedom of Information Act in the US (or the Wet Openbaarheid Bestuur in the Netherlands). In its wake, almost every government institution in the Western world felt obliged to begin its own information service to handle the enquiries of the press and the public. Something similar happened in the business world.

At this point in time, the combined manpower and resources of these information services and public-relations departments vastly exceed the media's capabilities to gather and check information – particularly in the field of international affairs and in crisis situations. Information officers have often become the prime definers of news. Let us take a closer look at the agenda-setting and prime-definition capacity of the major Western government, that of the US, and its main bureaucracies.

THE WHITE HOUSE   The number one news-maker in the world is the White House. In their study *The Age of Propaganda: The Everyday Use and Abuse of Persuasion* (1992), the American social psychologists Anthony Pratkanis and Elliot Aronson quoted political science research indicating that since the early 1960s, US presidents have averaged over twenty-five speeches a month. Many of these speeches are devised so that they will generate news coverage both at home and abroad (even Dutch television evening news has, on average, an item on the US president every other day or so). The psychologists concluded: 'By speaking frequently on certain issues and gaining access to the nightly news, a president can create a political agenda – a picture of the world that is favorable to his or her social policies' (p. 55). On many occasions, this does not affect only the American public, but the Western (or indeed the world) public as a whole.

THE STATE DEPARTMENT The second major news-maker is the State Department, with its network of embassies around the world, doubled by the United States Information Agency and its cultural centres. Mort Rosenblum worked as an international reporter for the Associated Press news agency for decades. He wrote: 'the State Department's noon briefing is an institution. Each day, press officers gather early to scour the papers. During the morning, they huddle with desk officers and their bosses to make up a briefing book. By 12:30, they have defined the world' (1993: 215–16). This definition of the world situation will often trickle down to the front pages of the daily newspapers, the cover stories of the weekly news magazines and the opening reports on the evening news at home and abroad – particularly when there are no authoritative alternative sources at hand.

THE PENTAGON The third major news-maker is the Pentagon. It is one of the largest conglomerates of information gathering and information processing, information withholding and information release in the world – embracing movies, television, radio, newspapers, magazines, books, etc. Its influence on American and Western opinion is immense, for instance by its continuous update on who is a threat to whom. At the time of the Vietnam war, the chairman of the Senate foreign affairs committee, William Fulbright, wrote a book attacking *The Pentagon Propaganda Machine* (1970), saying that it spent more on information than the two major American press agencies, the three major broadcasting networks and the ten major newspapers combined.

Under President Reagan, the Pentagon used to publish a 'factbook' on *Soviet Military Power*, which was updated every few years and became the fundamental source of reference for Western politicians and journalists. The military expert Tom Gervasi thoroughly reviewed its text, figures, pictures and published a completely annotated version. He concluded that every single page contained a number of gross distortions: in terminology, in pictures, in claims, in comparisons. After the end of the Cold War, it turned out that he had been right all along, and that the Russian army had never been the mighty fighting machine that had been portrayed.

Of course, the US government is not the only major Western government which has considerable agenda-setting and prime-

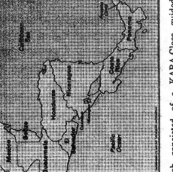

Figure 5.2 The world's prime news-makers. The Pentagon is the major global 'agenda setter' in 'security matters' to politicians, the media and audiences of the US, the West and much of the world. Military expert Tom Gervasi provided detailed 'comments' on a major 160 page Pentagon publication (this figure shows a sample; the notes are outside, the original text is inside the box). (Source: Tom Gervasi (1988) Soviet Military Powers: The Pentagon's Propaganda Document, Annotated and Corrected.)

Soviet delivery of military equipment to Nicaragua set a record in 1986, with numerous seaborne deliveries to Corinto. The 23,000 metric tons included six HIND helicopter gunships, three patrol boats, and numerous armored personnel carriers.

Castro had his first two meetings with Gorbachev. Despite manifestations of close relations at the two congresses, Soviet-Cuban relations continued to be plagued primarily by economic differences. Cuba's hard currency shortage has forced Havana to seek even more financial support from Moscow, but the USSR may not be willing or able to satisfy its partner.

Nicaragua

The Soviet Union's primary objective in Central America is to consolidate the Sandinistas' control of Nicaragua without taking the risk of provoking the US. To this end, the USSR devoted considerable political, economic, and military resources in 1986. Shortly after the US Congress voted to provide $100 million to the Nicaraguan guerrillas, the Soviet Union sent Deputy Foreign Minister Viktor Komplektov to Peru and Venezuela, where he criticized US policy in Central America. The Soviets also launched a propaganda campaign claiming that the US is preparing to invade Nicaragua.

During 1986, the continuing decline of Nicaragua's economy and of non-Communist financial support for the Sandinistas forced the

which consisted of a KARA-Class guided-missile cruiser; a KASHIN-Class guided-missile destroyer, a FOXTROT-Class submarine, and a BORIS CHILIKIN-Class oiler, conducted antisurface, antisubmarine, and antiair exercises with Cuban naval units during the month-long deployment. The Soviet-manned intercept site at Lourdes, the largest outside the USSR, enables Moscow to monitor sensitive US maritime, military, and space communications as well as US domestic telephone calls.

The first session of the 3d Congress of the Cuban Communist Party and the 27th Congress of the Communist Party of the Soviet Union last February highlighted a renewed closeness in Soviet-Cuban political relations. Yegor Ligachev, the second most powerful Kremlin leader, headed the Soviet delegation to the 3d Congress, and President Fidel Castro led the Cuban delegation to the 27th Congress. In Moscow,

Our Navy conducts similar exercises from our own naval base in Cuba—at Guantanamo.

Our National Security Agency has a network of 4,120 intercept sites around the world.

The propagandist's purpose here is to obscure recent history by creating the impression that the Sandinista revolution merely follows a Soviet agenda. Readers who do not know any better might assume from this that the Sandinista revolution was inspired by the Soviet Union, or could not have taken place without Soviet help.

The massive US troop exercises regularly held in Honduras are clearly intended to threaten the Sandinistas with the prospect of a US invasion. Here, the authors try to blame Soviet propaganda, not US troops, for this threat.

definition power with the major Western media and news-gathering organizations. Britain does (for example, on Northern Irish affairs) and France does (for example, on the affairs of certain African countries). The ideological and contingent nature of the statements of their political leaders and their spokesmen is further obscured by the media practice of identifying them with the anonymous institutions as a whole, through the anthropomorphic treatment of the buildings in which they are housed: The White House says and the Pentagon says, Downing Street or Whitehall says, the Élysée, Matignon or the Quai d'Orsay says.

Propaganda and censorship

We need a few words on propaganda and censorship at this point. The traditional conceptualization of these phenomena is extremely deterministic: it is related to the absolute power of a government to get certain things published by all media, and other things by none. This conceptualization limits propaganda and censorship to the brutal and primitive practices of totalitarian and authoritarian governments. A more modern understanding of propaganda and censorship should rather be probabilistic: it should be related to the relative power of a government to get certain things more or less into the public view and to keep other things more or less out of it. This is called information management, news management or issues management. In the US, for instance, it has long been a highly sophisticated practice. Let us take a quick look at the general outline.

PROPAGANDA AND MEDIA MANIPULATION Toward the end of the Vietnam war, US congressional committees launched various investigations into suspicions of repeated media manipulation by the CIA and the FBI. The official reports were censored (at the insistence of former CIA directors William Colby and George Bush, later the US president, among others), but investigative journalists were able to reconstruct the suppressed information anyhow.

The former *Washington Post* reporter Carl Bernstein wrote in *Rolling Stone* magazine (20 October 1977: 55–67), that 'more than 400 American journalists' had 'in the previous 25 years secretly carried out assignments for the Central Intelligence Agency'. This included only those who were 'tasked', not the even larger numbers who 'occasionally traded favors' with the agency. Media which knowingly cooperated, he said, included all major news agencies, AP, UPI and Reuters, major daily newspapers such as the *New York Times*, the major Hearst and Scripps-Howard newspaper groups, both major news weeklies, *Time* and *Newsweek*, all major broadcasting networks,

ABC, CBS and NBC. Assignments ranged from spying to 'planting subtly concocted pieces of misinformation'.

After this publication, two reporters from the *New York Times* itself delved into the issue as well. They wrote that

> The CIA has at various times owned or subsidized more than 50 newspapers, news services, radio stations, periodicals and other communication entities . . . Another dozen foreign-based news organizations, while not financed by the CIA, were infiltrated by paid CIA agents. Nearly a dozen American publishing houses, including some of the most prominent names of the industry, have printed at least a score of more than 250 English-language books financed or produced by the CIA . . .
>
> Since the closing days of World War II, more than 30 and perhaps as many as 100 American journalists employed by a score of American news organizations have worked as salaried intelligence operatives while performing their reportorial duties . . . At one time, according to agency sources, there were as many as 800 such 'propaganda assets', mostly foreign journalists. Asked in an interview last year whether the CIA had ever told such agents what to write, William E. Colby, the former CIA director, replied: 'Oh, sure, all the time' . . . Almost at the push of a button, or so Mr. Wisner [the first chief of the agency's covert action staff] liked to think, the 'Wurlitzer' became the means for orchestrating, in almost any language anywhere in the world, whatever tune the CIA was in a mood to hear.

One CIA man said: 'We "had" at least one newspaper in every foreign capital at any given time' (*New York Times*, 25–27 December, 1977).

After all these publications, official promises were made that this would never be allowed to happen again. Or at least, that media manipulation would be limited to foreign journalists and foreign media, and would not be allowed to affect American policy-makers and the American public. Yet, under the Reagan and Bush presidencies (1980–92) the practice flourished again. One insider report was later published by the man in charge of the PR department and media manipulations in favour of the anti-Sandinista Contra's in Nicaragua (Chamorro, 1987).

The successive American interventions in Cuba, Chile, Grenada, Nicaragua and Panama were all preceded, accompanied and followed by massive campaigns of media manipulation, as was the allied intervention in the Gulf. In such situations, the world's media prove to be extremely vulnerable because of their heavy dependence on just a few official sources. Furthermore, they are rather reluctant to look back upon such instances and draw conclusions from them.

CENSORSHIP AND SELF-CENSORSHIP But since many of these stories did come out (in the end), there is certainly no effective censorship or self-censorship in the US. When the US was divided over Vietnam, the *New York Times* did indeed publish the Pentagon papers and the *Washington Post* did indeed expose the Watergate scandal. But times have changed. The *New York Times* shied away from its muckraker image, and the *Washington Post* toned down its investigative journalism.

Around the mid-eighties, the latter's executive editor Benjamin Bradlee defended himself on this issue.

> First, we do consult with the government regularly about sensitive stories, and we do withhold stories for national security reasons, far more often than people think. The *Washington Post* has withheld information from more than a dozen articles so far this year for these reasons. Second, we do not allow the government – or anyone else – to decide what we should print. (*International Herald Tribune*, 11 June 1986)

That sounds like a strong position, but if we suppose this was an average period, it would mean that the most critical newspaper in the US routinely suppresses such information every two weeks on average, or twenty-five times a year. The well-known investigative reporter Scott Armstrong quitted the paper because of such attitudes. He explained: 'I should make clear that the *Post* is one of the better organizations; they did bring five Freedom of Information lawsuits on my behalf, for example. But there were 200 other instances when the *Post* was illegally denied access to information and did not challenge the government' (Lee and Solomon, 1990: 20).

In spite of all the fuss about the Iran-Contra scandal and the Iraq scandal in the American media, for instance, many of the key issues related to covert drugs smuggling, weapons smuggling, armed intervention, etc. were covered up. Although the major American media were the only ones in a position to find out, none of them really pursued these issues in their entirety. Only bits and pieces were cleared up.

Similar observations can be made in Great Britain, where all major media and foreign correspondents were manipulated for decades on Northern Ireland, as became clear in the Wallace affair, for instance (see Foot, 1990). Philip Knightley wrote an impressive overview of *The First Casualty* (1989) in war: the truth. He said the war correspondent had been a hero, but also a propagandist and myth-maker, from the Crimean war to the Falklands. One might add that this does not hold only for actual war, but also for all affairs stamped 'security matters'.

The problem is, if the major US, UK, French and other media often make themselves subservient to the proclaimed security interests of their own countries, whereas these same media heavily influence coverage in the rest of the world, do they not get a slanted view of who is threatened and who is a threat? This problem is not limited to military matters: it extends to political, economic, social and cultural issues as well.

Experts

If official sources often take the initiative in accessing journalists and media, journalists and media often take the initiative in accessing the other major authoritative voice in the media: experts. Over the years, experts have said a lot of silly things, as highlighted in a hilarious anthology by Cerf and Navasky: *The Experts Speak: The Definitive Compendium of Authoritative Disinformation* (1984). One illuminating example was the optimistic statements of economic authorities and experts (almost unanimous) on the eve of the stock-market crashes of 1929 and 1987 (Van Ginneken, 1993b). Yet journalists keep returning to the same experts again and again. The CBS anchorman Dan Rather, for one, admitted that – like so many other journalists – he always kept going back to 'a shockingly small . . . circle of experts [who] . . . get called upon time after time after time'.

The American authors Martin Lee and Norman Solomon have published a book called *Unreliable Sources: A Guide to Detecting Bias in the News Media* (1990). In the late eighties, at the time when the conservative President Ronald Reagan handed over power to the conservative President Bush, Lee and Solomon were members of the staff of the liberal media watch group for Fairness and Accuracy in Reporting, with offices in New York. FAIR commissioned two Boston College sociologists, William Hoynes and David Croteau, to carry out an 'objective' quantitative-empirical study on 865 instalments of, and 2,498 guests on, one of the most influential American television shows: ABC's *Nightline*. The results were revealing.

The study noted that of all commentators on the programme 97.5 per cent were American, 95.5 per cent white and 90 per cent male. The guests were 92 per cent white, 80 per cent were government officials, corporate representatives or professionals, and only 5 per cent spoke on behalf of 'public interest' constituencies (consumer organizations, environmental groups, peace movements, etc.).

> The leading guests, with 14 appearances each, were Henry Kissinger and another former secretary of state, Alexander Haig. Next came State Department official Elliot Abrams and the Moral Majority's Jerry Falwell (12 appearances each). Out of 19 American guests who could be termed *Nightline* 'regulars' (more than five appearances), all were men, all but two were white, and 13 of the 19 were conservatives.

The presenter, Ted Koppel, defended himself by saying that 'if you want to critique US foreign policy, you don't bring on the opponents of US foreign policy and let them speak their minds. What you do is bring on the architects of US foreign policy and hold them to account.' That is one point of view, of course. Lee and Solomon (1990: 17, 26–31) also report another point of view:

a former editor at the *Washington Post*, who has been one of the few black commentators to reappear on television, attests that in TV discussions 'the left is just left out. I've never seen Noam Chomsky on television. I don't even think I know what Chomsky looks like, though I know from his writing he's an extremely articulate critic of US foreign policy.'

Chomsky is a 'world-famous' professor of linguistics at the prestigious Massachusetts Institute of Technology, but also a controversial radical intellectual (see also Cohen and Solomon, 1993).

Although American commercial television is under tighter control than European public television, basically the same Rolodex (card index) system applies there. Almost every issue is covered by an extremely limited number of experts, who appear and reappear time and again. In foreign policy matters, a rather small range of area and security experts cover most of the ground. Foreign affairs, defence and related ministries in various countries have in recent years organized their own think tanks, which can conveniently supply newscasters with authoritative experts within hours or even minutes, so that they won't have to fall back on a wider range of university scholars, who have proved to be more unpredictable.

But even the academic world itself has its obvious limitations. There is a general tendency to consider middle-aged white male Westerners to be the supreme experts on almost anything under the sun. Edward Said pointed out that 'orientalists' quoted in the Western media are hardly ever people from Arab or Islamic countries, for instance. Nor are 'Indologists' people from India. An 'old China hand' is almost never a Chinese. A learned Arab, Indian or Chinese may know more about his culture than a Western academic, but the idea is apparently that he or she is probably not able to explain it to a Western (or a global) audience. That remains to be seen.

Jonathan Benthall has shown that in reports about non-Western natural disasters, too, the 'experts' interviewed are usually Westerners. The strong overseas 'helpers' would typically be filmed against a backdrop of miserable huddled masses, who are – once again – not able to play a significant role in solving their own problems. The individual white doctor or nurse would explain what is going on, the anonymous non-whites will largely remain speechless. Thus the Western expert frame on the world is constantly upgraded, and the non-Western frame downgraded.

Vox populi

It has been pointed out time and again that the 'ordinary local people' who are usually quoted in intercontinental news, particularly by roving reporters, are often guides, translators, taxi-drivers, bar-keepers, chambermaids and their like. They are not often identified by this role,

Table 5.1 *Herman and Chomsky's study of selective use of sources and related emphasis in themes in the* New York Times

First phase: 1 February–30 March. Total percentage of sources (and percentage of direct sources) used, with regard to news coverage of the El Salvador elections of 25 March, and with regard to the upcoming Nicaragua elections[3]

Sources (and direct quotes)	El Salvador	Nicaragua
Local officials	39.2 (20.2)	39.5 (08.0)
US officials	41.1 (16.0)	28.9 (18.4)
Opposition, rebels and others	19.8 (12.9)	31.6 (15.8)

Second phase: 1 September–6 November. Total percentage of supportive topics (+) or unsupportive topics (–), in news coverage of the Nicaragua elections of 5 November, compared to that of the Salvador elections in the earlier period (NA = not applicable)

Topics		El Salvador	Nicaragua
+ 1	Democratic purpose and hopes	21.4	4.8
+ 2	Rebel disruption	53.6	0
+ 3	Turnout	25.0	23.8
+ 4	Election mechanics	32.1	0
+ 5	Personalities and political infighting	35.7	14.3
+ 6	Official reflections on the election	35.7	14.3
+ 7	The army as protector of the election	17.9	0
– 8	Public relations purpose	10.7	33.3
– 9	Sponsors' investment in the election	7.1	9.5
– 10	Fraud in prior election	0	NA
– 11	(Limits on) free speech and assembly	3.6	38.1
– 12	(Limits on) freedom of the press	0	28.6
– 13	(Limits on) organizational freedom	0	9.5
– 14	Limits on ability of candidates to qualify and campaign	0	52.4
– 15	Prior state terror and climate of fear	10.7	14.3
– 16	Power of armed forces	3.6	14.3
– 17	Legal obligation to vote	14.3	NA
– 18	Legal penalties for not voting	7.1	NA
– 19	Marking voter's fingers	3.6	4.8
– 20	Stamping ID cards	7.1	NA
– 21	Legal requirement to check that voters voted	0	NA
– 22	Non-legal threat to nonvoters	0	4.8
– 23	Use of transparent voting urns	3.6	NA
– 24	Legal right of security force presence at voting stations	0	NA

though, nor by their full identity. This is not because journalists are particularly lazy or shy, but because the logistics of covering crises are such that they simply do not have the time or the opportunity to strike up even the most elementary relationships with other local people. Needless to say, the groups mentioned usually belong to social strata which are very specific in their social backgrounds and aspirations (for instance, more oriented towards the outside world in general and the West in particular), and will seek to please their clients.

In radio and particularly in television, the street interview is a standard format in which 'ordinary people' can also be heard and seen. At first sight, it seems that this is an opportunity to sample the opinion of average persons. Upon closer inspection, however, it turns out that this genre is often staged. There is an implicit preference for certain well-defined 'colourful' places and people and accents such as 'characteristic' markets with outspoken salesmen or women and folksy expressions. Microphones and cameras return to the same places time and again.

Most of the time, reporters also have very definite ideas about what they want to hear in advance, and will continue conducting interviews until they have one or two statements that fit the bill and then 'wrap it up'. It has little to do with real sampling of unexpected opinions. Nor could it have, because time is short and there is room for only one or two such statements anyway. Ordinary people are also often pictured in crowds, for instance, in crises and demonstrations. In such cases, however, they frequently just function as 'lively backdrops' for an interview with a spokesman or a 'stand-up' by the reporter.

Here is one more brief intermediary illustration of 'loud and whispering voices' worldwide. The 1992 Unesco *Statistical Yearbook* gave data on the 200 most translated authors throughout the world. Of this total, 57 originated from Great Britain (and 1 from Ireland), 52 from the US (and 1 from Canada). That is to say, two countries and one language account for the larger share. Of the rest, 22 came from France and its French-speaking neighbours, 19 from Germany and its German-speaking neighbours, and 17 from Russia and its Russian-speaking neighbours. By contrast, there were only 3 from India, 1 from Japan and none from China; only 3 from the whole of Latin America and none from Africa.

The same mechanisms of the selective accessing of the life experiences of some over others also holds for the transcontinental media industry as a whole. Upper- and middle-class authors, songwriters, composers, directors, actors, etc., from the major capitals of the OECD, G-7 or Anglo-Saxon countries – whether long-dead classical ones or avant-garde modern ones – stand a thousand more chances of getting worldwide exposure than do equally talented people from the least developed countries and rural areas. And so do their everyday problems and preoccupations. Whereas the former voices are made to be loud and omnipresent, the latter ones are reduced to a whisper or even completely drowned out. What holds for novels and songs and films also holds for news.

The question is, of course, if – and under what circumstances – the major Western news media are really interested in the story of illiterates speaking another language. In early February 1994, the major French news weekly *Le Nouvel Observateur* carried a report entitled 'In the skin of an untouchable: I was a beggar in Benares'. The introduction said: 'This journalist came back from hell. During more than two months, grease-painted and dressed like an Indian, after having learnt Hindi, and having carefully composed himself in the role of an untouchable beggar, Marc Boulet has lived the life of the poorest men on earth.'

Earlier, the best-selling author Dominique Lapierre wrote a novel about white helpers among the poorest people of Calcutta: *La Cité de la joie*. It was made into a major film, which was criticized as stereotypical by some of the local population though. Mother Teresa was also occasionally heard speaking on behalf of the untouchables of Calcutta. But when are the untouchables of Benares and Calcutta ever heard speaking for themselves through the transnational media industry? Does anyone help them to tell their own stories, to get them out, to make an impact, to convey a sense of urgency to the rest of the world? Only when there is an earthquake or flood, and the chronic situation suddenly gets covered as a sudden crisis.

Quotes and quotation marks

As we have seen, it is not only official sources from the First World which get quoted in the news. Unofficial sources get quoted as well, as do sources from Second and Third World countries. This, however, does not always mean that their point of view is presented *in extenso*, coherently, or even fairly. Although quoting seems a rather straightforward technique, there are subtle and less subtle differences in the way sources get quoted. In some instances, this validates their claims; in others, it invalidates them. This is done primarily through two devices: the strategic placing of the actual quotation marks, and the keynoting of the quote by putting a label on the source.

The actual accessing of sources within the framework of a media text is usually done by various forms of quotation. There are two extremes. One is that the actual source of the news and views is completely obscured. The piece is wholly or partially based on 'deep background information', but there is no hint of such sources, nor of their approximate identity. At the other extreme, the source is on the contrary highlighted in such a way that the responsibility for what is said is explicitly made to rest with him or her alone. Tuchman (1978) calls this 'relocating facticity'. It is a favourite technique of news agencies. They do not say 'this or that is the case,' but 'so-and-so said there and then that this or that is the case.' In this way, the statement of someone's point of view may be transformed into a 'fact' or factoid, which can then go on to lead a life of its own and elicit reactions.

Every critical reader knows, of course, that it is important to take careful note of where precisely the quotation marks are, or in broadcasting terms, where a change of intonation occurs to indicate that the spoken words are no longer those of the journalist but those of the source. This may or may not be accompanied by the emphatic words 'quote . . . unquote' or by an equivalent gesture of both hands. At least, that is the theory, but the practice is considerably more complicated. There is some kind of implicit hierarchy in who gets quoted both literally and *in extenso* (often that is to say who really gets interviewed), who gets quoted literally but only in bits of text and soundbites, and who gets paraphrased. Certain sources are quoted in ways to make them highly believable; others are quoted in ways to make them highly unbelievable.

When we hear or see an interview on radio or television, we should be aware that: (1) the interview taped was probably much longer than the interview broadcast, that considerable parts have been omitted; (2) that the order of the utterances may have been radically altered to fit the interviewer's hidden agenda; and (3) that the drift of what was meant may therefore have been radically changed as well. This can also be done by interspersing the literal quotes with short comments, sub-conclusions and sub-introductions. In all media, this cutting and editing process is obscured, and in television the altered interview is renaturalized, by separate counter-shots of details, the environment or the interviewer (the 'noddy'). These shots are often made for this specific purpose, sometimes at a different time and even a different location.

When we read an interview in a newspaper, similar things apply. In this case, furthermore, whatever is put between quotation marks may on occasion not literally be what was said, but the journalist's rendering of what (he or she thinks) was said or even intended. Rather than taping an interview, newspaper reporters working on a highly topical story often prefer to make brief notes, which then serve as a subsequent reconstruction of what was probably said or intended.

There are also subtle differences in quotation practices, which may give the readers subliminal cues as to the veracity or falsity of a statement. One may write: President So-and-so said a hostile country had violated the internationally recognized border. Or one may write: President So-and-so said 'a hostile country had violated the internationally recognized border.' Or even: President So-and-so said 'a hostile country' had 'violated' the 'internationally recognized' border. In the first two examples, the statement is treated more or less casually. In the last, considerable doubt is cast on each element of the claim. The former procedure is often spontaneously chosen for rendering quotes from friendly sources, while the latter procedure is often spontaneously chosen for rendering quotes from hostile sources.

Literal and paraphrased, elaborate and truncated quotes are then woven together in the piece. As John Hartley says, in *Understanding News* (1989: 110):

> All the individual voices, like individual notes in a musical score, are then orchestrated together within the overall news story. The effect of this on the narrative is to provide it with authenticity, the reality effect. This is not to say that outside voices are simply accepted into the narrative as 'right', or as definitive. Far from it. All quoted material or interviewed voices are treated as highly provisional in status. They are open to reinterpretation in the light of other voices in the story, particularly those of the professionals themselves.

Keynoting quotes

Hartley (p. 108) also draws attention to another major aspect of this whole process of composition, which is the keynoting of quotes through the labelling of sources. Just before or after the quote, sources are usually identified by their name, a qualification or a combination of both. This gives the reader (listener, viewer) another subtle hint at the veracity or falsity of the statement. Hartley cites Brunsdon and Morley (1978), who said this kind of nomination is for 'clueing the audience in as to the identity of extra-programme participants or interviewees; establishing their "status" (expert, eyewitness, etc.) and their right/competence to speak on the topic in question – thus establishing their proposed degree of credibility/authority within the discourse'. This may also be done by superimposing a title line with their name and role.

This setting of quotes to a major or minor key does of course implicitly tend to validate or invalidate the claims made in the statement itself. Even speaking about the representative of a 'regime' instead of a 'government' gives us a subtle clue as to his or her legitimacy. Thus the quasi-factual process of giving quotes from all interested parties suddenly turns out to carry a series of value judgments as well, with the effect of indicating who is probably right and who is probably wrong. This procedure is particularly obvious in reports on social or national conflicts to which the West is (implicitly or explicitly) a party. Let us take a closer look at some of the more common categories of labels used under such circumstances.

POLITICAL CONVICTION LABELS Who is a 'militant' and who is not? A 'radical' in the US is someone of the 'extreme' left, a radical in France is someone belonging to one of the various centrist parties (which have been in existence for over a hundred years). A 'federalist' in the US is someone in favour of more centralization, in France of less. A 'republican' in France is simply a good democrat, a republican in Great Britain is a threat to the established order. A 'liberal' in Great

Britain is a progressive, a liberal in France is generally ranked as more of a conservative (at least on economic and social matters, not necessarily on moral and cultural ones). If such problems arise in the translation of political conviction labels between Western countries which have so much in common, the problems are even greater in the translation of political conviction labels between Western and non-Western countries.

Saying someone is a moderate or a radical in this context often simply means that someone is seen as pro-Western or anti-Western (rather than the other way round). During the 'Iranian' hostage crisis (or the 'American' hostage crisis), considerable confusion arose because one faction was labelled 'moderate' and another 'radical'. Later, these labels were simply inverted: it turned out that the moderates had 'in reality' been the radicals, and the radicals had instead been the moderates. This is a perfect illustration of the arbitrary and often tautological nature of such labels.

This even holds for seemingly obvious ones. What does it mean to say that someone is a fascist or a communist, for instance, or – in the current context – a former fascist or a former communist? Many of the older German or Italian politicians did once belong to one fascist organization or another in their youth. Yet the stigma was always selectively stuck on some and not on others. Many of the Russian or Eastern European politicians of today did belong to communist parties and administrations not so long ago. Yet the stigma is currently selectively stuck on some, not on others – whenever it is politically convenient. Gorbachev was not called a communist, for instance, although he did not officially break with that ideology at the time. Allende, by contrast, was always portrayed as a communist and consistently labelled a 'Marxist' in many Anglo-American media, although he called himself a socialist and was a member of the social-democrat international.

Meanwhile, no major Western politician is ever identified as an ex-colonial, although the vast majority of the older generation in England, France, the Netherlands, Belgium, Portugal, etc. did initially resist decolonization and thus shared political responsibility for the bloody wars which ensued and often made hundreds, thousands, hundreds of thousands or even millions of people victims.

POLITICAL ROLE LABELS   White or 'coloured' royalty and nobility are often treated differently by the Western media, as well as heads of state or heads of government. To identify a leader with such a formal political role is usually legitimating, to identify him or her with a previous non-political role is often delegitimating. Most of the time, the Western media spoke of President Eisenhower, President Kennedy, President Reagan, President Bush, not of General Eisenhower, the millionnaire Kennedy, the movie actor Reagan, the CIA head Bush.

There is a strong tendency, however, to reserve the use of legitimating labels for pro-Western heads of state or government and delegitimating labels for anti-Western heads of state or government.

Fowler (1991: 112–19), for instance, took a closer look at the reports of the 1986 air raid on Libya by US planes taking off from UK bases. In these, Gaddaffi was consistently referred to as 'colonel', whereas Reagan was referred to as president and Thatcher as premier or prime minister. These epithets were accompanied by contrasting terms of abuse and endearment. The point here is not whether someone is 'really' legitimate or not, but that the nominating process is supposed to be neutral – whereas in fact it is subtly evaluative. Other examples may illustrate this point, because these mechanisms are not at all limited to the Arab world or Africa. A string of dozens of pro-American leaders from Latin America to South-east Asia were and are military men who came to power through coups or highly questionable elections, but they are usually just identified as 'president' or 'prime minister' – as long as they are considered friendly. Once such a leader is set on a collision course with the US, however, the media spontaneously revert to the label 'general' or 'major' or 'colonel' – as in the case of Panama's Noriega.

GENDER LABELS Something similar applies to women leaders 'nominated' by male journalists. There is a general tendency to emphasize the macho qualities of women who have become political leaders in their own right. This applied to Margaret Thatcher as well as to Golda Meir, for instance, but also to Indira Gandhi and many others. If women have come to prominence through their romantic involvement with powerful men, however, there is often an opposite emphasis on their feminine qualities. This is accompanied by derogatory labels such as 'the former cabaret dancer' or 'beauty queen' in cases such as those of Eva Peron.

Similarly, there have been dozens upon dozens of examples of the succession of postwar Third World leaders by close family members. Yet in some cases this is glanced over as natural, whereas in others it is emphasized as unnatural.

Thus the choice of sources, of modes of quotation and labelling of sources play a major role in 'the creation of the world in the news'.

Research indicates that the front-page news stories of even the very best daily newspapers in the world rely very heavily on official national sources. The criteria of authority, credibility and (most of all) availability drive journalists back to these same sources time and again. This gives them a disproportionately large agenda-setting and definition power. One clear series of examples is provided by the major news-maker in the world, the US government, and by its major institutions: the White House, the State Department and the Pentagon. In the past, furthermore, both the CIA and the FBI have run extensive campaigns of media manipulation. Military interventions abroad are increasingly accompanied by psychological warfare and misinformation campaigns. Similar things can be said about Great Britain and France. Whereas the leaders of the great Western powers can be heard almost daily, furthermore, billions of people around the world are never heard at all speaking about their life conditions or outlook.

Notes

1 Chapter 1 in Robert Karl Manoff and Michael Schudson, *Reading the News* (1987), pp. 15, 27–8. See also an earlier similar statement in Leon Sigal, *Reporters and Officials* (1973), p. 189.

2 J.D. Brown et al., 'Invisible power: Newspaper news sources and the limits of diversity', *Journalism Quarterly*, 64 (1987), pp. 45–54. D.C. Whitney et al., 'Geographic and source biases in network TV news', *Journal of Broadcasting*, 33 (1989), pp. 159–14.

3 From Edward Herman, '"Objective" news as systematic propaganda: The NYT on the 1984 Salvadoran and Nicaraguan elections', *CAIB*, no. 21 (1984), pp. 7 ff.; Edward Herman, 'Diversity of news: Marginalizing the opposition', *Journal of Communication* (Summer 1985), pp. 135–46. See also Edward S. Herman and Noam Chomsky, 'Legitimizing versus meaningless Third World elections', ch. 3 in *Manufacturing Consent: The Political Economy of the Mass Media* (1988), pp. 132–6.

Further reading

Sources: Gitlin (1980); Lee and Solomon; Sigal. *Agenda-setting*: B. Cohen; Protess and McCombs. *Propaganda*: Herman and Chomsky; Jowett and O'Donnell; Knightley; Pratkanis and Aronson.

6 WHEN DOES SOMETHING BECOME WORLD NEWS?

THE HISTORY OF RUPTURES AND CONTINUITIES

....

> Today we live in an environment where . . . news comes like a
> shock every few hours; where continually new news programs keep
> us from ever finding out the details of the previous news. . . .
>   Might it not be that we do not build experiences it was possible
> to do decades ago, and if so wouldn't that have a bearing upon all
> our educational efforts?
>
>   Paul Lazarsfeld, 'Remarks on communication research'.[1]

*As we have noted before (in Chapter 2) there is something very ambivalent
about news, in its relation to discontinuity and continuity. Identifying
something as news somehow implies a discontinuity, a rupture, even an
eruption. Yet this foregrounding only acquires its meaning against an
implied background of continuities. Note this is once again related to
selective articulation: certain continuities are heavily emphasized, others
completely ignored. How is this done in everyday news-gathering? What
about the live reporting of world history as it unfolds: is that possible, or is
it an illusion? Who generates the prime definitions of global events, which
then tend to stick? To what extent does the eternal focus on sudden events,
and the concurrent blurring of underlying processes lead to serious
distortions? And what role do news planning and calendar journalism play?*

We love to be surprised, and we are continually being surprised by
the news, by the headlines on the front page of the newspaper every
morning, by the announcement of the subjects of the television news
every night, by the flashes of breaking news on the radio every hour.
It is both fascinating and hypnotizing. It is like a drug, it is like a
kick, it alternately strikes us with awe and horror. It keeps us on our
toes, or so it seems, because it may also prevent us from standing
back from this steady stream, from thoroughly reflecting on what is
really going on.

   In *The Book of Laughter and Forgetting* (1982), Milan Kundera noted:
'The bloody massacre in Bangladesh quickly covered over the
memory of the Russian invasion of Czechoslovakia, the assassination
of Allende drowned out the groans of Bangladesh, the war in the
Sinai Desert made people forget Allende, the Cambodian massacre

made people forget the Sinai, and so on and so forth' (quoted in Middleton and Edwards, 1990: vii). By emphatically bringing the late, the latest news to our attention every hour and day, the media also make us continually forget the old events; they produce recurring bouts of amnesia. The continuous barrage of new clues may actually help to disorient us further, rather than the reverse. Closely following the news might therefore be compared to (eternally) 'reading a detective story with the last page ripped out', say Wallis and Baran (1990: 226).

The news presents itself to us as a natural succession of unrelated events. Yet the words and images which report them invariably evoke the past, the present and the future, because they also selectively imply some of the probable causes, relevant contexts and possible consequences of the reported events. They may do so explicitly or implicitly, and we will fill in the gaps from our standard knowledge of the world. Even a minor cue may thus help us make historical sense from a seemingly ahistorical report. An act of violence can be described and depicted as 'gratuitous provocation', for instance, or as an 'understandable reaction'. In this way, the 'spiral of conflict' is arbitrarily cut off at one point or another, and responsibility is selectively assigned to one party rather than the other.

Although the media seem to report isolated events, they never report in a vacuum. There are always a thousand threads which connect them to other equally (un)isolated events. Some of these lines are uninterrupted, others are dashed or dotted or only vaguely hinted at, as in the Burda model discussed before. Some are immediately visible to the naked eye, some only gradually become apparent, while most remain hidden from sight. Carlin Romano (1987) quoted Reinhold Niebuhr (1963) in this regard:

> Facts consist of hardly more than names and dates. There are events in history, and these events cannot be understood except in relation to a whole stream of previous causes. Every record of events is therefore also an interpretation of this stream of causes. In the strict sense, there is therefore no unbiased account of either past or contemporary history.

As an illustration, the German theologian pointed to 'factual' Nazi films about the US, consisting of a succession of authentic newsreel material of mud fights, pie-eating contests and beauty contests (Manoff and Schudson, 1987: 73–4). It is through such mechanisms of selective articulation that images and bias are created.

The weaving together of certain facts, and pointing to relations with other facts, the implicit construction of continuities and ruptures, is another way of making sense. It actively makes the acts of certain actors seem understandable and those of others incomprehensible, some acts laudable and others despicable. It thereby achieves the normalization of those acting within the norms of one's own society, and the 'pathological impression' of those acting outside those norms. Other authors speak about the 'rhetorical organization of remembering and forgetting' in this regard. 'Primarily it can be seen in argument about contested pasts and plausible accounts of who is to blame, or to be excused, acknowledged, praised, honoured, thanked, trusted and so on, that occur as part of the pragmatics of everyday communication' (Middleton and Edwards, 1990: 9).

Media – along with education and science – not only note and remember: they choose to forget and blot out even more. They contribute to the production and reproduction of our sense of historical continuity or eruption (that is to say, an absence of it). A civilization will tend to form a certain collective perspective and ignore its shadow. Whatever fits into the pre-established configuration is acknowledged; whatever does not is conveniently overlooked. The construction of historicity and ahistoricity, of synchronicity and asynchronicity, is therefore a central mechanism of the news. In this chapter, we will take a closer look at selective articulation through time frames.

World history live?

Journalism has been labelled the first draft of history. With the emergence of the electronic media this first draft has become particularly sketchy. One of the particularities of radio and television is that they can broadcast live. The announcer stereotypically says: we (in the news-room) are discovering this at the same time as you do (at home). Film cannot be shown live, for it has different rules, but television can. We are told on such occasions that we can witness 'world history live', as it unfolds on news channels such as CNN. But there is no news genre which is more ahistorical than precisely this one. At best, raw emotions outdo rational analysis. At worst, we see images which seem to make no sense at all: explosions, flames, smoke, wrecks, people lying on the ground, bleeding; other people running around, screaming. It is only the added commentary which imposes a certain meaning on these chaotic impressions. Live news coverage is presented as a virtue; often it is a vice. But most of the time it pretends to be something which it certainly is not.

Live news coverage is often planned long in advance: TV resources have to be deployed to a spot where the event is going to happen. Live news coverage is usually even announced in advance: the appetite of the audience has to be whetted. The first international live broadcast in several European countries was the coronation of Elizabeth II of Great Britain, which celebrated the monarchy. Yet, on such occasions, the unexpected is but a minor element within a larger framework of the expected. We do not know exactly what the

American president is going to say in his or her speech or press conference or interview, but we surely have a pretty good idea of it beforehand. Live news coverage if often not all that surprising, but largely predictable.

Things become more interesting when cameras are covering an ongoing event and something unpredictable happens. Sometimes camcorders record a weird occurrence, usually minor events such as embarrassing mistakes, not major events. Assassination attempts on President Reagan and Pope John Paul II were recorded live – but they were not broadcast live. There were many foreign reporters in Peking to cover the Gorbachev visit, when student protesters peacefully occupied Tiananmen Square. There were many national and East Coast reporters in California covering a major sports event when a major earthquake struck. Yet even on these occasions, very little of the original news event was really covered live.

Very often, live coverage of an unexpected event is really live coverage of the *aftermath* of an unexpected event, because time is needed to redeploy cameras and news teams. The typical commentary in live disaster coverage is, for instance: 'rescue workers are doing all they can to locate survivors and free them from under huge piles of rubble.' Or: 'experts and material will be flown in from elsewhere.' Or: 'the authorities say they are on top of the situation now.' All this is extremely predictable; it is like mechanically going through a script which was written long before, and had already been used dozens of times.

Only ongoing news events, which were unannounced but which may last several days, seem to lend themselves to live coverage. This is particularly true for certain gross acts of violence. Take terrorism. International pressure through hijacking and hostage-taking was almost (re)discovered to be covered live. It serves the purposes of television, it serves the purposes of terrorists, it even serves the purposes of the authorities. But terrorists hardly ever succeed in getting their message across, whereas authorities do. The role of the security apparatus and the state is very much validated by live coverage of hostage-taking of innocent civilians. Television crews will position themselves at a safe distance and register the alignment of superior force, which prevails nine times out of ten. Live coverage of terrorist acts is often like a protracted commercial for police, army and intelligence services: something the insurgents do not seem to understand.

The other gross act of violence which lends itself particularly well to live television coverage is a 'just' invasion (or 'counter'-invasion). The cameras will usually cover their own side of the story: the deployment of forces, distant skirmishes, safe returns. What they will not be able to cover well and in time is the other side of the story: the civilian casualties behind enemy lines, the inevitable excesses.

Cameras will often be denied direct access during the first twenty-four or forty-eight hours for 'security reasons'. They will therefore cover such situations (the Falklands, Grenada, Panama) from a secure spot, and automatically give more airtime to spokesmen from their own side than to the actual battle and its aftermath – let alone to spokesmen from the other side. Live coverage is therefore usually the exact opposite of investigative journalism: there is no time or opportunity to check a certain version of events. We will return to these questions later.

Prime definition

When events first announce themselves, particularly in the domain of breaking international news, their true historical meaning is often not immediately apparent. What might be the immediate and distant causes, what might be the immediate and distant consequences? Which aspects of the context are trivial, and which aspects are essential? Who are the heroes and who are the villains? Selection and interpretation start right away, even in the reporting of the basic facts of the event itself.

This is where the process of prime definition plays a key role. The prime definition is the first and/or most influential early definition of an event. Research in psychology, social psychology and sociology has demonstrated that such prime definitions tend to stick. If people or groups are presented with an ambiguous stimulus, which can be seen in two different but incompatible ways, they can be cued to one of the two perceptions. This is called 'set'. Once they are locked into this one perception, there is a certain resistance to change. The Gestalt or configuration will tend to perpetuate itself.

How does this relate to international news reporting? In two different ways. On the one hand, news-gathering is a stopwatch culture. The head of one major news agency proudly recalled in an interview that they had beaten the competition by ten minutes on one major story more than a decade ago. This may be of great interest to speculators and investors, but less so for the general public. On the other hand, only such major news agencies and global news-gathering organizations do indeed have the organization and resources, the worldwide distribution and reactive capability, to actually be first. This is particularly true if an event takes place in the news periphery far from the major news centres.

The practical consequence is that the three major world news agencies, the major American, British and French news-gathering organizations, have a quasi-monopoly in providing prime definitions of breaking news in the world periphery. Even if they are not actually the first on the spot, they are usually the first to inform the rest of the world. But these few news-gathering organizations are primarily responsive to the interests and frames of the major media and audiences in the major Western countries. Their prime definitions of events grow out of, and cater to, the greatest common denominator of these groups. They are extremely reluctant to come up with prime definitions that go against these views, let alone hurt the sensibilities of these groups.

Even major quality newspapers themselves apparently recognize this. Lee and Solomon (1990: 23) report: Associated Press 'is often on the scene first, covering for virtually everyone until other media outlets can get their people there,' a *Los Angeles Times* analysis concluded in 1988. But AP rarely digs deep into stories, they concluded. The *Los Angeles Times* (which teams up with the *Washington Post* to operate a news service marketed as a supplement to Associated Press), reported that 'clichés and superficiality often abound' in AP copy. And:

> Reporters who like to write investigative stories or other stories that challenge the Establishment generally complain the most about AP; many walk away from AP unhappy, convinced that AP is reluctant to break ground on certain kinds of controversial stories for fear of being criticized by editors of member newspapers – who are simultaneously AP's employers and its paying customers.

Shortly before these conclusions were reached, I witnessed this mechanism in full operation. In the spring of 1986, I attended a sensational trial in San José, Costa Rica. The judge threw out the libel suit which a local American 'covert operations' manager had launched against two foreign correspondents. The hearing produced a string of highly credible witnesses, which confirmed his involvement in multiple murder, and an arms-for-drugs smuggling operation from a farm in the North. They turned out to be early signs of the Iran-Contra affair. I do not know what the local AP representative reported to headquarters. But the AP story which was put on the wires and published in the newspapers had just a few extremely bland and ambiguous lines. Its prime definition did in fact cover up and hide the significance of the entire event.

Timeliness, process and event

News has a very particular way of inserting itself into our views of history, whether explicit or implicit. As Galtung and Ruge (1965) pointed out, and others have corroborated since, news is not about long-term processes but about short-lived events. It is not about decades of deteriorating trade conditions, but about a sudden price hike. It is not about decades of harsh exploitation and cruel repression, but about a few days of violent disturbances. It is not about decades of unsafe building in the wrong places, but about the sudden occurrence of a 'natural' disaster. Processes are subliminal: they do not make a 'just noticeable difference'. Events are supraliminal: they cross the threshold of news perception. Events trigger a run: often on the very same persons, institutions and conditions which have been ignored for years. Suddenly, every second counts, or so it is made to seem.

Manoff and Schudson note (1987: 81):

> No one in the audience gives a damn if ABC beats CBS by two seconds or not. The journalist's interest in immediacy hangs on as an anachronistic ritual of the media tribe. Getting the story first is a matter of journalistic pride, but one that has little to do with journalistic quality or public service. It is a fetishism of the present . . . [It] serves, in part, to cover up the bureaucratic and prosaic reality of most news gathering. The news organization is, as Philip Schlesinger put it, a 'time machine'. It lives by the clock. Events, if they are to be reported, must mesh with its temporal spokes and cogs.

Practising journalists and communication experts have noted time and again that the media of the Northern and Western centres of the world seem to be interested only in the very worst of crises as far as the Southern and Eastern peripheries are concerned. The British author Evelyn Waugh eloquently depicted this in his 1938 novel *Scoop*. The American journalist Mort Rosenblum analysed it in his 1981 book *Coups and Earthquakes: Reporting the World to America*, for instance, in its introductory chapter on 'The West Malaria Rebellion' (and also in a later version of the same book).

We are continually made to forget that at any point in time there are more than a dozen armed conflicts under way in each of the major areas of the Second and Third Worlds (Latin America, Africa, the Arab world, Asia). Each brings scores of killings and atrocities with it. Yet only very few of these killings and atrocities make the front pages and the evening news in the First World. Some are hardly reported at all, if they concern peripheral areas alone and there are no immediate central interests at stake (for example, in the South and South-east Asian interior).

Some conflicts are reported, but only intermittently and casually: if coloured people are fighting on a huge scale but there are no white parties involved, or at least not visibly so (for example, in the Iran/ Iraq or rather Iraq/Iran war, or in the Angolan and Mozambican civil wars – which took hundreds of thousands or even millions of lives, without people in New York, London or Paris getting terribly excited about it). Some are reported insistently and dramatically, by contrast. The French anchorman Patrick Poivre d'Arvor (of the evening news on the major TV channel TF-1) described this as the 'funnel effect'. 'There is only room for one overwhelming emotion a day or week . . . There'll always be forgotten countries,' he said (Benthall, 1993: 28). Of course such a common choice of the outrage of the week or month is never entirely innocent; there are always good reasons why that particular drama does not or does fit in with preconceptions or preoccupations.

Something similar can be said about natural disasters. Jonathan Benthall recently published a major study of *Disasters, Relief and the Media* (1993). He said: 'The vast majority of natural disasters such as floods and earthquakes are not reported at all in the international media. Some cases of warfare and civil strife might be happening on the dark side of the moon for all we read or hear about them.' He considers that

> the coverage of disasters by the press and the media is so selective and arbitrary that, in an important sense, they 'create' a disaster when they decide to recognize it. To be more precise, they give institutional endorsement or attestation to bad events which otherwise have a reality restricted to a local circle of victims. Such endorsement is a prerequisite for the marshalling of external relief and reconstructive effort. The endorsement is not decided by some mysterious Moloch but by quite small numbers of professional editors and reporters, whose decisions on whether or not to apply the 'hallmark' of recognition can have far-reaching chains of consequences, both positive and negative. (pp. 11–12)

This was particularly clear in the case of the 1984 famine in Ethiopia (see Figure 6.2, p. 118), and as a matter of fact in all the major famines ranging from the Sahel to East Africa, which preceded and followed it over the last few decades, and which immediately affected tens of millions of people. One might add, somewhat provocatively, that there are no such things as 'natural' disasters – or at least much less so than the media make people believe. As Benthall says:

> It is now generally recognized that even the 'sudden elemental' disasters nearly always include a human element ... Buildings are the principal cause of death from earthquakes. According to the USA's Overseas Development Council, agricultural modernization and demographic pressure push six out of ten poor people to live on land which is specially vulnerable to disasters. (pp. 12–13)

Also: 'World Health Organization statistics show that the mortality rate for disasters in rich countries is far less than that in poor countries.' In the latter it is 48 times higher per square kilometre than in the former, 27 times higher per disaster and 3.5 times higher per thousand inhabitants (p. 37).

Particularly eloquent are the minor disasters which take place every year, and the major disasters which take place every few years in Bangladesh: along the major rivers, in the estuary and along the coast. News reports in the Western media invariably relate these floods (or droughts) to 'bad weather'. Yet they are related to dozens of other causes, ranging from deforestation in the Himalayas to failed land reforms, which push poor peasant families to try and subsist on the mud flats and salt marshes. The overarching cause is extreme

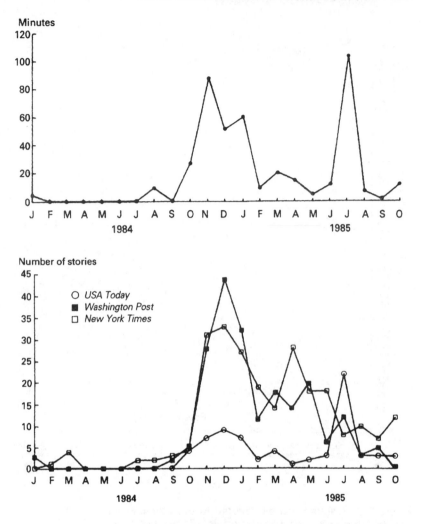

Figure 6.1 *Non-coverage and coverage of the Ethiopian famine by American TV networks and newspapers. (Sources: Above, Vanderbilt Television News Archive; Below, Annual index for each newspaper.*

poverty, with no end in sight. If the people of Holland (or England or France or Louisiana) lived on the lowlands outside the dikes along the main rivers, in the major estuaries and along the coast, they too would risk drowning in massive numbers during recurrent spring and autumn storms. Labelling these as natural disasters is therefore a highly ideological operation, which shifts the blame to the weather gods and away from anyone who might be in a position to do anything about the situation.

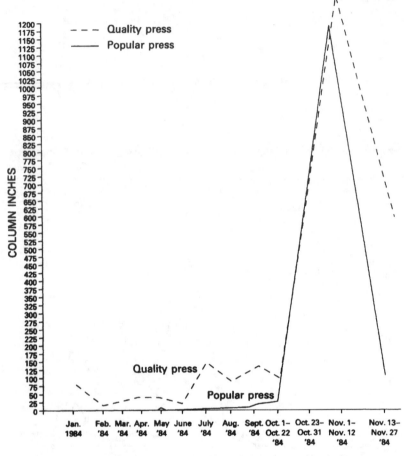

Figure 6.2 *Column inches devoted to the Ethiopian famine in the British quality and popular press. (Reproduced by permission of Routledge from G. Philo in J. Eldridge, Getting the Message: News, Truth and Power, 1993.)*

News rhythms and synchronization

In relation to news and history, ruptures and continuities, there are other mechanisms which tend to affect news reporting. The occurrence of some events fits in rather well with news reporting, while the occurrence of others does not. Some categories of events and voices therefore tend to be over-reported, others are under-reported. Synchronization or its opposite tend to respect or disrupt the organization of certain discourses, and to affect their capacity for making sense. How does this come about?

News planning, by both media and their sources, requires constant attention to news cycles: cycles of the production and consumption of news for and by the major audiences. Rather than being completely unpredictable, the emergence of certain news items – and the interest in certain broad subjects – closely follows predictable patterns. The world news machine is like a giant clock, with a wide variety of smaller and larger cogwheels all together driving the mechanism. There are cycles of an hour, a day, a week, a month, a quarter, a year and more. In general, the news rhythms of the Western world dominate the global media agenda and the formation of public opinion. The news rhythms of the non-Western world may often be out of sync. That is to say that both their technical and semiotic transmission is hampered by a lesser fit.

THE NEWS DAY   Since most news comes from official sources, most news is produced during office hours, and most major news reports are prepared during office hours as well. Few are gathered (although some are prepared) during the evening, still fewer are gathered or prepared during the night. Thus the ebb and flow of news production and news reporting falls and rises with night and day in the Atlantic. This also has certain consequences for the interaction between sources and journalists, between actions and reactions.

One cluster of groups which were long out of sync with many news-gatherers were certain 'alternative' social movements. The feminist movement pointed out, for instance, that many of their activists were tied up by work, home or children during weekdays. The activities of volunteers, meeting in their spare time in evenings and weekends, often went un- or under-reported, they claimed. On the one hand, their activities were often judged not newsworthy enough; on the other hand, few reporters were particularly keen on working odd hours to cover them. Some of this has changed in recent years though, and on both sides.

THE NEWS WEEK   In many countries there are no real daily newspapers on Sunday: there is less home distribution and only a limited number of news-stands are open at all. This situation leaves a huge black hole in newspaper reporting between Saturday and Monday. As a matter of fact, Saturday morning and afternoon papers are often almost entirely produced on Friday evenings, and only part of the staff resumes work on Sunday evenings, so that expensive overtime work is limited to a minimum. Radio and television broadcasters may also work with a reduced news staff and reduced news formats over weekends. The black hole in weekend news coverage tends to become even larger in international communication, not only because of time-zone differences, but also because of cultural mechanisms, for instance, between the West and the Middle East. Christians have their day of rest on Sunday, Jews on Saturday and Muslims on Friday. If a major event takes place on Thursday, it may often take three or four days before both Israeli and Arab reactions become available in a European or American daily.

THE NEWS YEAR Similarly, there are news rhythms related to the electoral cycles of years within major Western countries: certain international decisions are accelerated or postponed with an eye on major elections being just around the corner or still far away. This is particularly true of American elections, and most of all presidential elections, which stick to a steady schedule of four years. Political scientists have shown that certain types of foreign-policy decisions (such as new military commitments abroad) are highly improbable at one point in the cycle and much more probable at another. Psycho-historians such as Lloyd DeMause have even tried to prove that there are parallel cycles of public opinion and media moods in the US: at the beginning, middle and end of each presidential term. This would then supposedly affect the Western and the world's political and news agendas as well.

News planning and media events

We have seen before that timeliness is often an optical illusion. Totally unexpected news events stand to expected news events as the few fresh food departments in the supermarket stand to many alleys with prepackaged and deep-frozen, dried and vacuum-packed foods in plastic and cardboard, bottles and tins. The former demand more resources; the volume of the latter is many times greater. But most important: the former tends to legitimate the latter. It is the same with news. Most news is carefully planned. We may not know when a head of state or a head of government or a minister or a party leader will die, but we know for sure that she or he will, sooner or later. Journalists therefore continually update their obituaries – even though it may take decades before they are used as such. What is served up as news, on such occasions, therefore largely consists of old information.

NATIONAL POLITICAL PROCESS On many occasions, an endless succession of seemingly topical news items is carefully planned and even more or less staged through a tacit understanding among all those involved. This is the case in the run-up to elections in major Western countries, for instance. It is not the elections themselves which are staged, but the horse race in the three or six months which precede them. This staged race comes about, for instance, through a daily succession of initiatives and reactions which would have been ignored at other times, and through repeated opinion polling and a wilful misreading of the results.

In itself, polling is a more or less scientific technique in which a more or less representative sample of citizens (usually ranging from a few hundred to slightly over a thousand) are asked about their voting intentions. But the staging occurs through the way in which the results are continually reported and commented on. All insiders (politicians, pollsters and even some journalists) know that these results never mean what they are made out to mean. But they all have good reasons to go along with the play, or at least good reasons not to be seen as the spoiler (or bad loser).

Why is the race largely a staged play? Long before the elections take place, most people are not yet familiar with the candidates and the issues. One may force them to express a preference, but it has little validity. When the media report that candidate A has x per cent of the vote and candidate B has y per cent of the vote at that point, they usually do not emphasize that half or a quarter of the people have not yet made up their mind in these early stages. One may publish these results, but they have little reliability. Saying that A has lost a few percentage points to B during a particular week makes no sense either, since the margin of error usually consists of several percentage points. Yet everyone loves to play along and pretend that all this makes sense.

The overall effect is highly legitimating of the electoral process itself. It creates the impression that everyone has a chance, that the odds change all the time, and that there is real suspense about the outcome. In some cases, this is highly exaggerated, and power-broking in the wings is at least as important. Whereas the race in major countries such as the US, the UK and France is reported worldwide and thereby underlines the democratic process in such countries, there is usually only little attention for genuine democratic processes in non-Western nations. This reconfirms the stereotype of democracy as being an exclusively Western invention, which has hardly ever taken hold anywhere else.

Between elections, too, the political process in the major Western countries is given considerable exposure in the global media. Whether programmatic (the state of the Union speech in the US, the opening of parliament in the UK and other European nations) or ceremonial (coronations in the UK and other European monarchies, royal weddings and births and deaths), there is a general tendency to over-expose political processes, leaders and controversies in the media, and to under-expose economic processes, leaders and controversies. Yet worldwide, and increasingly, the latter set the margins of action for the former. According to some radical critics, the growing per-vasiveness of global free-market mechanisms (for money, that is, not for labour) even tends to empty national sovereignty and political democracy of most of their meaning – particularly in smaller and more peripheral countries.

INTERNATIONAL POLITICAL MEETINGS The world's news media also devote a large part of their reporting to the public diplomacy of the major Western news powers. Their judgment of others, their threats and promises, bilateral and multilateral meetings, often get extensive coverage. Excessive deployments of media resources are made to cover such events. Being there is what counts, not whether this serves the quality of the ensuing information.

The great summit meetings between the American President Reagan and the Soviet President Gorbachev, or between Clinton and Yeltsin, for instance, the official peace negotiations concerning the Middle East and the former Yugoslavia, were covered by thousands upon thousands of journalists. Yet few meetings have such tight security, so little access to major players as these. There even seems to be an inverse relation between the number of journalists present and their utility. The real negotiations take place outside the limelight. Thus the presence of scores of journalists reporting live is often a completely empty ritual and a gross squandering of scarce resources. It serves a legitimating function, but no real purpose of information. The situation is somewhat different in major international conferences with large national delegations, by contrast: in such cases it may indeed be useful to try and tap the perspectives of many people present.

Stewart Purvis of the British Channel 4 News summed it up this way:

> What is tending to happen is that the cost of the big stories is so enormous in this competitive business that it doesn't leave a lot of money for what some people would call second-division stories, but what we would call fascinating middle-ground stories. By the time you've covered an Olympic Games and a royal tour, you've spent a lot of money and you're not looking to say: 'Let's go and have a look at Africa' (Harrison and Palmer, 1986: 78).

While this book was being finished, the commercial US TV network NBC paid 2.3 billion dollars for the American broadcasting rights of the Olympic Games from 2004 through 2008 (though the site for them has not even been decided yet). At the same time, commercial TV networks complain that overseas news-gathering has become too expensive and try to cut back on their staff of correspondents.

The *ne plus ultra* of news planning is the creation of a pseudo-event such as a staged competition or rivalry. Certain events have little or no significance in themselves: their only significance lies in their planned media impact. The sociologist and historian Daniel Boorstin identified the rise of this phenomenon in his landmark study *The Image: A Guide to Pseudo-events in America* (1980). A pseudo-event, he said, 'is planted primarily (though not always exclusively) for the immediate purpose of being reported or reproduced'. They seem to multiply. 'In the last half century a larger and larger proportion of our experience, of what we read and see and hear, has come to consist of pseudo-events,' Boorstin wrote. 'They flood our consciousness' (pp. 11–12).

Calender journalism and commemorations

Present-day commemorations are increasingly planned events and pseudo-events of symbolic political significance, particularly because they explicitly insert the present into a highly ideologized perspective on the past and the future. In commemorations, according to Middleton and Edwards in their book *Collective Remembering* (1990), 'people recall and celebrate events and persons that are part of their jointly acknowledged generational and cultural identity and common understanding. In the gunfighters of the Western, in the statues of eminent citizens and places named after the famous, people "in society" with each other evaluate their culture by establishing what is notable or notorious.' But at the same time, they add, 'commemoration silences the contrary interpretations of the past.'

Our primary ideological socialization takes place in school, particularly in history and geography lessons, but also in many of the routines and rituals surrounding education. As Middleton and Edwards point out:

> The morning recitation of the Pledge of Allegiance in American schools exemplifies both the joint and commemorative nature of the *social foundation and context of individual memory*. The unison of voices provides an environment of collectively realized performance within which the novice can bridge any gaps of individual incompetence. At the same time each re-performance consolidates the authority of this commemorative practice, and the authority of those who obligate the children's performance. (p. 8)

Annual holidays and certain media events act as reminders to adults of what they have learned in their youth. They are a renewal of patriotism and pride in one's civilization.

Think of the American Fourth of July or Independence Day, or the French Quatorze Juillet (the date of the storming of the Bastille prison). Both events have been highly mythologized, to the extent that most children in school and parents at home share a version of these events which has long been debunked by historians. The Americans and the French have been rivals in putting up 'the greatest show on earth' on the occasion of the bicentenary of their respective revolutions. Both succeeded in having their festivities reported and broadcast worldwide, as a kind of protracted global commercial for their respective constitutions.

Both claimed to have invented and introduced the democratic system of 'one man, one vote' on these occasions, to have invented and introduced civil rights. Yet the slavery of blacks was permitted to persist for a long time after that. (The bicentenary of the subsequent revolution in Haiti, which did put an end to slavery, was largely ignored by the international media.) But even women in the US and France did not really get the vote until a century or more later. Great Britain, in turn, was one of the very last Western countries to introduce fully universal suffrage at home – not to speak of introducing it in the colonies. After having ruled Hong Kong for almost ninety-nine years, the British introduced democracy there on the very eve of its return to China. After having long maintained that such territories formed an integral part of the Empire, non-whites were refused European passports upon secession. These three democratic regimes – as well as many others – were often built on the blood, sweat and tears of non-white peoples in colonial and neo-colonial times, which is often forgotten by the media and the public on the occasion of all such commemorations.

A particularly vivid example of the limited historical perspective of the Western media was the quincentennial celebration of the supposed discovery of America and its Indian inhabitants by Columbus. Was it a discovery, was its name America, were its inhabitants Indians, and was Columbus the first overseas sailor to set foot there? None of the four elements of this standard phrase is probably true. Was there reason to celebrate? Only for the Western world, because 1492 proved the turning point in world history: only from that moment on did its wealth, trade, industry, technology and science definitely come to outstrip that of the Eastern world. But at what cost?

Shohat and Stam put it rather bluntly (1994: 66–70):

> For many native Americans, to be asked to celebrate Columbus is the equivalent of asking the Jews to celebrate Hitler. Not only did Columbus inaugurate the transatlantic slave trade (in reverse) by taking six shackled Tainos back to Spain on his second voyage, his brief rule of 'Hispaniola' accounted for the deaths of some 50,000 people. Indeed, twenty-one years after his first landing, 8 million people had been killed by violence, disease or despair . . . [The priest] De las Casas described nothing less than a massive genocide, which reduced the native population in the first thirty years after Cortès' landing from 25 to 6 million souls.

In forty years, he estimated, the 'infernal actions of the Christians' had led to the unjust slaying of 'more than twelve million men, women and children'. And this was only the beginning.

I am aware of the fact that there was some critical media attention given to the event as well, but it was in no proportion at all to the gravity of the event. Nor was there any serious soul-searching about the causes and consequences of the emergence of the successive colonial empires. A spate of Hollywood movies and television documentaries celebrated the genius of Western explorers. Some tried to be balanced – but without offending Western audiences, let alone questioning their world system. (A global analysis can be found in Shohat and Stam, 1994: 61–77.)

Spot news and historical discourse

Underlying commemorations of this kind, heavily exposed by the Western and thus by the global news media, there seems to be a very particular vision of the past. Every group, institution, regime, country, civilization tends to construct its own vision of history. One can easily do so by selectively emphasizing certain historical continuities and discontinuities, by highlighting some aspects and obscuring others. The same holds for Western civilization and its preferred rhetoric on the inevitable progress of freedom and wealth for everyone. Here is a brief outline in a few points.

1 The West sees itself as the legitimate heir of all liberal and enlightened episodes in its own past, but disowns all illiberal and obscurantist episodes in that same past. It emphasizes continuities with the former, but constructs discontinuities with the latter developments (or tries to ignore them altogether).

2 The unstoppable progress of civilization (science, wealth, democracy) is consistently over-emphasized, and constructed as a more or less continuous development: leading from ancient Greece and Rome to early Christianity, Renaissance Italy and the Iberian explorers. One element which is consistently blotted out, for instance, is that the achievements of these periods were closely related to those on the other side of the Mediterranean: the Orient, that is to say Persia, Turkey and the Arab empires of West Asia and North Africa.

3 The shadow side of this same European expansion in Africa, Asia and America is under-emphasized and constructed as a succession of isolated incidents of little consequence: the Crusades, pogroms, the Inquisition and witch hunts, the near-extermination of native Americans, the taking of precious metals and other raw materials, the slave trade, the coolie trade, the wars of colonization, the imposition of unequal trade conditions, poverty and famine in colonial times, repression abroad, resistance to decolonization, armed interventions – which cost dozens of millions of lives.

4 The unconditional integration of peripheral countries into the Western-dominated world system is presented as the only legitimate choice. Today, consent to the global policies of the major powers is often implicitly taken as a sign that a country or regime or politician is civilized, liberal, enlightened, modern, moderate. Resistance to these worldwide policies of the major Western powers is implicitly

taken as a sign that the country or its leader is uncivilized, authoritarian, obscurantist, traditionalist, extremist. There is little recognition that they might have good historical reasons to mistrust *laissez-faire* in the economic sphere, subordination in the political sphere (Nederveen Pieterse, 1990, 1992; Shohat and Stam, 1994: 2–3).

Although this is hardly ever said in so many words, let alone in spot news coverage, it is often the underlying logic guiding the choice of words and images for describing unexpected international events. Incidents are implicitly or explicitly related to this wider hidden discourse. We will return to this same subject of discourse and ideology in the chapters on words and images, on linguistics and semiology.

The Burda model tells us that mediated information may make certain patterns stand out and may ignore others. As far as time-frames are concerned, the social construction of discontinuities and continuities is such a process. The disproportionate emphasis on instantaneous reporting of sudden events hides the fact that most news is carefully planned. Sudden news from non-dominant subcultures and cultures may also find it difficult to fit in with the cogwheel of Atlantic day-time hours. What the fireworks of international news illuminate or leave in the dark is the historic panorama beyond them. This becomes obvious on the occasion of the commemoration or non-commemoration of certain historical events (for instance, in the relative amounts of attention devoted to the bicentenary of the American and French revolutions, as compared to the Haitian one). It makes clear that without being aware of it, the global media often promote a highly ideological version of world history.

Notes

1 In *Studies in Philosophy and Social Science*, 9 (1) (1941), pp. 2–16 (12). See also Wallis and Baran (1990): 3.

Further reading

Construction of the past: Lorenz; Middleton and Edwards. *News and pseudo-events*: Boorstin. *News ideology*: Hartley; Manoff and Schudson. *Disasters*: Benthall.

7 WHERE DOES WORLD NEWS COME FROM?

THE GEOGRAPHY OF CENTRES AND PERIPHERIES

> There is a significant difference between the capacity of a blanket and that of a net to gather fodder for daily newspaper columns and television air time . . .
> The narrower the intersections between the mesh – the more blanketlike the net – the more can be captured . . . Instead of blanketing the world by their independent efforts, the news media and the news services leave the same sorts of hole in the news net, holes justified by a professionally shared notion of news.
>
> Gaye Tuchman, 'Space and the newsnet'.[1]

Another dimension of social construction is the unequal coverage of geographic space. Are journalists and other observers evenly distributed around the globe? Or do they crowd together in certain world centres such as New York and Washington, London and Paris, and stay away from large areas in the periphery such as the interior of Africa, Asia and Latin America? If this is the case, what are the consequences for news flows and the world of the news which results? To what extent do the handful of foreign journalists in distant outposts stick together and how does it affect their reporting? And what about sudden crises, and the parachuting of a pack of reporters into an unfamiliar area? To what extent is this conducive to collective derailment?

Selective articulation is a function of time-frames and historical perspectives, but also of spatial grids and (social) geographical emphasis. Potential news reports may be compared to zillions of fish in the ocean of time and space. The media's news net is organized in such a way that it tends to fish certain news reports out of this ocean and lets countless others slip through.

One may extend this metaphor further by saying that there is often only a distant relation between the original news item and the news report ultimately carried by the media. Compare it to live fish being caught, killed, cleaned, cut, preserved. Many characteristic parts such as the head and tail, the fins and bones are thrown away or ground into fish-meal. The colour, taste, smell and substance of the rest may be standardized even further in the food-processing plant. It may be compressed into uniform blocks, coated with breadcrumbs, deep-frozen and packaged before being distributed and sold. Finally, it will be fried, served with a touch of lemon, parsley and mayonnaise on reaching the consumer. It is still the same fish – but then it isn't. Something similar is the case with the news.

As Gaye Tuchman suggested, the net with which the world's news media catch their fish is a rather curious contraption. At certain locations it closely resembles a blanket: its meshes are not even a tenth of a millimetre wide. It will fish out even the smallest fish eggs and the most inconsequential events. The White House press corps, for instance, will invariably report on major events in the life of the president's favourite . . . pet. His cat or dog is the subject of ongoing media attention, and most people in the world will hear about such stories every now and then.

At other locations, however, the news-net may be hardly recognizable as such: its mesh may be tens of metres wide. It may only catch the largest whales and events of a staggering magnitude. News on major African droughts and famines affecting millions, for instance, may take months or even years to break worldwide. It will attract worldwide media attention only under very peculiar sets of circumstances, and for a limited amount of time.

The world news net is woven by the tens of thousands of foreign journalists and news-gatherers, stationed around the world. They are distributed quite unevenly, although in recognizable patterns. In certain areas, their density is ten, a hundred or even a thousand in a few square miles, for instance, in the metropolitan areas of the North and West, in downtown Washington and New York, London and Paris. In other areas, the density fails to reach even ten in 100,000 or 1 million square miles, for instance, in the interior of the Southern and Eastern continents, in the Sahel or Amazonia. This chapter will look at how the world news net covers socio-geographic space, what patterns of news flow result, and what makes the world of the news.

The news centres

The global centre–periphery system is at the same time very complex and relatively simple. In each domain, there is something like a tree, or an inverted tree, with branches of unequal relations between clusters of centres and subcentres, peripheries and sub-peripheries. This is so in the political, the economic and the cultural domains. In most domains, the major world centres can be found in the major nations and the major language areas of the West. New York, London and Paris are major multidisciplinary centres of the diplomatic, financial and entertainment fields, and others too.

In North America, Washington is another major diplomatic centre, Chicago another major financial centre, Los Angeles (and the nearby Hollywood and Beverly Hills) another major entertainment centre. In

Western Europe some major countries are highly centralized, such as Great Britain and France. Other major countries, such as Germany, are more decentralized: it has a financial centre in Frankfurt, a political centre in Bonn and Cologne, an industrial centre in Düsseldorf and the Ruhr area, a foreign trade centre in Hamburg, and at least one major other cultural centre in Munich. Soon, however, Berlin may recentralize many of these functions again. Some other countries, such as Belgium, Switzerland, Austria and Italy, still have the permanent seat of major international organizations in Brussels, Geneva, Vienna and Rome. That may be an additional reason to base a correspondent there, who may then also report on local events. No other areas of the world traditionally have such a density of 'world news-makers' as the American north-east and the European north-west.

The media themselves follow a more or less parallel tree pattern. The most influential news-gathering organizations have their headquarters in New York, London and Paris. This holds for the major press, photographic and film agencies. The major headquarters have a permanent staff of something like a thousand people or more, of whom many hundreds are journalists, and a hundred or more may work on foreign affairs at all times. The most influential media have their headquarters in these same three cities and a few others. These headquarters process the news they receive from elsewhere. They receive some of the information indirectly through (other) news agencies, media and other institutions, and they receive some directly from their own correspondents. The paradoxical situation is that they have by far the most people in the very same cities which are also extensively covered by the competition, and very few people in distant outposts which hardly anyone covers at all.

The world news net is extremely dense in the centres. Hamid Mowlana counted 1,262 foreign correspondents in the US some time ago (mostly in New York and Washington) – the overwhelming majority from highly developed countries and not one from Black Africa. Almost a thousand correspondents are accredited to the European Commission in Brussels. The 1993 press list of the information service of the French prime minister has eighty pages and 607 names of foreign correspondents alone, in and around Paris. Whenever there is a major event in Latin America or Africa in which the US, Great Britain or France are involved, input from Washington, London or Paris will often be greater than from the news locations themselves.

There is an even grosser mechanism whenever centre interests are at stake in a peripheral event. In such cases, there will also be a heavy input of centre spokesmen or women (government officials, business managers, academic experts) commenting on faraway occurrences – whenever these are considered relevant. In doing so, they help to frame the issue until it fits their own perspective. There are always more foreign journalists at hand to cover the views of major Western spokesmen and experts in the centres than there are foreign journalists covering the actual events in the periphery.

During a conference on the Gulf war, Ed Cody of the *Washington Post* observed, for instance:

> An avalanche of information comes out of the U.S. government. They do it with such intensity and such volume that almost automatically it becomes the definition of what's happening. Anyone in Saudi Arabia, in Kuwait, in Baghdad who has the temerity to approach the problem from a different angle, to say wait a minute, this is the situation, I'm here, I'm talking to this person Mohammed and he tells me that's the way it looks from his point of view – that voice is not rejected, it's simply ignored or its volume is not at a level that can compete with the volume of information coming out of what is essentially the U.S. government and its agenda. (Rosenblum, 1993: 222)

The news periphery

Since maintaining foreign correspondents is expensive, only very few countries and media organizations can support really strong independent news-gathering networks abroad. The most extensive network in the world is obviously maintained by the US and its major media. In spite of (or maybe because of) its hegemonic position, however, this network is relatively modest in comparison to that of some others. The AP veteran reporter Mort Rosenblum deplored this limited interest in the outside world in two successive and highly revealing memoirs: *Coups and Earthquakes: Reporting the World to America* (1981) and *Who Stole the News? Why We Can't Keep up with What Happens in the World and What We Can Do about it* (1993).

Shortly after the Second World War, he says, a study estimated that there were 2,500 full-time American reporters abroad for newspapers, magazines and radio. From then on, the figure went down. After the end of the Vietnam war, a study by Ralph Kliesch of Ohio University counted a low of only 676 people working for US news organizations abroad. In 1990 this figure was back up again to 1,734 people, of whom 820 were Americans and 914 foreigners. These numbers were inflated, though, by the emergence of television – where individual reporters may be surrounded by an entire crew, often consisting of locals. Compare this figure, furthermore, with the sum total of 211 foreign correspondents for a small and marginal country like the Netherlands (16 million inhabitants) around the same time – no crew members included. The figure excludes overlap, but probably includes a number of part-timers.

Yet it should be acknowledged that the central position and scale of the US have enabled some American media to become some of the best staffed in the world, with some of the best and brightest among foreign correspondents. The *New York Times* has some thirty bureaux abroad, the *Washington Post* about twenty. Correspondents are often assisted by local staff. These two papers also participate in the *International Herald Tribune*, which thus boasts a network of thirty foreign bureaux: some its own, some shared with the others. *Le Monde*, the much smaller and poorer French daily, claims fifty corresponents abroad plus a few in French overseas territories (although a number of these are probably part-timers, without assistance). Some of the difference can be explained by the fact that American postings across the US are not labelled foreign, whereas French postings within neighbouring European countries are. So the contrast may be slightly smaller than it seems.

No matter how international such news-gathering networks are, they always cater primarily for the home audience of one nation. This holds even more for television coverage, which has overtaken the press as the prime definer of world news. American public opinion, for instance, is highly dependent upon American television news. The problem with some commercial network television news is that in its battle for ratings it caters mostly to the greatest common denominator. It hardly bothers its audience with background and analysis any more. This leaves room for only a few hyped-up, snappy foreign news flashes which inevitably project an extremely stereotypical image of the outside world.

The major world news agencies may have people in close to a hundred foreign locations. But – as we have seen before – major quality papers have correspondents in a maximum of fifty and a minimum of twenty capitals abroad. Television networks may have even fewer. As a rule of thumb, somewhat less than a third of agency correspondents are stationed in North America, somewhat more than a third in Western Europe and roughly a third cover the entire rest of the world: Eastern Europe, Africa, the Arab world, Asia, Oceania and Latin America.

In recent years there has been a noticeable shift, particularly to East Asia, now identified as a major current and future growth area, and therefore an important producer and consumer of news. Yet major intercontinental news media continue to cover entire continents with only one or two correspondents. Where are these other correspondents stationed? Oliver Boyd-Barretts's study of *The International News Agencies* (1980: 152–3) identified a number of interrelated factors which help explain differences in the strength of agency representation in different countries, as well as disparities in wire content:

> The most important of these can be categorized as (i) *historical*, referring largely to the continuing influence of the old agency cartel practices; (ii) *logistical*, referring to differences between countries in their importance as possible strategic or communication centres for coverage of wider geographic regions; (iii) *political* factors arising from controls or restrictions

imposed by given countries on visiting correspondents; (iv) more important than these others, *commercial* or *cost/revenue* factors arising out of
differences in market-pull between different areas in the world, and differences in the responsiveness of the agencies to the news requirements of
different markets; while (v), a category of *'temporary'* factors, relates to
news crises in centres which are not otherwise well represented.

Similar factors apply to media correspondents in general. Cultural
values and ideological affinities play a role, as well as available facili-
ties to sustain a larger foreign community (housing, schools, leisure).
Japanese media and correspondents would thus prefer a capital which
already has a significant Japanese community – if there is one at hand.
Islamic media and correspondents would prefer a capital with a significant Islamic community. And most Western correspondents prefer
a capital with a significant Western community.

All other things being equal, a more congenial environment is
obviously preferred over a less congenial one. Wherever there is a
choice, most Western media correspondents would rather reside in a
capital or country which is considered more or less (pro)-Western in
outlook. From that vantage point, they will also report on other
nearby capitals and countries which are considered more or less non-
or anti-Western. Whenever there is a crisis, they therefore have easier
and wider access to information and sources which tend to present
one side of the story. This tends to reinforce other tendencies in the
same direction.

The everyday life of an alien

When a news medium claims it has a foreign correspondent somewhere, this may mean a variety of things. The first possibility is that it
has one or several foreign correspondents there, with a real bureau,
that is to say, an office with a small staff of assistants. This is often the
case for the larger American media. The second possibility is that it
has a full-time salaried correspondent, who works largely on his or
her own. This is often the case for the larger European media. The
third possibility is that it has a part-time salaried correspondent, who
is shared with other (non-competing) media. This is often the case for
the smaller European media (where a journalist from one country
simultaneously works for a daily and a weekly, a radio and a
television broadcaster). The fourth possibility is that it has a free-lance
correspondent or a stringer, who gets paid only whenever they order
or accept a news item or feature. He or she may have other activities
on the side, which may or may not be in the field of journalism.
Finally, a large variety of helpers may play some role too: technicians,
researchers, typists, drivers, etc.

In general, these five levels form some kind of implicit hierarchy,
not only because full-time correspondents with competent assistants

will work for the more powerful foreign media at the most important overseas locations, whereas free-lancers and stringers may work for less powerful media and/or at less important locations. Those higher up in the hierarchy often tend to be well-educated, well-connected, slightly more mature white middle-class males, usually from the media home country itself (or its nearest equivalent); whereas those lower in the hierarchy are more often younger or non-whites, often from the correspondent's assigned country (or its equivalent).

Maintaining a full-time foreign correspondent abroad is an extremely expensive proposition for a medium. It takes a decent salary, considerable surcharges to enable the correspondent and family to have social security and a lifestyle comparable to that in the home country, office and documentation costs, communication and travel allowances. For full-time correspondents from most Western countries, this easily amounts to 100,000 dollars a year or more. For a large amount of say a hundred items a year, this still amounts to 1,000 dollars an item. It is much cheaper to take these from a news agency or syndication service. Usually therefore, this expenditure is worthwhile only if (1) the correspondent is based in a place which generates many possible items, and (2) the correspondent can deliver them custom-made for the home medium and the home audience.

It is rather rare for a full-time salaried correspondent to be based in one foreign location for a full decade, several decades or a whole lifetime, even if she or he knows the local language and customs better than anyone else. There are a few such exceptional cases, for instance, when he or she is married to a local and cannot or will not move for other reasons. The standard objection is, however, that the journalist will gradually lose the perspective of the home country, adopt that of the host country, come to identify too closely with it and may even become complacent or subject to pressure. The most widespread practice is, therefore, to move correspondents every few years, or even to require them to spend a few years back in the home country on the editorial staff itself every now and then to regain a better understanding of new procedures and altered perspectives.

In the context of this book, it is important to consider the implications of this policy. Even if many correspondents do indeed learn the language, study the culture, learn the ropes, strike up new relationships with each new posting, the chances that they can completely blend in are rather limited. This is not even the goal, since it is judged as important that they retain the perspective of the home country, or at least that they mediate the perspective of the host country for it.

The more alien the host country, the higher the chances that Western correspondents stick closely together to maintain a Western perspective on the alien reality. Even in most First World capitals, Western correspondents from one particular home country or even one particular group of home countries (North Americans, Anglo-

Saxons, West Europeans), meet quite regularly and exchange information. In major Second and Third World capitals, however, this contact is more intense, even if there is no formal foreign press club. Not only do they maintain intense contacts among themselves, but also with possible sources of information from their own country or group of countries.

There may be religious and humanitarian sources, for instance, clergymen from church organizations and laymen from charitable organizations; experts, for instance, development aid workers or consultants; economic sources, for instance, bankers or traders, or managers of foreign companies; political sources, for instance, representatives of various embassy departments; army and intelligence sources, for instance, defence attachés or military advisers. In Third and Second World capitals, First World journalists often share a large part of their social life with this entire expatriate community, and come to share information and views. They often live in the same neighbourhoods, belong to the same clubs, send their children to the same schools. (The same, of course, often applies to Third or Second World journalists living in the First World or, for instance, Japanese in America and Europe.)

In Nairobi, the capital of Kenya, for example (long perceived as a more or less pro-Western country from where many Western journalists cover East Africa or even larger parts of the black continent), they often tend to work closely together. In their book *The Known World of Broadcast News* (1990), the radio journalists Roger Wallis and Stanley Baran quoted the BBC stringer Lindsey Hilsum in this regard:

> Other journalists passing through are sometimes surprised at how much we do collaborate with each other. I think it's vital, simply because it's so difficult to get any information out of anybody. Getting anything out of Government is really getting blood from stone. If you do get anything, you will obviously want to get it first, but then you will want to share it . . . Obviously you check out the information as far as possible, but it's the same here as anywhere else; you know who the good journalists are. You know who not to trust as well. The local papers, for instance, are the seed of many stories, but you never take them as truth. (p. 231)

This also points to another important fact. Not only do journalists often get a considerable part of their information or perspective from other journalists, but the media often get a considerable part of their information from other media as well. The national press, radio and television often provide raw material for foreign journalists. The degree to which they trust it differs in Third and Second World countries, and even within First World countries themselves. If they do not trust the local media, Western journalists will also try to tap other major international media or news-gathering organizations for more background. They may be able to buy major international newspapers, to listen to BBC World Service radio or the Voice of America, or to receive CNN. On occasion, they may also have access to material from the major wire services, either directly or through contact with their home staff. The important thing to note is that this may then decisively influence their perceptions of what is happening around them, supposedly under their own eyes.[2]

Parachute journalism and pack journalism

Recycling information and a circular reaction among foreign journalists (that is, a self-reinforcing reaction to events) have become increasingly common phenomena, particularly in major crisis situations. They may have several serious consequences. One is that certain rumours may be taken to confirm or corroborate other rumours, since it looks as if they come from a different source, whereas ultimately they come from the same source. A second consequence is that certain relatively arbitrary definitions of the situation may come to be seen as absolutely trustworthy ones. And a third consequence is that one particular world-view may come to dominate the entire spectrum. In recent years, there have been a few major cases where dozens of Western journalists reported that they had seen the most dramatic things with their own eyes, whereas it later turned out they had not. How is this possible?

Whenever a major crisis breaks out at a considerable distance from places which are routinely covered by correspondents, large numbers of foreign journalists may try to get there as fast as they can. Such parachuted journalists may range from experienced reporters sent on their umpteenth assignment to young free-lancers covering their very first stories. The more acute the crisis, the more exotic the location and the parties involved, the greater the risk of massive derailments. There are basically two groups of reasons for this: one related to the limits of the local infrastructure, the other to the nature of the patterns of interaction which follow.

The limits of the local infrastructure relate to the resources reporters need. There may be only one or two major hotels nearby which can accommodate large groups of unexpected and demanding clients, therefore journalists may end up in the same accomodation, sharing food and drink and conversation. There may be only a limited number of cars for hire, with or without drivers, therefore, many journalists may try to share costs and transport and rides. There may be a dearth of leads; hearsay, rumour and gossip may therefore easily come to dominate their daily exchange of information.

There may be only a limited number of improvised guides and translators, many of them too strongly motivated by money, kicks, ideology or a volatile mixture of all three. Official sources may

Missiles at Iraqi Nuclear Site

Clinton Supports Attack, Calling It 'Appropriate'

By Paul F. Horvitz
International Herald Tribune

WASHINGTON — United States warships launched a concentrated cruise missile attack Sunday night against what was described as a nuclear installation near Baghdad as a confrontation with Iraq escalated sharply.

A total of 40 to 50 "smart" cruise missiles, carrying 1,000-pound conventional warheads, were launched, according to the CBS and ABC television networks.

[At least three people were killed during the attack, Reuters reported from Baghdad, quoting a hospital doctor. "I know of three dead and 19 wounded in my hospital alone," said Dr. Fawzan Nuun, head of surgery at Yarmouk Hospital in Baghdad.]

Marlin Fitzwater, the White House spokesman, said that the target was a suburban, multi-building, nuclear-reprocessing and fabrication plant at Zafaraniyah, on the Tigris River about 20 kilometers (13 miles) from the center of Baghdad.

He said the attack was launched to "demonstrate our determination to demand Iraq's compliance" with United Nations resolutions passed during and after the Gulf War. He declined to say which ships had launched the missiles, but it is known that American surface ships, and probably submarines, are on station in the Gulf.

President-elect Bill Clinton, who takes office on Wednesday, immediately issued a statement supporting the U.S. action.

"Saddam Hussein's continuing provocation can been met by appropriate and forceful response," his statement said. "I fully support President Bush's action."

"Saddam Hussein should be very clear in understanding that the current and the next administration are in complete agreement on the necessity of his fully complying with all relevant United Nations Security Council resolutions."

The cruise missile attack came three hours after American officials announced that warplanes had shot down an Iraqi fighter that had violated the "no-fly" zone in northern Iraq earlier in the day. U.S. planes attacked an Iraqi radar site that had the coalition pilots.

"Noncompliance with UN Security Council resolutions will not be tolerated," Mr. Fitzwater said after the missile attack. He strongly indicated that more such attacks would be

considered unless Baghdad adheres to the terms and spirit of all UN resolutions.

"The purpose, the goal of that operation is to seek compliance with UN resolutions," he said. "We do not have that yet, and I don't believe that you can assume that these kinds of episodes are over until we get compliance."

Aides to President George Bush and Mr. Clinton were in close contact throughout the day, and Mr. Bush, spending the day at the presidential retreat in Camp David, Maryland, was said to have discussed the situation with Prime Ministers John Major of Britain and Brian Mulroney of Canada as well as President

See RAID, Page 4

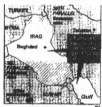

François Mitterrand of France and Turkish officials.

As the attack was mounting, at about 10 P.M. Baghdad time, anti-aircraft fire and tracers filled the night sky over the Iraqi capital. The Iraqi nuclear complex reported to have been singled out... U.S. and allied warplanes during the Gulf War, which began precisely two years... that was not destroyed. Later, it was visited by UN inspectors.

CNN quoted its map statement Sunday, saying that the missiles hit a mechanical engineering plant, not a nuclear site. The network said the statement, from the Iraqi Information Ministry, asserted that the plant made molds and dyes. The White House said earlier that the plant was a nuclear fabricating plant which made components for nuclear weapons.

An Iraqi-born journalist working for a British newspaper was caught, tried and hung in Baghdad a few years ago after he was found

---

ton, Here Comes the Hard Part

...Pfiffner, a professor of government and public policy at George Mason University who has studied past transitions, gives Mr. Clinton high marks. "As the public and symbolic level, it's been a success," Mr. Pfiffner said.

But a prominent Democrat from outside the capital had a different view. "All sorts of alarm bells have been going off," he said. "I

1 a crisp and White House. son arrived in nch of loungeiced anew was s of his candidg the econo-

brought some ment of good stimating outd a skillfully sis. But conpointees' eth- parties, ques- a campaign economy pos- ing that do- the transition

NEWS ANALYSIS

looks to me like they've violated half a dozen of their campaign pledges. They really have given the impression that they're approaching business as usual. I think they've got a real challenge now to demonstrate that they really can govern with something new and different and innovative."

Aides say they believe the coming week of celebration and symbolism will drown out whatever negative commentary may be swirl-

ing about — just as the Democratic convention last summer gave the Clinton ticket an enormous lift at a time when the candidate was being challenged by the press. "The inaugural is a direct form of communication, just like the convention," said a Clinton pollster, Stan Greenberg.

Aides admit Mr. Clinton will be in trouble unless he can discipline himself to establish a handful of priorities and a timetable for action — and then delegate much of the rest.

Mr. Clinton faces difficult decisions on the economy and health-care reform. Foreign-policy crises, meanwhile, cry out for action even before Mr. Clinton has put in place a team big enough to handle them all.

One Clinton adviser was recently asked to describe the difference between Mr. Clinton as a candidate and Mr. Clinton as president-

See CLINTON, Page 4

IHT   18-1-93

Reporters' Favorite Hotel Is Damaged During Raid

Reuters

BAGHDAD — The Rashid hotel in con... chairs everywhere. There was broken glass and puddles of water on the floor.

Ir. Saddam's address, in which he restated Iraq's claim to Kuwait and his defiance toward the West.

Karen Schlossberg-Frans-Press

Figure 7.1 *Selective attention. On the second anniversary of the beginning of the Gulf War, the US bombarded an Iraqi site. One of the front page headlines in the* International Herald Tribune *following the raid said 'Reporters' Favorite Hotel Is Damaged During Raid', it did not say if other civilian targets had been hit as well. (From the International Herald Tribune, 18 January 1993 and reproduced by permission of the New York Times Syndicate.)*

be inaccessible and/or not credible, opposition sources may be just as inaccessible and/or not credible. A number of ordinary people may claim to be in the know, but they too do not distinguish between what they have seen and heard, between first- and second-hand information, which may turn out to be tenth-hand and distorted. In short: it is hard to sift fact from fantasy.

Several conditions may aggravate this situation. The first is if the events take place in a country with an unfamiliar culture and an unfamiliar language: in such cases, observers often do not have a clue as to what is really going on. The second is if the events take place in a country with a peculiar political system (totalitarian, for instance), which may or may not be breaking down, permanently or temporarily. The third is if the journalists themselves have strong feelings about the past, present and future of this political system (such as the perceived 'emergence of democracy').

Such conditions were united when a host of Western journalists reported that they had seen thousands of students killed under their own eyes, crushed by tanks in Tiananmen Square, victims of government repression in the Chinese capital of Beijing. (Considerable numbers have probably been killed elsewhere, before and after that, but no mass killings took place there and then, as it turned out.) Such conditions were also united when a host of Western journalists reported that they had seen a mass grave with many thousands of mutilated bodies, victims of government repression and torture, in the Romanian city of Timisoara.

These two are extreme cases, which became well known and have since been thoroughly studied. There were many similar cases which were not as extreme or clear-cut, which have not become as well known and have not been studied as thoroughly. They were related to gross over-dramatization or gross under-dramatization of both negative and positive events. They were related not only to the news net, news flow and the world of the news as painted by the media. They were also related to other factors, to which we will return.

News flows

The debate about the worldwide news net is closely related to the debate about the worldwide news flow and the debate about the world of the news which (in part) results from it. The debate about the intercontinental flow of information goes back to (at least) the end of the Second World War, to the establishment of the United Nations Organization in New York, and of its educational, scientific and cultural branch UNESCO in Paris. At the time, these organizations were comfortably dominated by the Western allies, which had just defeated the fascist Axis powers, and were bracing themselves for a cold war with the communist Eastern bloc. They believed in a free flow of information between countries.

Whereas the US favoured a rapid decolonization, the West Europeans long resisted the independence movements throughout their former empires at the time. But between the late forties and the late sixties, scores of 'new' countries emerged in the Third World all the same. They tried to steer clear of the East–West (or West–East) confrontation, and gradually formed the so-called non-aligned movement. They complained that global exchanges of news and views were still dominated by the North, and demanded a more balanced flow of information with the South.

Neutral observers such as President Kekkonen of Finland conceded that they had a point. He said:

> The traditional Western concept of freedom, which states that the state's only obligation is to guarantee laissez-faire, has meant that society has allowed freedom of speech to be realized with the means at the disposal of each individual. In this way freedom of speech has in practice become the freedom of the well-to-do. A different judicial system would not just be content at guaranteeing freedom of action to its citizens. It would define basic rights in a positive way. The state would be obliged to arrange for its citizens the practical possibility towards the realization of their rights . . .
>
> In the world of communication it can be observed how problems of freedom of speech within one state are identical to those in the world community formed by different states. At an international level are to be found the ideals of free communication and their actual distorted execution for the rich on the one hand and the poor on the other. Globally the flow of information between states – not least the material pumped out by television – is to a very great extent a one-way, unbalanced traffic, and in no way possesses the depth and range which the principles of freedom of speech require. (Gerbner et al., 1993: x–xi)

The issue was taken up at the summit meetings of non-aligned countries in Algiers (1973), Colombo (1976), Havana (1979) and repeatedly put on the agenda of the UNESCO General Conference and its committee meetings in Paris and abroad. At the time I covered several of these summits and meetings on the spot as a journalist, which forcefully confronted me with other views of world communication. The Tunisian secretary of state for information, Mustapha Masmoudi, for one, presented a key document calling attention to:

> 1. A flagrant quantitative imbalance between North and South . . . 2. An inequality in information resources . . . 3. A de facto hegemony and a will to dominate . . . 4. A lack of information on developing countries . . . 5. Survival of the colonial era . . . 6. An alienating influence in the economic, social and cultural spheres . . . [and] 7. Messages ill-suited to the areas in which they are disseminated. (*Journal of Communication*, Spring 1979, vol 29, no. 2: 172–85)

As the debate heated up, there was an explosion of studies on the subject. One major scholar of the field noted that he had been able to identify no more than 318 publications in the broad category of the 'international flow of information' between 1850 and 1969, whereas he found no less than 447 different items dealing with the flow of news for the period from 1973 through the early part of 1983 (Mowlana, 1986: 19). Another scholar summed up the conclusions of such studies, saying that:

Quantitatively it may be estimated that the total flow of communication taking place between the industrialized part of the world (inhabited by some one-third of mankind) and the Third World (comprising about two-thirds) takes place at least a hundred times more in the direction from the industrialized to developing countries than vice versa. (Kaarle Nordenstreng, quoted in Frederick, 1993: 128)

Meanwhile, the UNESCO General Conference had appointed a broad International Commission for the Study of Communication Problems headed by Sean MacBride, a former Irish minister of foreign affairs, a founder of Amnesty International and winner of the Nobel Prize. It also included Hubert Beuve-Méry, founder of the respected French daily *Le Monde*, the famous Colombian novelist Gabriel Garcia Marquez, the well-known Indonesian journalist Mochtar Lubis, Jan Pronk later the Dutch minister of development cooperation and eleven others. Their 1980 report *Many Voices, One World* summed up all aspects of the debate, and reinforced the call for 'a new world information and communication order' (NWICO for short). When Third World countries, supported by Second World countries, tried to follow this up with concrete proposals, however, the major First World countries proved sceptical.

They feared new charters and rules might lead to licensing journalists, to limitations on international news-gathering and ultimately to a suppression of press freedom, since many of the NWICO advocates had a dubious track record in those fields. They also felt highly critical about the UNESCO organization and its director-general, M'Bow, their supposed inefficiency and nepotism. The counter-offensive was led by the administrations of the Conservative Prime Minister Margaret Thatcher and the Republican President Ronald Reagan, and supported by the major Anglo-American media organizations. A recent series of studies claims that this resulted in a rather one-sided reporting of the entire UNESCO debate. (See Gerbner et al., 1993, particularly Part III.)

The Western political and media offensive resulted in the temporary withdrawal of the UK and the US from the international organization, and a refusal to pay their dues. It also precipitated a financial and a policy crisis, leading to the dismissal of the old director-general and the election of a new 'more moderate' one. In the process, the NWICO debate became largely side-tracked and stalled. Today, only limited technical and professional assistance to Third World media and journalists is still under consideration.

The world of the news

The question is, of course, do geographical news net and news flows make a difference in what reaches politicians and the public elsewhere,

in the emphasis on certain problems cum solutions and not on others?
As Bernard Cohen (1963) says:

> The 'map-making' function of the press is very easy to overlook, because
> the newspaper is so much a part of our everyday life, like the morning cup
> of coffee with which it is intimately associated. It is overlooked also
> because of a general tendency to regard the news as objective or factual,
> and hence to think of the possible impact of the press largely in terms of
> editorial persuasions. Yet, this map-making function is . . . central to the
> real impact of the press in the foreign policy field. (p. 12)

One early and illuminating study of the world of the news, by
George Gerbner and George Márványi (summarized in Gerbner and
Márványi, 1977) was done when the Cold War was still on. They
compared foreign news coverage from all over the world in its scope
and emphasis. They selected three countries from each of the three
worlds. They analysed the relative space devoted to foreign news in
general and to these various regions in particular. For each of the
countries and blocs, they then produced world maps, in which the
(inflated or deflated) volume of the various regions corresponded to
the relative attention given to them by the media. This visual device
(related to the procedure discussed in the introduction to this book) is
a good illustration of the fact that the world of the news differs from
country to country – but still has certain traits in common.

Over the years, there have been various such attempts to settle
questions on the supposed geographical and topical one-sidedness of
news with the help of the well-known formal technique of content
analysis. A selection of a representative (or composite) period may be
studied, for instance, the Monday of week A, the Tuesday of week B,
etc.; and/or a full week or month of the year. A selection of countries
and media is also made, for instance, some representative élite and
popular newspapers plus (tapes or transcripts of) the major radio and
television news programmes on the main channels.

The researcher acquires the help of a panel (usually students), who
are briefly trained and tested for objectivity. They are then asked
to measure the length of the news items, to note from where and
whom they came, to score the topic(s), the actor(s), the source(s), etc.
One may even try to evaluate both the event and/or the report as
positive or negative or neutral. These variables can then be related to
each other and analysed. For instance, do certain Western media
devote much more attention to Western events than to non-Western
ones, more attention to negative non-Western topics than to positive
ones, etc.

At the height of the NWICO debate, the UNESCO General
Conference had asked the (old) director-general to arrange for a major
study of how countries with different social systems and at various
developmental stages were portrayed by the world's mass media. He
assigned it to the representative International Association for Mass

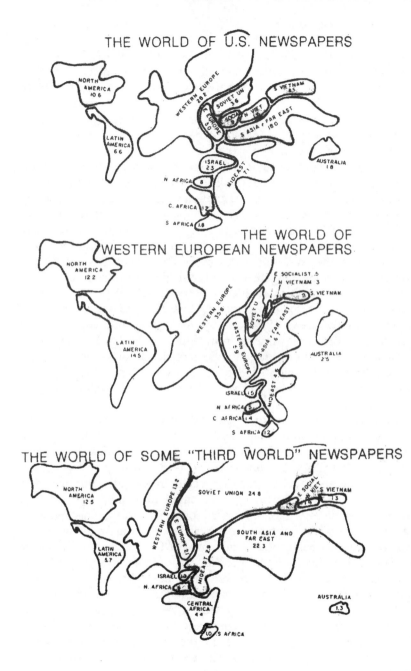

Figure 7.2 *The relative importance of foreign news about various regions in a sample of newspapers from around the world. (From 'The many worlds of the world's press',* Journal of Communication, *27, 1: 52–66 and reproduced by permission of Oxford University Press.)*

Communication Research (IAMCR), whose president at the time was Professor James Halloran, director of the Centre for Mass Communication Research at the University of Leicester in the UK. Everyday coordination and reporting was at first in the hands of Paul Hartmann, then in those of Annabelle Sreberny-Mohammadi. More than a dozen national groups of scholars took it upon themselves to assemble data on foreign affairs coverage by a selection of daily newspapers and major broadcasting channels in twenty-nine different countries over a total of two weeks.

They used the same categories and shared the resulting material for further comparison and analysis. The 1984 final report identified six major conclusions: (1) selection criteria in international news reporting have become almost universal; (2) all national media systems emphasize regional events and actors; (3) the US and Western Europe are consistently news-makers in all regions; (4) after the US and Western Europe come the 'hot-spot' stories; (5) Third World countries not covered as 'hot spots', together with the socialist countries, remain the least covered areas in international news reporting; (6) the national news agency or the 'own correspondent' is the most important source for international news, followed by the major international news agencies. At the same time, it turned out to be hard to prove or disprove some of the major contentions of the debaters with the help of traditional techniques of content analysis alone. (See the conclusions and debate in the *Journal of Communication*, Winter 1984, vol. 34, no. 4: 121–42.)

Meanwhile, the American national group, headed by Robert Stevenson and Donald Shaw of the School of Journalism at the University of North Carolina at Chapel Hill, had set out on a course of its own. It enlisted the financial and technical help of the United States Information Agency (the overseas opinion and communication branch of the State Department) and some individuals, and was thus able to cover no less than seventeen countries – some on continents that otherwise could not have been included. But the American group also chose to emphasize that it felt some of the criticism of the major Western news media and agencies was highly exaggerated and remained unconfirmed. Third World editors themselves, it said, proved just as one-sided in spontaneously ignoring items from other Third World continents and from Second World countries, in emphasizing items from First World countries, in favouring negative over positive news, in using terse prose inviting readers to fill in the gaps, etc. Yet none of this could be attributed to a deliberate skewing of reports.

Since those days, a host of other studies have been published, based on content analysis and a systematic comparison of news reports in various countries. Some focus on particular media, such as Wallis and Baran's study on *The Known World of Broadcast News*;

others focus on particular subjects, such as Cohen, Adoni and Bantz's study of *Social Conflict and Television News* (both published in 1990). The problem is that purely formal content analyses often cannot resolve all controversies that remain – for epistemological and semiological reasons we will return to in Chapters 8 and 9. Even the same statistics may lead to widely divergent interpretations by scholars from various nationalities and persuasions. Some very basic observations may well be made, however.

As AP's Mort Rosenblum said (1993: 270):

> From 1960 to the 1980s, forty independent African countries joined the world community. In 1989, US news organizations paid less attention to all of them put together than to the trial of Zsa Zsa Gabor for slugging a Beverly Hills cop. Or to a few California grey whales trapped in Alaskan ice. And that was when we were watching closely.

Since then, we have been treated to the Clarence Thomas/Anita Hill confrontation, the Tonya Harding/Nancy Kerrigan affair, the O. J. Simpson trial. Neither the race issue, nor the sports, nor the celebrities in question were particularly recognizable for overseas audiences beforehand. Yet increasingly, such American news soap operas conquer the whole world.

The unequal coverage of geographical space seems to be intertwined with a vicious circle: certain areas have more foreign journalists because they generate more foreign news, but they also generate more foreign news because they have more foreign journalists. Events in the world peripheries are often even refracted and reframed through the lenses of the world centres. Thus, the perspectives of the great mass of the world population are under-represented in global news, while those of relatively small élites are over-represented. After the non-aligned countries' and international organizations' debates on the desirability of a New World Information and Communication Order, various researchers have investigated the world of the news. They found that selection criteria have become almost universal.

Notes

1 Ch. 2 in *Making News: A Study in the Social Construction of Reality* (1978), pp. 21, 23.

2 Content analyses claiming that only a certain percentage of international news comes from news agencies, whereas the rest comes from 'our own correspondents' often tend to forget that the latter often derive their prime definition and frame from initial reporting by the former as well.

Further reading

News net and agencies: Boyd-Barrett. *News flows and Unesco debate:* Frederick; Hamelink; MacBride; Mowlana; Reeves. *World of the news:* Gerbner and Siefert; Wallis and Baran.

8 HOW ARE NEWS MESSAGES FORMULATED?

THE LINGUISTICS OF LINES AND BETWEEN THE LINES

··

> Briefly put, the way an object is described and the manner in which a course of action is presented direct our thoughts and channel our cognitive responses concerning the communication. Through the labels we use to describe an object or an event, we can define it in such a way that the recipient of our message accepts our definition of the situation and is thus pre-persuaded even before we seriously begin to argue.
>
> Anthony Pratkanis and Elliot Aronson,
> 'Pre-persuasion: Setting the stage for effective influence'.[1]

In our common-sense and everyday life, we consider language a simple instrument for the neutral reflection, the mirroring of the world. But is this realistic? Is there not always more than one synonym at hand, with a slightly different connotation? Is not the use of euphemisms and metaphors commonplace, particularly by influential spokesmen or women (see Chapter 5). And even if journalists themseleves strive for unambiguous language, is this an attainable ideal? How can evaluations become imperceptibly woven into descriptions, through various ordinary means of sentence formulation and narrative construction? How do news items relate to mega-stories about particular issues, to the central myths and unacknowledged ideologies of our society?

Both media producers and media consumers can only perceive and render the world in terms of meaning systems, in terms of pre-existing frames. The sociologist Erving Goffman observed in his book *Frame Analysis* (1986) that 'each primary framework allows its user to locate, perceive, identify and label a seemingly infinite number of concrete occurrences defined in its terms. He is likely to be unaware of such organized features as the framework has and unable to describe the framework with any completeness if asked' (p. 21). One of our primary meaning systems is language. Language is not a mirror but a frame.

The social psychologists Pratkanis and Aronson recall some familiar examples of linguistic framing (1992: 46):

> Early American patriots were able to increase revolutionary fervor by terming a minor skirmish with the British the *Boston massacre*. Adolf Hitler

used the same technique to mobilize the German people by explaining Germany's economic troubles in terms of the *red menace* and the *Jewish problem*. Those opposed to abortion call their position *pro-life*, whereas those supporting a women's right to elect an abortion call their position *pro-choice*.

The Defense Department (formerly the War Department) uses the term *low-intensity conflict* to refer to wars the United States supported in Nicaragua and El Salvador during the 1980s; this is a curious term when one considers that these have been very intense experiences for those innocent civilians caught in the crossfire – estimated at 50,000 in Nicaragua and 70,000 in El Salvador. Similarly, those opposed to the war with Iraq talked about 'bringing home our sons and daughters in body bags', whereas the military used more sanitized terms, such as *collateral damage* and *BDA* (bomb-damage assessment). Politicians interpret social problems and invent the national agenda by such phrases as *the Cold War, the domino theory of creeping communism, perestroika and glasnost, the war against drugs, Japanese protectionism,* and, now, *the new world order.*

Others had drawn attention to the key importance of political language well before. George Orwell's novel *Nineteen Eighty-four*, first published in 1949, was a warning against totalitarianism of either the left or the right, in which Big Brother continually had history rewritten in the language of the day: Newspeak.

> The purpose of Newspeak was not only to provide a medium of expression for the world-view and mental habits proper to the devotees of Ingsoc, but to make all other modes of thought impossible. It was intended that when Newspeak had been adopted once and for all and Oldspeak forgotten, a heretical thought – that is, a thought diverging from the principles of Ingsoc – should be literally unthinkable, at least so far as thought is dependent on words. (p. 241)

The continuous production and reproduction of language comparable to Newspeak within each political culture, however, is also a spontaneous process.

In the present-day Western world, for instance, some newspeak does result from the selective importation of strange words. At the outset, they were meaningless, in the new language that is. But subsequently they began to signify something entirely new. Since they were associated with strangeness, this often resonated heavily with the moral superiority or moral inferiority dimension. From Eastern Europe we selectively adopted terms such as: dissident, glasnost, gulag, perestroika, samizdat, securitate, Solidarnosc, Stasi and others. From Latin America we have adopted campesino, caudillo, contra, guerrilla, macho, latifundia and others. From the Middle East we have adopted ayatollah, jihad, mullah, mujahedin, shalom, sheik, sultan. It is interesting to note that the labels imported from various regions belong to entirely different political registers. But their alien character invariably tends to give them an added negative or positive afterglow.

The choice of words

Reality is largely continuous and unstable; language and thought impose most discontinuity and stability. They help us make sense. Sign systems are largely built from oppositions and categorizations: white and black, instead of a hundred shades of grey; a dozen colours instead of a thousand. This cutting up of reality into bits and pieces implies the application of a cultural grid. The more meaningful a certain sphere of reality and practice is within a certain culture, the more detailed and complex the language dealing with it will be.

Furthermore, words have denotations and connotations, and provoke associations as well. The denotation is the literal meaning, as it can be found in any dictionary. The connotations are the various figurative and other collateral meanings which have also been attached to it. The associations may or may not be related to the original meaning; they may be based on pure coincidences which made an impression (between sounds or images or both, for instance). One classic is Raymond Williams's study *Keywords: A Vocabulary of Culture and Society* (1983). It illustrates the fact that the meaning of a word to someone (or to an entire group) is never simple and straightforward; it is always complex and layered, ambiguous and contradictory, with certain elements placed in and others hidden from immediate sight. This is most obvious for various categories of suggestive and colourful language, of which we have quoted examples before. Two pertinent forms are euphemisms and metaphors.

EUPHEMISMS William Lutz (1989) has published a hilarious book about euphemisms, jargon, gobbledegook and other forms of inflated language. He gave examples:

> There are no potholes in the streets of Tucson, Arizona, just 'pavement deficiencies'. The Reagan Administration didn't propose any new taxes, just 'revenue enhancement' through new 'user's fees'. Those aren't bums on the street, just 'non-goal oriented members of society'. There are no more poor people, just 'fiscal underachievers'. There was no robbery of an automatic teller machine, just 'unauthorized withdrawal'. The patient didn't die because of medical malpractice, it was just a 'diagnostic misadventure of a high magnitude'. The US Army doesn't kill enemies any more, it just 'services the target'. And the doublespeak goes on.

He explained: 'Doublespeak is language that pretends to communicate but really doesn't. It is language that makes the bad seem good, the negative appear positive, the unpleasant appear attractive or at least tolerable. Doublespeak is language that avoids or shifts responsibility, language that is at variance with its real or purported meaning' (p. 1). Doublespeak increasingly permeates press releases and news accounts, particularly when there is a conflict or crisis going on.

METAPHORS   Another pertinent category is that of metaphors; those referring to illness, natural disasters, wars may be particularly evocative. In the Flemish case, Christ'l De Landtsheer (1987) set out to demonstrate that the rise and fall of such metaphoric language in the newspapers corresponded with the rise and fall of (a sense of) crises. In his study of the 1986 'Tamil panic' in the Dutch press, Teun Van Dijk (1988b: 244) noted that the sudden influx of a relatively small group of refugees gave rise to a range of highly dramatic wording and imaging. One paper even spoke of

> an 'invasion', which suggests the imminent presence of a hostile foreign army. In The Netherlands, which has a long nationalistic tradition of struggle against water, the flow metaphors are particularly revealing and effective. The remedy against such tidal waves is to build dikes, and much of the reception of the Tamils can be interpreted in that metaphorical context. To keep them out, we must build dikes, dams or barriers against the flow of foreigners.

Another paper spoke of 'a "gigantic stream" of Tamils that the authorities in Amsterdam can no longer handle. The number associated with this torrent appears to be 1,200 in a city of more than 700,000 people and which annually receives millions of tourists.'

UNAMBIGUOUS LANGUAGE   It should be acknowledged, though, that the use of such blatantly tainted language is the exception rather than the rule in news reporting, for instance by press agencies. News-speak, the language of journalists, often sets out to be very straightforward. As John Hartley (1989) put it:

> News discourse is hostile to ambiguities and seeks to validate its suppression of the alternative possibilities intersecting its signs by reference either to 'the facts of the story' or to 'normal usage'. Many of the explicit 'values' of journalistic codes are concerned with unambiguity, clarity, etc. And, as we shall see, one of news discourse's most consistent (self-imposed) tasks is to *prefer* particular meanings for events over against other possible meanings. But since signs are necessarily multi-accentual, any discourse which seeks to 'close' their potential and to prefer one evaluative accent over another is ideological: such discourses present *evaluative* differences as differences in *fact*. (p. 24, italics in original)

News agencies such as the Associated Press, for instance, for a long time instructed their journalists to shun adjectives and prefer nouns, since the former look more openly evaluative/subjective and the latter look more openly factual/objective. Yet it is an illusion to think, that substantives may not be just as subjective. As a matter of fact, there seems to exist a double vocabulary in English and all other major languages: in economic, social and political matters, for instance. One vocabulary is legitimating, the other is delegitimating (Hartley speaks of 'hoorah' and 'boo' words). Journalists instinctively prefer one alternative over the other, depending on their split-second judgment of the situation.

In his book about 'the construction of the past', the Dutch historian Chris Lorenz (1987) illustrates this with the example of the events which took place on 21 January, 1793, on a square in Paris which was later renamed the Place de la Concorde. Some observers might claim that King Louis XVI was then and there murdered by the mob. Other observers might claim that Citizen Louis Capet was beheaded by the executioner. There are no adjectives here, just substantives and verbs. Yet the very choice of words implies a choice of legitimacy: of the victim, of the act, of the actor. One may try to rephrase the item to get around the problem. But whatever one does, one has to make choices from alternatives, and limit oneself to certain aspects of the situation (pp. 28–30). Not surprisingly, every subsequent regime has since favoured a different history of the French Revolution to serve its own political needs (Van Ginneken, 1992: 36–7).

Exactly the same mechanisms are at work in everyday news reporting. This is particularly obvious whenever some kind of conflict or violence is involved, whether national or international. As Gary Marx and Douglas McAdam (1994: 21) describe: 'For example, what should we call the actions in urban black areas from 1964–1968 – riots, civil disorders, rebellions, crime, or protest? Was the 1964 sit-in at the University of California administration building in Berkeley during the Free Speech movement a valiant act of protest against the denial of civil liberties, or was it criminal trespass?' Who is 'disturbing' order, and who is 'restoring' order? What order and whose order, anyway? Yet, in everyday news reporting such terms are used as if they provided simple and unproblematical descriptions of events.

Murray Edelman (1988: 98) elaborates the same problem:

> Words like 'public', 'official', 'due process of law', 'the public interest', and 'the national interest' have no specific referent, but induce a considerable measure of acceptance of actions that might otherwise be viewed with skepticism or hostility. Such terms invoke a sacred aura, as do inaugurations, flags, imposing buildings, and judicial robes.

Similarly, words like 'freedom', 'democracy', 'human rights' are continually used in foreign news as if they were entirely clear-cut and unambiguous.

In national discourse, it is easy to see that one can take various points of view, which imply various degrees of (acceptance of) legitimacy. The voices of 'the other side' get through, every now and then. In similar international cases, however, this is even more problematic, as Frederick (1993: 131) describes: 'Vietnam "fell to", but Afghanistan was "liberated from", the communists. Ronald Reagan called Nicaraguan Contras "freedom fighters", whereas the Sandinistas referred to them as "mercenaries". Palestinians are "terrorists", whereas Israelis carry out "retaliation raids".' And so on. Once again there are no adjectives, only nouns, but a lot of value judgments, implicit legitimation and delegitimation parading as factual description.

Grammar, idiom and style manuals

Standard English and other major Western languages abound in special treatments of non-dominant groups, critics say, both grammatically and idiomatically. In his *Language in the News*, Roger Fowler (1991: 95–6) observes, for instance, that:

> in languages such as English . . . gender is thoroughly encoded both in language used by women, and, perhaps more so, in language used about women. This coding is found in almost every dimension of linguistic structure, so thoroughly engrained is it. Linguists and feminists have been concerned with observations such as the following (not all of which are strongly documented, but the overall picture and case are overwhelmingly plausible):
>
> - the use of male expressions generically to include reference to females . . . : 'man', 'chairman', 'spokesman';
> - similarly, the use of the masculine pronoun 'he' to refer to females in a generic context: 'a writer must ensure that *he* does not make libelous statements' . . .;
> - the use of marked expressions containing extra morphemes or words to refer to females, implying deviance or irregularity . . .: 'actress', 'poetess', 'lady doctor', 'female accountant' . . .;
> - the use of dimunitive or juvenile forms . . . 'sweetie', 'girl';
> - titles and address forms: the choice between 'Mrs' and 'Miss', forcing a woman to declare her marital status (sexual availability) . . .;
> - the over-lexicalization of women: there are many more terms for women than for men, thus indicating that the culture regards women as having abnormal status; many of these terms are sexually abusive.

Of course this comes on top of the fact that women are much less often presented as serious speakers in newspapers, on radio and television. The Glasgow University Media Group noted in *Bad News* (1976: 15) that during the dozen weeks of the Women's Year they happened to analyse, only one out of sixteen news-readers on the three national channels, and only 65 out of 843 people interviewed 'by name' were women. I am aware, of course, that some of these things also apply to texts and quotations in this book, and indeed to many other forms of everyday communication. This is a further illustration of the fact that it is extremely hard to simply break out of such conventions, and start to write and speak a radically different language and discourse.

As far as nationality and ethnicity are concerned, standard English and other major Western languages have a host of current idiomatic expressions which are derogatory towards other groups – groups

Developing Nations Threaten to Sabotage Nuclear Treaty

By R. Jeffrey Smith
and David B. Ottaway
Washington Post Service

WASHINGTON — The Clinton administration has launched a last-ditch diplomatic campaign to overcome objections of a loose group of about 90 developing nations and win a permanent extension this spring of the global treaty that restricts the spread of nuclear arms.

The Third World countries are resisting the U.S.-led effort because they do not see why they should promise never to seek nuclear weapons when, in their view, the United States and other nuclear powers have not sufficiently pursued nuclear disarmament.

Their stance threatens a proposal by the Clinton administration for unconditional, in-

definite removal of the 25-year-old Nuclear Nonproliferation Treaty, which comes up for review at an international conference in New York in April.

President Bill Clinton was to discuss the treaty in a speech Wednesday evening, underlining what his aides say is now one of the administration's top foreign-policy priorities. He plans to echo pleas for the treaty's unconditional extension that he made in recent letters to the heads of Mexico, Colombia, Indonesia, South Africa and other nations.

But U.S. officials said the developing world's position may force Mr. Clinton to settle for a compromise, making it more feasible for countries now committed not to developing nuclear weapons to someday change their mind.

U.S. officials said that Washington needed the votes of 71

more countries to get a majority at the 172-nation conference and extend the nonproliferation treaty forever. But Washington would consider that a foreign-policy failure because it wants support from a large portion of the estimated 80 or so undecided countries.

Otherwise, U.S. officials said, they fear the treaty could lack sufficient moral and political authority to preserve global support for nonproliferation.

Many developing countries, including U.S. friends such as Egypt and Mexico, say they object to unconditional extension of the treaty because it turned out to be a bad deal. When they signed it 25 years ago, they promised not to seek to obtain nuclear weapons. In exchange, the United States, the Soviet Union and a handful of other countries with nuclear arms promised both to pursue disarmament and to provide a steady supply of peaceful nuclear technology.

Now, the developing countries claim, the treaty appears to have permanently enshrined the nuclear powers' military and political superiority. Today, the overall number of U.S. and Russian strategic nuclear

arms is more than double what it was when the treaty was signed. And even if arsenals are cut as foreseen in recent arms treaties, the number of U.S. and Russian long-range nuclear weapons will be reduced only to roughly the same level prevailing in 1970.

As a result, developing nations want to link the treaty's extension to new steps by the nuclear powers toward disarmament. While they have yet to agree on a specific proposal, their overall strategy is to exert leverage on the nuclear powers by extending the treaty only for a limited period, or a series of periods. That would deliberately create uncertainty about whether the treaty was permanent, leaving open the possibility that Third World nations would obtain nuclear weapons in the future.

An alternative proposal being raised by Egypt and some other critics of the treaty is that the New York review conference should be postponed at least until a global ban on nuclear testing is completed. That possibility alarms some supporters of disarmament.

"A short-term extension or a recess would cripple nuclear

arms-control efforts," said Joseph Cirincione, executive director of the independent Campaign for the Nonproliferation Treaty, a Washington-based coalition of 18 arms-control groups. "Many countries would feel compelled to maintain or start nuclear weapons programs — if only as a hedge against possible designs of rival states."

In the Middle East, another issue has complicated the U.S. drive. Egypt and other countries are upset that Israel, which has a substantial, undeclared nuclear arsenal, has not signed the pact or signaled any intention to do so.

Nevertheless, Israel is the one country in the region that the Clinton administration is not pressuring to endorse the treaty.

Following long-standing U.S. practice, the administration is keeping its hands off Israel's nuclear policy.

U.S. officials say it is a waste of time to urge Israel to back the treaty, because the country has long relied on its nuclear arsenal as the ultimate security guarantee and is highly unlikely to sign the treaty.

As Washington tries to build support generally for extending the treaty, some Clinton administration officials have criticized senior Clinton aides for failing to act earlier to bolster the U.S. position.

The result has been an intense last-minute, rear-guard U.S. lobbying effort in concert with other developed nations such as Canada, Australia, Britain, and France.

Washington's position is supported by three of the other declared nuclear powers — Russia, Britain, and France — by all other members of the Organization for Security and Cooperation in Europe, Scandinavian countries, Japan, and a scattering of Third World nations. While China, the only other declared nuclear power, has not yet stated its position, officials expect it to support indefinite extension by the time of the conference.

Thomas Graham, the chief U.S. negotiator, has estimated that 76 of the 172 nations that are now treaty adherents favor indefinite extension. Only 13 countries — including North Korea, Thailand, and Venezuela — are on record as opposing the U.S. plan.

Mexico Becomes a Drug Power With Help From On High

By Tod Robberson
and Douglas Farah
Washington Post Service

MEXICO CITY — Mexico, for decades a key transshipment point for cocaine entering the United States, has expanded its role over the past year as a clearinghouse for worldwide drug shipments and money laundering with the active help of business leaders and government officials, U.S. and Latin American narcotics experts say.

The Mexican narcotics organizations, which sprang up as franchises of the Colombian cocaine cartels, are now viewed by U.S. and Mexican authorities as independent entities that maintain business ties with other criminal organizations but are strong enough to operate on their own.

Experts say they have built a financial empire using the country's booming tourist industry and stock market, converting billions of dollars in drug profits into legitimate forms of capital that are integral to Mexico's financial health.

Bankers in Mexico do not discount the possibility that the December financial crunch that led to the peso's devaluation was the result, at least in part, of a massive transfer of drug money from the country.

As in Colombia, where the Medellín and Cali cartels pioneered large-scale shipments of cocaine through a combination of ruthless violence and huge bribes, the Mexican organizations depend on protection from members of government, the police and the judiciary.

In both countries, officials are often offered the choice of "silver or lead" — money or a bullet — allowing traffickers to build empires that often endanger the highest levels of government and law enforcement.

Remarkable similarities are emerging in the pattern of corruption and violence — including an unusually high-profile series of killings — that has characterized Colombia for years and marks Mexico today.

The former deputy attorney general, Mario Ruiz Massieu, is under arrest in the United States as authorities investigate links between him and the Gulf of Mexico drug cartel based in northern Tamaulipas State.

A Mexican source close to the investigation said tens of millions of dollars that Mr. Ruiz Massieu kept in several U.S. bank accounts had been traced directly to the Gulf cartel. Meanwhile, Mexican authorities say the assassination of Mr. Ruiz Massieu's brother, José Francisco, also appears to be linked to the cartel.

Investigators say they have tied the notorious Arellano Félix cartel, based in Tijuana, directly to the May 1993 shooting death of Cardinal Juan Jesús Posadas Ocampo. Now they say they are looking into the possibility of drug tie to the March 21 assassination of the governing party presidential candidate, Luis Donaldo Colosio.

A U.S. drug official said the recent political assassinations were characteristic of muscle-flexing by major drug gangs and have coincided with a number of shoot-outs between rival Colombian-allied cartels in Mexico.

As Mexico's major gangs consolidate their control and expand their alliances with Asian and European organizations, he said, there will come a time when they challenge Colombia's Cali cocaine cartel for control of the transshipment market here. The Cali organizations control about 80 percent of the world's cocaine market.

"The Mexicans in five years just might be more powerful than the Colombians," the U.S. official said. "For now, they are partners out of necessity, but it won't stay that way for long."

Evidence of the new strength acquired by the Mexican gangs has been the recent use of specially equipped Boeing 727 jets to fly tons of cocaine from Colombia to points in rural Mexico. Several jets were seized in Cali in January after making runs to Mexico.

Part of the reason that drug organizations have been so successful, U.S. officials say, is that they devote millions of dollars in profits for payoffs to Mexican officials.

A senior Mexican official said that as the chief anti-narcotics officer, Mario Ruiz Massieu held one of the most coveted positions in Mexican law enforcement.

"He decided which police chief got which region to 'enforce,'" the official said. "That is not a professional appointment based on merit, it is from special treatment."

Eduardo Valle, an anti-narcotics adviser to former Attorney General Jorge Carpizo, said: "One of the good airports, like Tamaulipas or the other border states, can sell for $1 million or $2 million. That is what you get from your own police, on top of what you get from the cartels."

Figure 8.1 *Selective legitimation and delegitimation. Two questions. Are the US and the EU (consistently the major importers and, therefore, financiers of the international drug trade) ever labelled 'drug powers'? Do the developed nations themselves not 'threaten to sabotage' the nuclear treaty by refusing to share their knowledge, and by refusing to give up their monopoly (as the article indicates)? (From the International Herald Tribune, 2 March 1995 and 14 March 1995 and reproduced by permission of The Washington Post.)*

which used to be considered hostile, different or inferior at one point in time. In some cases, this may not be a real problem. English used to have (and sometimes still has) a series of derogatory idiomatic expressions about former British rivals on the European continent, for instance, such as the Dutch and the French. Since they are more or less on a equal footing today, this may not be particularly serious. Furthermore, the Dutch and French languages may include similar derogatory idiomatic expressions about the English.

It is somewhat different for other labels, like those identifying 'Chinese' with 'funny, weird'. And it is fundamentally different with typical ethnic slurs. In recent years, therefore, there have been various attempts to draw attention to the unconsidered use of such expressions. Even the sign language for deaf people (another contested label) has recently been purged of certain gestures, like those identifying Japanese with slit eyes (*International Herald Tribune*, 2 January 1994).

Major quality papers in various countries – such as the *New York Times* in the US – have published style manuals, carrying recommendations to their contributors on correct language and identifying labels. Late in 1993 there was a row, when the editor of the *Los Angeles Times* had a 22-member committee draw up a 19-page booklet with *Guidelines on Ethnic, Racial, Sexual and other Identifications*. The booklet advised against certain stigmatic labels: birth defect, deaf (= an individual who cannot hear), crippled, handicap, invalid. They all seem to place a crude and excessive emphasis on a shortcoming, thereby denying full personhood to the people in question.

Gender labels such as coed, divorcée, mailman, mankind were prohibited because they unnecessarily make men the norm and women the exception. Geographic labels such as the 'new world' and the 'dark continent' were not recommended because they betray a Eurocentric view of history and geography. Derogatory expressions such as 'Dutch treat' and 'Chinese fire drill' were prohibited. Things became more complicated the closer one got to the ethnic and/or racial divide in Los Angeles itself. The word 'nigger' was out, of course, as was the word 'negro', although the latter is Spanish for black, and the English 'black' is acceptable. The words African American were preferred to Afro-American.

Yet some of these shifts seemed conditioned by cyclical trends and a continuous search for some kind of euphemism. Thus the labels 'slum' and 'ghetto' had evolved into the more neutral 'inner city'. But these were then considered 'weasel words' and the same label, 'slum', was reintroduced on occasion. It is not surprising, then, that the entire purge was met with ridicule by some, and with accusations of 'thought control' by others. This news-speak reminded them of the Newspeak in Orwell's *1984*, they said. The editor and his committee countered by saying that these were only recommendations for consideration, and there was no absolute taboo on certain labels. The whole debate once again drew attention to the importance of language in highlighting or blotting out certain social realities.

From words to sentences

The ideological nature of language is easiest to understand for separate words and labels. Yet this is only the very first and most elementary level on which linguistic choice manifests itself – often unconsciously. Without going into the full technicalities of a more advanced linguistic analysis, let us briefly review a few other elements which are somehow obvious, but easily overlooked. Words are linked between themselves, for instance, they are organized into sentences and accounts in definite ways.

WORD COMBINATIONS Words do not appear separately but in pairs and clusters. If one takes a close look at the words which are commonly associated with certain people or groups within published texts, definite patterns become visible. Men and women, younger and elderly people, upper-class and lower-class people, whites and non-whites are routinely associated with entirely different sets of words, and with different aspects of everyday life as well. Men may often be associated with professional roles, for instance, and women with household roles and children. Minority groups and Third World countries are constantly associated with social problems and violence.

A vocabulary should therefore be conceived not so much as a list, but rather as a (multidimensional) map. Certain words are often associated with each other – in the first, second, third and other degrees. We can make an elaborate 'mind map' of such associations. For instance: desert – sand – Africa – poor; or: desert – oil – Arab – rich; or: OPEC – cartel. In his book *Covering Islam* (1981), Edward Said comments on the extremely widespread use of the word 'oil crisis' in the media, as if it had been the only price hike in world history: 'Words like "monopoly", "cartel" and "block" thereafter achieved a remarkably sudden if selective currency, although very rarely did anyone speak of the small group of American multinationals as a cartel, a designation reserved for the OPEC members' (p. 33). As a matter of fact, the constant deterioration of terms of trade for other raw materials is usually passed over in silence, or presented as a natural fact of life.

ACTIVE/PASSIVE FORMS It is not only combinations of words which suggest a certain reading of a text, but also the ways in which the sentences are constructed. They may accentuate or mitigate responsibilities, for instance, by foregrounding participants or keeping them in the background, or by using active or passive forms. This is particularly obvious in headlines, which are usually incomplete sentences, thereby permitting very particular mechanisms of emphasis and obliteration. See Van Dijk (1988b: 11):

> A headline like 'Police kills demonstrator' puts police in first, subject position and expresses that the police has agent role. In the passive sentence 'Demonstrator killed by police', the police is also agent, but in this case, the phrase referring to the demonstrator is in first, subject position, which means that police is assigned a less prominent role.
>
> Finally, the headline 'Demonstrator killed' may make the role of the police implicit. At the same time, the headline becomes syntactically ambiguous: It could also be read as a description of an event in which the demonstrator was the killer or more generally associate demonstrators with killing. Grammatical research on newspaper syntax has shown that this is indeed the case: Negative roles of the elite tend to be dissimulated by this kind of syntactic downgrading and implicitness. (See also Fowler et al., 1979; Fowler, 1991)

This is a very important aspect of selective articulation. But note that most of the time this is not a conscious choice by the journalist, but rather an unconscious reflex.

TENSES AND VERBS   The widespread use of the present instead of the past tense by journalists is meant to enliven the description of a dead event and to convey a false sense that it is happening while we read about it. The widespread use of conditional forms such as 'would be' and 'would have been' by journalists enables them to suggest facts which have not yet become realities and may never materialize (for instance, a supposed threat). Certain sets of verbs have very peculiar ideological roles in the organization of sentences and accounts. The various modalities of want, must, can, etc. imply a grid of possibilities and impossibilities taken for granted. 'Already' or 'still' may imply forwardness or backwardness. We usually overlook such assumptions, which are included in sentences and articles in most casual ways.

WE, US, OUR VERSUS THEY, THEM, THEIRS   We have already mentioned that news journalists have learned to shy away from the (openly) subjective, therefore journalists shun the use of the word 'I'. At the same time, however, words such as we, us, our and they, them, theirs regularly recur in newspaper texts. Each and every time such a word is used, humanity is implicitly chopped in half. At this point I must admit once again that throughout this book I have often used such terms in inconsiderate ways too. Sometimes it means: we First Worlders, as distinguished from those Second and Third Worlders. Sometimes it means: we journalists and/or academics, as distinguished from others and non-professionals. Sometimes it means: we, the writer and the reader, as distinguished from outsiders not sharing this text. But it is important to note that the use of such terms (explicitly or implicitly, consciously or unconsciously) constantly defines and redefines the world, often in highly ideological ways. There is no way around that. We will return to this subject in the Chapter 10 on the psychology of media effects.[2]

Standard elements and configurations in news formats

In recent years, news conventions have increasingly been subjected to closer scrutiny within a new sub-discipline alternatively labelled critical linguistics (Fowler et al., 1979, Fowler, 1991) or discourse analysis (Van Dijk, 1988a, 1988b). It tends to build on a wide range of older traditions: Russian formalism, American microsociology, French structuralism, German *Textwissenschaft*, British media studies (particularly of the Birmingham, Leicester and Glasgow schools) and – most recently – cognitive psychology.

News is, of course, a very peculiar kind of text. News items are usually small, isolated and self-contained pieces. The emphasis is on singularity and objectivity, that is to say on those aspects that relevant audiences might inter-subjectively agree upon. Dominant readings are usually inscribed into it, alternative readings are closed off. Very often, the item is stripped of those elements which would make an oppositional reading possible at all. The news items are selectively de-contextualized. They may of course be re-contextualized by the reader – but only with the help of *idées reçues*.

Another observation is that it is a genre of text ruled by its own schemata. Aspiring journalists learn, for instance, that (the opening of) their text will always have to contain the same handful of elements, the famous five Ws: who, what, where, when and why? The first four are simple: they locate the event in space and time, define the actors and the act, and construct its singularity. This reminds us of the news reporter's device of focusing on those aspects of an event, on which the relevant readers might be able to agree. They may be marginal aspects, but they can at least be treated as given objectively. The fifth element, the why, is much more complicated: selective pre-interpretation does inevitably emerge here.

Not only key elements of a news item are predefined in this way, however, and only have to be filled in as with a standard form. Various dimensions of the structure too are predefined. This is not unique for news items, but holds for any self-contained text fragment, which has to 'make sense'. In his book *News as Discourse*, Van Dijk says (1988a: 49):

> Stories, for instance, have a narrative schema, consisting of conventional categories such as Summary, Setting, Complication, Resolution and Coda ... Everyday conversations also have schemata. These may also be

Figure 8.2   'Our troops are doing a great job', headline from the
Daily Mail, 25 February 1991. (Reproduced by permission of Solo
Syndication Ltd., London.)

functionally analyzed in global units that may be conventionally categorized. Many conversations, for instance, begin with some kind of Greetings
exchange, and may be terminated by a sequence of closing turns and
leavetaking formulas. Scientific discourse, such as journal articles and
lectures, may also have a conventional form, which often features an
argumentative schema: a number of Premises followed by a Conclusion.
Psychological articles may even have a fixed, normative form, which
requires an Introduction or Theory section, an Experimental section that
itself has subcategories such as Design, Materials, Subjects, and a final

Discussion section. In this way, many discourse types in our culture have a more-or-less fixed schematic organization. Language users learn such schemata during socialization, although for some schemata, such as those used in professional discourse, special training may be required.

In news formats, one such 'structuring principle' is the so-called 'inverted pyramid'. Van Dijk notes that it is not really inverted at all, but rather an ordinary pyramid. One of the key elements of news discourse, he says (p. 48), is that it has a 'thematical realization structure that is basically (1) top down; (2) relevance controlled; and (3) cyclical (in installments)'. What does this mean? It means that the supposedly most relevant information is given first, and that small packages of less relevant information are given in subsequent paragraphs. In contrast to other genres, a news item usually carries its summary as an introduction. The underlying reason is that until the very last moment it may remain uncertain how much space can be devoted to the news item. Thus it should be possible to chop off an arbitrary number of paragraphs from the tail-end without harming the main message and its understanding.

It is interesting to note, in this regard, that the very first element of a news item is the headline. It is the summary of the summary, so to say, it sets the tone for the entire piece. Yet it is rarely chosen by the writer, particularly in international news. It is often produced by a specialized editor, who has only glanced over the article quickly. Very often, therefore, the headline is much more stereotypical than the news item itself, and sometimes it even contradicts it. Yet it primes the reader as to the interpretation of the rest of the text.

Apart from the headline, Van Dijk identifies a number of other elements in the average news text. First the 'lead' which is a more elaborate summary of the major topics, sometimes printed in different type and/or across several columns. Then an 'episode' with the main events, occasionally embedded in (some) context and with (some) background. Other categories are the (real or possible) 'consequences', verbal 'reactions' from relevant people and (usually indirect) comments, related to evaluation and expectation. In his related book *News Analysis* (1988b), Van Dijk has applied such principles to some elaborate case studies of national and international news, such as press reporting about squatters, immigrants and race in the Netherlands (for instance, the 'Tamil panic' of 1984/5) and the assassination of the Lebanese President Gemayel in 1982.

News narrative and myth

We have seen that a news item implies a choice of words and the construction of sentences, the inclusion of certain standard elements and their organization into a certain standard configuration. More

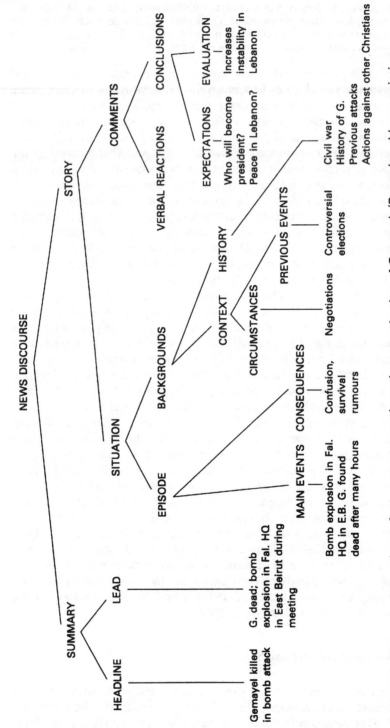

Figure 8.3   Superstructure schema for a news report about the assassination of Gemayel. (Reproduced by permission of Lawrence Erlbaum from T. van Dijk, News Analysis, 1988b.)

than anything else, however, a news item is a little story. Several observations may be made in this regard.

COMPRESSION The story has to be brief (most of the time). Both the production process and the resulting product are severely constrained by limitations of time and space. Since a considerable part of the story is already taken up by basics (such as the first four Ws), this leaves little room for other elements (such as the fifth W). If it is an ongoing story, furthermore, some of these basics will have to be repeated every day, rather than taking them for granted and moving ahead. In introducing other elements, the journalist will try to convey the maximum amount of information using the minimum number of words. That is to say she or he will refer to information already available to the reader, by using certain words and labels which may evoke existing stereotypes. The veteran reporter Martin Bell, for one, complained in his newly published memoirs (1995) that the BBC forced him to sum up the Bosnian war in (literally) no more than a hundred seconds per night, whereas directives also forbade the showing of blood on the main evening news. He felt this was a *reductio ad absurdum* of an extremely complicated conflict. It is a further illustration of how journalists are often put into an impossible position by their own employers.

COHERENCE This information, furthermore, is to be embedded in a little story, with a captivating beginning, middle and end. This often means imposing a logic which is not really (the only one) inherent in the reported facts themselves. We have already quoted Goffman, who noted that: 'Human interest stories are a caricature of evidence in the very degree of their interest, providing a unity, coherence, pointedness, self-completeness, and drama only crudely sustained, if at all, by everyday living.' Journalists learn how to construct these stories, by emphasizing some elements and de-emphasizing others, and by shuffling the elements around until they form a neat configuration corresponding with pre-existing cultural conventions and expectations.

NARRATIVE In order to produce coherence, one also has to organize the piece. Walter Lippmann (1947: 347) said: 'in all but exceptional cases, journalism is not a firsthand report of the raw material. It is a report of that material after it has been stylized.' This styling of the story is the construction of a narrative. Manoff elaborates (in Manoff and Schudson, 1987: 228–9):

> narratives are organizations of experience. They bring order to events by making them something that can be told about; they have power because they make the world make sense. The sense they make, however, is conventional. No story is the inevitable product of the events it reports, no

event dictates its own narrative form. News occurs at the conjunction of events and texts, and while events create the story, the story also creates the event. The narrative choice made by the journalist is therefore not a free choice. It is guided by the appearance which reality has assumed for him, by institutions and routines, by conventions that shape his perceptions and that provide the formal repertory for presenting them.

The result, he says, is 'the impression that narrative seeks to convey: that there is but one story to tell and but one right way to tell it'. The apparent logic of the narrative helps produce ideological closure: it makes it harder to come up with an alternative account.

Stuart Hall went even one step further. He once said:

> When a journalist is socialized into an institution, he or she is socialized into a certain way of telling stories. And although individual journalists may perform operations (or what is called originality) on top of that, they are working within a given language or within a given framework, and they are making those adjustments which make the old and trite appear to be new. But they are not breaking the codes. Indeed, if they constantly broke the codes, people outside wouldn't understand them at all . . . I think that journalists learn them very habitually, rather unconsciously, and they are not aware that the mode in which you construct a story alters the meaning of the story itself. They think it is just a set of techniques . . . The stories are already largely written for them before the journalists take fingers to typewriter or pen to paper.

The story seems to derive almost automatically from a larger framework of cultural presuppositions (quoted in Benthall, 1993: 191).

DRAMA Increasingly, critical linguists tend to challenge the widespread claim that there is a fundamental difference between factual and fictional narratives. Both have a scene or setting, acts or occurrences, actors or dramatis personae, aims and motives, characters and styles, and – most of all – a scenario or plot-line. The American sociologist Robert Park had already noted that 'The ordinary man, as the *Saturday Evening Post* has discovered, thinks in concrete images, pictures and parables. He finds it difficult to read a long article unless it is dramatized, and takes the form of what the newspapers call "a story"' (Epstein, 1974: 241). Similarly, the political scientist Doris Graber (1988) noted that definite configurations often emerge only gradually, over three successive stages in the reporting of a crisis: first there are uncoordinated messages, then definite patterns emerge and a coherent story develops, and finally it is integrated into larger perspectives on causes and consequences.

MEGA-STORIES Thus the way in which news stories actively make certain things understandable (and other things incomprehensible) is not only related to the nature of the story itself but also to the nature of all similar stories that (might have) preceded it, and in a sense even to the nature of many similar stories that (may) follow it –

within a certain media culture. Stories about arms build-ups, conflict, devaluation, espionage, fundamentalism, guerrilla movements, hunger, the information explosion – and so on to z – do not usually stand on their own, but form part of an ongoing story. Manoff labelled such 'stories behind the stories' mega-stories, and compared a story to 'the faucet' of a mega-story briefly turned on. When we leave the realm of the story and the 'reported event' and move to the realm of the mega-story and historical 'sense-making', the evaluative aspects gradually emerge more clearly.

MYTHS   In these ways, news discourse refers to the commonplace views of certain issues, shared by (most members of) a society or culture. For instance, the Western common-sense idea that rapid demographic growth within a developing country is by definition a brake on rapid economic growth. The reverse might just as well be defended: namely that rapid economic growth within a developing country is a brake on rapid demographic growth. It just depends on the ways in which various hypothetical constructs are linked within a larger theoretical framework that makes sense. The French semiologist Roland Barthes chose to call such frameworks myths.

As John Fiske (1990: 88) said:

> A myth is a story by which a culture explains or understands some aspect of reality or nature. Primitive myths are about life and death, men and gods, good and evil. Our sophisticated myths are about masculinity, and femininity, about the family, about success, about the British policeman, about science. A myth, for Barthes, is a culture's way of thinking about something, a way of conceptualizing or understanding it. Barthes thinks of a myth as a chain of related concepts. Thus the traditional myth of the British policeman includes concepts of friendliness, reassurance, solidity, non-aggressiveness, lack of firearms.

Within Western culture, similar myths abound about the nature, causes, consequences and solutions to development and under-development in various parts of the world.

EXNOMINATION AND NATURALIZATION   In his *Mythologies* (1970), Barthes noted that one should not only look at what is present within a system of representations, but also at what is absent from it. Certain elements of the social structure (such as economic determinants) are systematically hidden from sight, he said: they are exnominated. Or they are presented in a very peculiar way. Fiske explains: 'Exnomination is the evacuation of a concept from the linguistic system with its structure of differences and alternatives. That which is exnominated appears to have no alternative and is thus granted the status of the natural, the universal, or that-which-cannot-be-challenged' (1993: 290).

If the government of a Third or Second World country takes certain measures to correct or regulate 'free' markets, for instance, the positive results are often automatically obscured and the negative results highlighted. First World media hold that government responsible for the shortages, black markets and price hikes which may ensue. If the governments of Third World countries refrain from taking measures to correct or regulate markets, however, the positive results are often highlighted, the negative results (for example, excessive financial speculation, market manipulation and profit-making) obscured or 'naturalized'. In another example, present-day media coverage emphasizes that certain countries, regions, cities or classes in East Asia have entered a period of accelerated growth. But there is little emphasis on the fact that the rift between the richest and the poorest 20 per cent of the population in Latin America has doubled over the last three decades. Or that per capita income in many (if not most) countries of Black Africa has consistently gone down during that same period. Thus global hope and despair are continually being constructed in a very peculiar way.

If millions of people die from malnutrition and poverty in the world, this is often depicted as a fact of life, which is the fault or responsibility of no one in particular – not even those who could have done something about it. If these same poor people stage an armed rebellion, however, they are held responsible for the ensuing bloodshed. Of course, this view might well be defended; that is not the point. The point is that it is a view which is unnoticeably woven into the 'neutral presentation' of 'objective facts' in the world news.

Ideology and discourse

Stories, mega-stories and myths do in turn coalesce in (and derive from) ideologies and discourses. Ideologies are literally more or less coherent and all-embracing systems of ideas. It is a widespread misunderstanding that some views are ideological and others are not. Strictly speaking, all views are ideological, in the sense that they have a place within a larger system of ideas. Ideologies are particularly relevant if there is more than one possible way of looking at things, and there usually is. This is especially true for social ideologies, systems of social ideas, constructed from different vantage points within an unequal society. O'Barr (1994: 2) therefore defines ideology as 'ideas that buttress and support a particular distribution of power in society', and Marx and McAdam (1994: 32) as 'beliefs that mobilize people for action' (to change or consolidate this same distribution of power).

Social power cannot rest only on external force, at least not for long. It must also rest on internalized ideas, which make the less powerful accept their domination by the more powerful as a 'natural' given. Women to a certain extent accepted their domination by men, non-whites to a certain extent accepted their domination by whites, the poor to a certain extent accept their domination by the wealthy. The former to a certain extent believed (and were made to believe) that the latter were preordained (by God, by nature, by science, by 'objective' qualities) to dominate the former.

The first major provocative statements about class ideology in modern times were made by Karl Marx. He noted (*Selected Writings*, 1970: 67, 93): 'The mode of production of material life determines the general character of the social, political and spiritual processes of life. It is not the consciousness of men that determines their being, but, on the contrary, their social being determines their consciousness.' Thus the dominant class decisively contributed to shaping the dominant ideology, and it did so in a variety of ways.

> The ideas of the ruling class are, in every age, the ruling ideas: i.e. the class which is the dominant material force in society is at the same time its dominant intellectual force. The class which has the means of material production at its disposal, has the control at the same time over the means of mental production, so that in consequence the ideas of those who lack the means of mental production are, in general, subject to it.

In the later works of Marx, in the works of his German collaborator Engels, the Russian revolutionary Lenin, and also in the works of many subsequent authors, particularly in Eastern Europe, the emphasis shifted to what has been named 'vulgar Marxism'. It claimed that the 'working class' had an 'objective interest' in overthrowing the 'capitalist bourgeoisie', under the leadership of mass organizations and a centralized party. This would lead to a socialist transition period of 'dictatorship of the proletariat', and ultimately to the creation of a communist 'classless society'. Those who 'understood' this and went along with it were supposed to be scientific and 'class conscious'; those who disagreed were ideological and had a 'false consciousness'. (One of the most elaborate discussions of the evolution of this whole tradition is a three-volume work by Leszek Kolakowski on *Main Currents of Marxism*, 1981).

Heterodox marxists, particularly in Western Europe, developed a slightly different view. The Italian Antonio Gramsci, for one, analysed the role of ideological 'hegemony' in society leading to 'mass consent' of the oppressed, and the role of critical 'intellectuals' in challenging it. Max Weber introduced the subject in non-marxist sociology, where it inspired the emergence of the field of the sociology of ideas. The encounter with notions derived from Sigmund Freud's psycho-analysis also inspired the critical theories of the Frankfurt School (Adorno, Horkheimer, Marcuse and others) about the ideological role of the 'culture industry', 'repressive tolerance', etc. within modern society, for instance (see Jay, 1973; Hughes, 1975).

In recent decades, the analysis of ideology and 'false consciousness' was reinvigorated by French structuralism and post-structuralism. One of the most interesting elements is a serious philosophical challenge to the entire notion of the free individual subject, as embedded in Western secular humanism and middle-class values. Two authors stand out: on the one hand the marxist-structuralist Louis Althusser, who claimed that 'ideological state apparatuses' or ISA's (such as school and university) guarantee the reproduction of dominant views in new generations; on the other hand, the 'post-structuralist' Michel Foucault, who claimed that various 'discourses' embed each individual person in social practices – discourses on gender and sex, for instance, on normality and deviance, on race and ethnicity. Discourses are strings of key ideas, melodies of central notions with regard to a particular field.

They also play a quintessential role in the news process. Certain repertories of discourses are implicitly treated in the news as falling within the consensual, common-sensical, acceptable realm. They are actively made to seem obvious, logical, coherent. Others are thought to be outside the 'limits of acceptable discourse'. They are actively made to look silly, irrational, weird. This is usually not a conscious choice of journalists, either as individuals or as a group. Try to imagine an average male journalist in the mid-nineteenth century, reporting about the claims of some that women should be treated as equal to men: socially, politically, economically. It would probably have been written in such a way as to highlight the absurdity of those claims. The same thing happens around us every day. The views of 'deviant' cultures and groups are often treated as if they were absurd, whereas they are just radically different.

Yet none of this is explicitly meant that way. In his *Understanding News* (1989: 61–2), John Hartley concludes that:

> 'the impartiality, objectivity, neutrality which form the bedrock of editorial ideology are no sham' and that there 'is no deliberate conspiracy to "dupe" the public'. [But] News re-produces dominant ideological discourses in its special areas of competence. Finally, the ideology of the news is not a 'partisan' ideology. On the contrary, the purpose of news ideology is to translate and generalize, not to choose this opinion or that. In other words, news naturalizes the (fairly narrow) terrain on which different sectional ideologies *can* contend – it constantly maps the limits of controversy.

News journalists usually work under time pressure, which reinforces their tendency to use language conventionally – in accordance with the dominant conventions of their own culture and society. The choice of words, the phrasing of sentences, the construction of narrative seem self-evident and are not identified as fundamentally problematic, as one choice out of many, with specific implications. News stories also follow strict rules: they are often like the mechanical filling in of a pre-printed form. The famous five Ws – who, what, where, when and why – frame the singularity of the event. The headline, the lead, the instalments in successive paragraphs organize a perspective. That perspective usually matches dominant views.

Notes

1 Part II in *Age of Propaganda: The Everyday Use and Abuse of Persuasion* (1992), pp. 44, 63.

2 It is interesting to note that 'the American founding fathers' . . . chose to label the country USA, to abbreviate it as US, and to note that this abbreviation has since been adopted by others. The fact that the Soviet Union used to be abbreviated as the reverse, SU, may be a pure coincidence. The habit of abbreviating Western Europe as WE also has welcome implications.

Further reading

News language: Fowler; Van Dijk. *Words:* Lutz; Williams. *Narrative and myths:* Barthes; Nimmo and Combs; Said. *Marxism:* Marx; Kolakowski. *Frankfurt School:* Jay; Hughes.

9 HOW DO IMAGES COME ABOUT?

THE SEMIOLOGY OF WHAT IS SEEN AND OVERSEEN

....

The first rule for understanding the human condition is that men live in second-hand worlds. They are aware of much more than they have personally experienced; and their own experience is always indirect. The quality of their lives is determined by meanings they have received from others. Everyone lives in a world of such meanings. No man stands alone directly confronting a world of solid fact. No such world is available.

The closest men come to it is when they are infants or when they become insane: then, in a terrifying scene of meaningless events and senseless confusion, they are often seized with the panic of near-total insecurity.

> The American sociologist C. Wright Mills, in an article on 'The cultural apparatus', published in the British BBC magazine *The Listener*.[1]

What seems true for words seems even more true for images: that they appear as simply a mirror of reality. Even photographers or camera people are not aware of all the decisions they have made in a moment. But they are dependent on many others as well for decisions about which events are to be covered, from what side, and what access, if any is given at all. Where to stand and where to aim, what to include and what to exclude? Distance and angle, exposure and lighting? As soon as sequences of pictures are involved, things become even more complicated. What comes first, second and last? How is the visual story constructed? Who are the main characters, and what are they made to show and say? What are the backgrounds and props? What do they convey?

News photographs and news film seem to provide us with a purely 'naturalistic' account of what has 'really' happened. Most of the time, we are unaware of the enormous amount of staging and composition this implies. Colin Morris, the former BBC head of religious broadcasting and later controller in Northern Ireland, once put it this way:

> In the book of Genesis, it is God who brings order out of chaos; in the modern world, television journalists have to make a stab at doing it. They subdue into harmony a mountain of telex printouts, miles of video tape and a pandemonium of ringing telephones. They organize into a coherent picture a riot of impressions, a chaos, a bedlam of attitudes and opinions

that would otherwise send us scurrying to the hills in panic. And they have to construct this world at lightning speed, in a welter of instant judgments. (Elridge, 1993: 4)

The problem goes even deeper. On some 'real events', television news staff receive huge amounts of 'attractive' footage which they cannot possibly refuse. On other events they receive no visual material at all. Let me illustrate this with a concrete example. When the French army (the Foreign Legion) intervened to stop the massacre in Rwanda (through Zaire), or when the American army intervened in Haiti to restore democracy, they were accompanied by professional spokesmen, information departments, satellite link-ups, television cameras and 'live TV feeds'. But the other side of the coin was never seen, and mentioned only in minor articles on the inside pages of the newspapers. For instance, the fact that the French military mission in Rwanda had secretly continued to supply the Hutu government and Hutu militias, even when they were already openly slaughtering 'rival' Tutsi civilians in many thousands. Or the fact that representatives of the American CIA had close links to the very death squads that had murdered hundreds of democrats in Haiti. So the noble roles of the French and the American defence establishments were presented extensively (and highly emotionally), while their more dubious previous roles were almost blotted out.

News producers and news consumers are hardly aware that cameras 'take position', register (and even stage) social power in very particular ways. In such cases, the 'north-westerners' are often presented as the helpers and saviours, whereas the 'south-easterners' are presented as both brutes and victims. News film is hardly ever analysed with any semiological sophistication, whereas feature films are. Yet there is every reason to scrutinize it critically every single day, because exactly the same mechanisms hold for both genres.

Shohat and Stam (1994: 208) discuss the depiction of 'ethnic' others, for instance:

The cinema translates such correlations of social power into registers of foreground and background, on screen and off screen, speech and silence. To speak of the 'image' of a social group, we have to ask precise questions about images. How much space do they occupy in the shot? Are they seen in close-ups or only in distant long shots? How often do they appear compared with the Euro-American characters and for how long? Are they active, desiring characters or decorative props? Do the eyeline matches identify us with one gaze rather than another? Whose looks are reciprocated, whose ignored? How do character positionings communicate social distance or difference in status? Who is front and center? How do body language, posture, and facial expression communicate social hierarchies, arrogance, servility, resentment, pride? Which community is sentimentalized? Is there an esthetic segregation whereby one group is haloed and the other villainized? Are subtle hierarchies conveyed by temporality and subjectivization? What homologies inform artistic and ethnic/political representation?

In April 1989 the General Assembly of European NGOs adopted its Code of Conduct on Images and Messages Relating to the Third World. This is designed to counter fatalistic images of the Third World by providing:

more realistic and more complete information, thereby increasing awareness of the intrinsic value of all civilizations, of the limitations of our own society and of the need for a more universal development which respects justice, peace and the environment. It is the duty of NGOs to provide the public with truthful and objective information which respects not only the human dignity of the people in question but the intelligence of the public at large.

The Practical Guidelines are quoted here in full:

1. Avoid *catastrophic or idyllic images* which appeal to charity and lead to a clear conscience rather than a consideration of the root problems;
2. All people must be presented as human beings and sufficient information provided as to their social, cultural and economic environment so that their *cultural identity* and *dignity* are preserved. Culture should be presented as an integral part of development in the South;
3. *Accounts given by the people concerned* should be presented rather than the interpretations of a third party;
4. People's ability to *take responsibility for themselves* must be highlighted;
5. A message should be formulated in such a way that *generalisations* are avoided in the minds of the public;
6. The internal and external *obstacles* to development should be clearly shown;
7. *Interdependence* and *joint responsibility* in underdevelopment should he emphasised;
8. The *causes of poverty* (political, structural or natural) should be apparent in a message in order to enable the public to become aware of the history and real situation in the Third World, and the structural foundations of these countries before colonisation. It is the situation today, coupled with a knowledge of the past, which should be the starting point for examining ways in which extreme poverty and oppression can be eliminated. Power struggles and vested interests should be exposed and oppression and injustice denounced;
9. Messages should avoid all forms of *discrimination* (racial, sexual, cultural, religious, socio-economic);
10. The image of our Third World partners as dependent, poor and powerless is most often applied to *women* who are invariably portrayed as dependent victims, or worse still, simply do not figure in the picture. An improvement in the images used in educational material on the Third World evidently requires a positive change in the images projected of Southern women;
11. *Southern partners* should be consulted in the formulation of all messages;
12. If an NGO calls on the services of other partners (institutions, organisations or private companies) for a fund raising activity, it should ensure that the recommendations of this Code are respected by all parties. Reference should be made to the Code in the *sponsoring* contract(s) between the NGO and its partner(s).

Figure 9.1 *General Assembly of European Non-Governmental Organizations' Code of Conduct. (Reproduced by permission of J. Benthall author of* Disasters, Relief and the Media, *1993.)*

The news media confront us with an uninterrupted cascade of images every day. Newspapers publish photographs and drawings. They may be maps or situation sketches – which both necessarily present a particular view of the world, in the guise of objective documentation. They may be editorial cartoons or comic strips, which are both openly editorializing, but once again reflect an unequal exchange, with the strongest media nations exporting their ironic views abroad, but importing relatively little of other views in return. This unequal exchange is even more obvious with photographs and moving pictures, with news films and television news.

Men are visual animals: they believe whatever they seem to be seeing with their own eyes. They believe photo and film cameras act as their substitutes, and that they can witness world history live. This is the major illusion of our times: that true reality simply presents itself to us in a relatively unmediated form. Let us take a closer look at how these images come about. First, in the case of news photographs for the press; then in the case of news film for television and in the daily presentation of the evening news.

News stills photography

Even more than with the writing journalist, we have the idea that the picture journalist simply registers the highlights of what is out there. We do not see that each picture that gets to us involves a hundred and one choices by the organization and the individual – largely made on an intuitive basis. Harold Evans, the former editor-in-chief of the *Times* and the *Sunday Times*, and author of a book on photo editing, said in this regard (1978: 2): 'The newspaper reader is unaware of the judgments that open and shut his eyes.' Let us take a closer look at some of these choices.

To be or not to be there is the first question. On the one hand, 99 per cent of the corruption and exploitation, repression and brutalities in the world go on outside the view of the camera. On the other hand, certain political leaders are well dressed and well trained to 'act their civilized part' in one of those many 'photo opportunities' which are staged every day. What we get to see is not a representative sample of events but a particular choice prearranged by others. Very often those others are the stagers of events, not the journalists. Once the photo reporter or 'snapper' does get assigned to an event and is admitted there, he or she will have to make scores of decisions a minute – mostly without being aware of them.

One series of choices is related to the point of view, taken literally, that is to say, the location and orientation of the camera with regard to the subject. Research of the last few years has found, for instance, that women are systematically portrayed in different ways from men, not only in advertisements and fiction, but also in documentary and news pictures. Their faces are less often shown in mere close-up; they are shown with more of their bodies. They are less often shown in serious poses, more often with smiling faces, etc. (see, for example, the *Psychological Record*, vol. 39, 1989: 325–31; the *European Journal of Social Psychology*, vol. 19, no. 4, 1989: 311–16). No one 'plans' it this way, it happens 'spontaneously'. The same holds for 'exotic' news pictures.

Three physical dimensions play a role in news framing. The first dimension is the direction in which the camera is pointed. In a confrontation between two sides, for instance, it makes a difference whether you are on the side of the police and photograph the actions of the demonstrators; or on the side of the demonstrators and photograph the police. Similarly, it makes a difference whether you are on the side of the army or the rebels. Think of the Palestinian Intifada in the territories occupied by Israel. The photographer does not always have a choice; it may be almost impossible, or extremely risky, to work on one side rather than the other. But choices are being made, usually implicitly rather than explicitly, and they may result in a specific orientation of the picture and the report.

The second dimension is the distance to the subject. The physical distance may or may not translate into a psychological distance, and vice versa. First World subjects are on the average pictured from a shorter distance than Second or Third World subjects: the former tend to appear more often in individual close-ups and medium shots, the latter more often in panoramic and long shots. The former tend to be more often identified as individuals, the latter remain largely anonymous. This adds to other mechanisms privileging our identification with the former rather than the latter.

The third dimension is the vertical angle. The picture may be taken head on, at the level of the head and eyes (of an average adult). It may take on a bird's-eye perpective, which might also be labelled a 'giant' perspective if the photographer can and will take a higher vantage point. Or it may take a worm's-eye perspective, which might also be labelled a 'dwarf' perspective, if the photographer can and will take a lower vantage point. I propose to replace the terms 'bird' and 'worm' by the terms 'giant' and 'dwarf', because it is once again not so much a matter of a physical perspective but of a psychological one.

The giant photographer is in control: this perspective often emphasizes the insignificance and/or helplessness of the pictured subject. Today I saw such a picture in the paper of a black orphan child sitting on the ground next to a parent's corpse, during another major African crisis. The child is being looked down upon from the perspective of the adult cameraman, which emphasizes its powerlesness. The dwarf photographer looks up to others, by contrast; this perspective often emphasizes the overpowering nature of the subject. The other day I saw a picture in the paper taken during a public speech of another Arab dictator – or so it seemed. He was photographed from below as he stood on a rostrum overlooking a crowd. Rather than benevolently smiling in the way we know of our Western leaders, his face was contorted angrily as he was apparently shouting.

These three dimensions (direction, distance and height) only relate to the point of view of the camera – before any picture is taken at all. Another series of decisions is related to the choice of the lens and the lens angle, which results in the frame. Some things are in the picture, some things are out. Whatever is to the left or the right of the frame, above or below, does not appear in the picture. Neither does whatever is hidden by the subject, or behind the camera itself. Therefore no picture can ever give the full picture. If we see a man apparently about to fire a pistol, it does make a difference if we also see someone else outside the frame charging towards him with a knife. Certain elements which are often present are usually kept out of sight by cameramen: for example, other photographers and cameramen, reporters holding microphones and notebooks. Because their presence in the picture undermines its claim to naturalness, it draws attention to the contrived aspect of many news situations and to the phenomenon of pack journalism.

These possibilities are also related to the sensitivity to light of both the lens and the film one has chosen. Shadows and bright spots, contours and contrast, the incidence of light and counter-light may all enhance the dramatic nature of the confrontation between people, objects and the environment in the photograph. This is related to the composition itself, which aligns and opposes, activates and deactivates certain elements. The solitude of an individual may be emphasized by having him or her stand out against a large open space. The unanimity of a crowd may be emphasized by having a large mass of similar faces or silhouettes, clothes or gestures – reinforced by a particular kind of lighting, as is often the case with lower-class and Third World crowds. This part of the 'interpretation' of the subject by the photographer is placed in full view, however, and may not need lengthy development here.

In sum: an event has been covered. The 'event' may have taken place over one or ten or hundreds of thousands of square miles. The photographer and his camera may have covered a few spots of a few hundred square yards. The event may have developed over an hour or a day, or months and years. On a major assignment, some photographers shoot as many as a hundred rolls of film, or a few thousand pictures. Three thousand pictures, taken at a normal shutter speed of one sixtieth of a second, makes a sum total of 50 seconds: not even a minute, which has been frozen in time. This is not gratuitous demagoguery, but an attempt to emphasize once

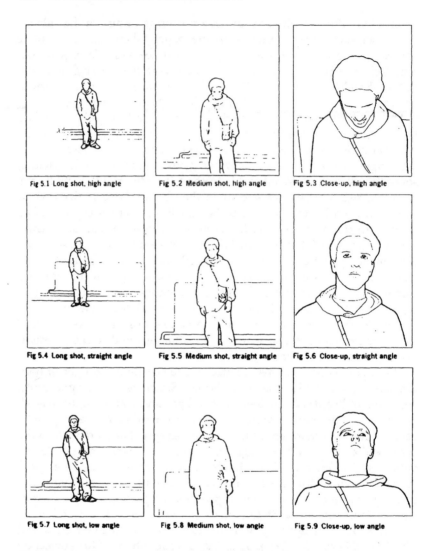

Fig 5.1 Long shot, high angle

Fig 5.2 Medium shot, high angle

Fig 5.3 Close-up, high angle

Fig 5.4 Long shot, straight angle

Fig 5.5 Medium shot, straight angle

Fig 5.6 Close-up, straight angle

Fig 5.7 Long shot, low angle

Fig 5.8 Medium shot, low angle

Fig 5.9 Close-up, low angle

Figure 9.2 Frame and angle. Different angles, for example, carry different suggestions and are often intuitively reserved for specific groups and situations. (Reproduced by permission of Addison Wesley Longman Ltd from S. Price, Media Studies, 1993.)

again that out of a zillion possible pictures and views of reality we get to see only a few.

One might, for example, take a closer look at the World Press Photo Award winners of the last forty years (Mayes, 1995) and analyse their commonalities in the choice and framing of news events. Of course, such award-winning photographers are well trained and highly experienced professionals: they know their trade and how to capture the moment which seems most significant and revealing. Often they agonize over a picture or report, how it may affect the subject and/or the audience, because whatever they do, their reportage necessarily represents a point of view, not the full picture of reality.

Picture editing

The editor narrows this choice even more. Out of a few thousand pictures, he or she may select only a handful which are fit to be printed. This also means that they fit into the world-view of the editor and supposedly into the world-view of the public. News media are quite selective, for instance, in their intermittent publication of horror pictures. There is a spontaneous tendency to say 'this is too gruesome to show' on some occasions, and to say 'the public must see this' on others. Think of the corpses in Timisoara: under normal circumstances we would never ever be shown such pictures, even if there is an almost daily supply of them.

Victims of our own social system, or of the brutalities of our allies, find it harder to get into full view than those of our enemies (see Baarda (1989), Knightley (1989), John Taylor (1991)). This is not a calculated one-sidedness; it is a spontaneous tendency at all places and times, in all societies and groups. The liberal system is much more self-critically inclined than others, but it is not exempt from self-defensive reflexes. The editor will thus often tend to choose the pictures which mesh with his or her preconceptions of normality, while at the same time standing out from it.

The next question is how the evocative power of the pictures can be optimized within this same framework. There are handbooks on photo-editing, such as *Pictures on a Page* (1978), by Harold Evans. They discuss the qualities of a good news picture, but also techniques such as cropping and highlighting. Cropping means cutting off 'superfluous' strips at the top and bottom, left and right of the picture, and reframing it to focus on an amended composition of the various elements which are considered most meaningful. Careful cropping improves a picture, careless chopping destroys it. On more than one occasion a photographer found that the editor had unthinkingly cut off major elements of his composition, which may on occasion just be empty space to suggest space and depth. Highlighting may involve correcting contrast in all the picture or just in key parts of it: making certain things stand out and others fade into the background.

This may go so far as to erase certain dissonant elements from the picture altogether. The Dutch photographer Wubbo de Jong, a veteran of many Second and Third World crises, gave some examples in a recent interview. He showed a picture of a family of victims of the Bangladesh war of independence, fought against (West) Pakistan, with the support of India. The faces of the elder family members fully express their sense of shock and tragedy. On coming home the photographer discovered that some of the children were laughing at the camera, one of them right in the centre of one of the best pictures. He chose to eliminate it, but acknowledged: 'The question then becomes: is that permissible? . . . Of course that is a major bone of contention within photography' (in Wesselius, 1994: 42–3).

Other corrections relate to colour. Increasingly, newspapers publish colour photographs just as news magazines and glossies do. Today, the colours of separate elements in a picture can be corrected much more easily than before. Since pictures are being digitalized they can be endlessly retouched and transformed – without this ever showing (see Wombell, 1991). Elements from one picture can easily be copied and added to another. Basically the difference between 'imaginary' images and 'real' images has been eliminated. One immediate result is that pictures not only become more evocative, but that they also get more stereotypical. The tropical sea will increasingly be made immaculate blue, some palm-trees may be added to the beach, to make the reality conform to our imagination – rather than the other way around.

It has been said that even the sensitivity of film and standards for lighting are 'racist', in the sense that they are based on average 'white' faces (for instance in ID photograph machines). Everyone has also seen reports from Africa or the Caribbean where the contrast shown within 'dark' faces is insufficient, so that they simply blur into a black blob. Even more interesting are those cases where photo editors chose to 'correct' skin colour in pictures before their publication. Here are two examples related to race, sex and violence: an older one and a newer one, both from some of the largest circulation magazines in the world.

The American monthly *National Geographic Magazine* had a rule that white women could not be shown with naked breasts, but 'coloured' women could. On one occasion, nude women in a nice picture taken somewhere in the Third World looked 'too white', and were therefore 'darkened' in the lab before publication. This would supposedly make them look less erotic in the eyes of white middle-class readers in the First World.

More recently, the American weekly *Time* did something similar. When O. J. Simpson was arrested on suspicion of the murder of his (white) wife, they decided to run a cover with his portrait. But when it turned out to be 'too light' they decided to darken it artificially. This was only discovered because its competitor *Newsweek* had decided upon a cover with exactly the same picture – 'uncorrected'. Of course, this whole continued obsession with 'skin colour' is far from innocent, as we have seen in our discussion of the outdated notion of 'race' in the Introduction.

This is not the place to go into the advertising and propaganda applications of these new techniques. I have elsewhere published a chapter in Dutch (in Wesselius, 1994) entitled: 'Look, you don't know what you see – Tampering with photographs and films in past and present'. It is a review of 'news' picture propaganda in liberal-democratic, communist and fascist societies, before and during the First and Second World Wars, during decolonization and the Cold War – up to the Grenada, Nicaragua, Panama interventions, and the Gulf war. That is not the subject of this book, which is not focused on bad-faith manipulations but on good-faith professionalism.

At the same time, we have to remind ourselves at this point that however strongly a picture seems to be oriented, it basically remains polysemic. That is to say, different meanings can always be read into it. In the previous chapter on words we have seen that the meaning of a text always depends on the context and the reader, that within each (sub)culture there may be a dominant or hegemonic, a negoti-ated or an oppositional reading of the picture.

One perfect example is a famous 1989 picture taken in Beijing, at the time of the crackdown on student protests in Tiananmen Square. It shows a frail man in civilian clothes positioning himself right in front of a tank: a column of tanks, to be precise. The series shows how the first tank tries to get around him, but he blocks it, climbs on the tank, admonishes the driver, etc. The arch-image of 'the man and the tank' was presented in the West as symbolizing the extraordinary courage and force of unarmed civilians standing up to a brutal military clampdown. The same image was presented by the Beijing authorities as symbolizing the extraordinary restraint of well-equipped soldiers in the face of stubborn provocations.

The picture does not carry either interpretation in itself: it is the reader who decides on the meaning of the image, by referring to certain notions which are taken for granted in his or her political (sub)culture. Something similar holds for identical pictures which were presented as showing the 'liberation' of the Falkland Islands in Western Europe, but also presented as showing the 're-occupation' of the Malvinas Islands in South America. They show neither: they just show soldiers and civilians, grieving or rejoicing; the 'true meaning' is not in the pictures themselves.

Yet there are certain ways, in which the editor can help to favour a certain preferred reading. The most important one is the knitting together of the picture with a heading, a caption and/or an article. It is only by labelling a photograph that an editor can attempt to anchor certain floating interpretations, to close off some, and open up others. Commentary plays a similar role in news films and television news. This is a lesson of the utmost importance to keep in mind. Contrary to a widely held belief, pictures almost never speak for themselves. And a different label can completely change the preferred reading by the public. This is one more reason why the slogan 'witness world history live' is utter nonsense. Pictures carry no meaning in and of themselves, but they can be made to elicit certain preferred readings, and to pass other things over in silence.

Television evening news

What holds for still pictures holds even more for moving ones, particularly on the TV evening news. Although it presents itself as a window on the world today, the news production process involves scores of arbitrary decisions and staging rules. Charles Bantz and colleagues emphasized that most items are 'technically uniform, visually sophisticated, easy to understand, fast-paced, people-oriented stories that are produced in a minimum amount of time' (Shoemaker and Reese, 1991: 87). In recent years, the style and pace of most TV evening news programmes has also shifted to meet the competition of other programme categories such as spots, clips, action movies, etc.

There was a time when television news was considered unprofit-able. US commercial networks would not easily interrupt their programmes for news. There was the famous case of Fred Friendly, who resigned as president of CBS News when his superiors would not interrupt 'a fifth rerun of "I love Lucy" to show Congressional Hearings on the growing US involvement in Vietnam' (Altheide, 1976: 20). Since CNN emerged as a successful specialized news channel, however, others have come to acknowledge that there is one thing the public adores even more than soap opera: that is, a real-life drama unfolding in real time. The major problem CNN and its rivals face is that there is not always a crisis at hand which can be covered 'live'.

The audience of CNN sags dramatically when there is no major news story breaking, therefore there is a great temptation to hype issues. Today, both CNN and other networks revel in live coverage of all aspects of real-life soap operas, such as the American cases around O. J. Simpson and their like. Every incident is exploited extensively and overshadows major world issues. On the occasion of Simpson's acquittal, the three major American TV networks were said to have devoted no less than 1,400 hours to the subject during the year of the (first) trial: well in excess of one hour a day, twice as much as the amount given to the simultaneous Balkan conflict and much more than to the Middle East 'peace process'.

News profitability is the result of two factors: generated income and cost expenditure. On the one hand, generated income can be extremely high. (CNN advertising revenue soared during the Gulf war, for instance.) Even ordinary evening news programmes still have rather high viewing rates, viewers with above-average purchasing power, and form a good *Umfeld* (advertising environment) for certain messages (for example, for all kinds of savings and insurance). Furthermore, they form the lead-in to the rest of the evening programme. On the other hand, expenditure has been brought under control. There is a heavy emphasis on technical support and know-how: a camera crew can fly out any minute to any spot on the globe, and can beam back satellite images within hours of its arrival. Of course this is extremely expensive, but at the same time it is relatively cheap as well.

Apart from a few journalists, none of the 'actors' needs to be paid. One has real-life drama with first-class authorities, with people dying on camera, or with massive disasters and high-tech rescue operations: all for free. This is 'good value for money', as producers would say. Overall, live coverage of such news is often considerably cheaper than producing a real 'attention grabber' of a television movie. Yet increasingly, the two types of stories are told in exactly the same way: highly personalized, with a heavy emphasis on individual fate, and very little on social causation and economic frameworks.

Still, television is the major news source for most people and the prime definer of emerging issues. TV news and its main anchors are often mentioned as the most trusted sources of news, particularly by less educated people. This is noteworthy because of the extreme brevity and highly stereotypical nature of television news. In many countries, 30 minutes of evening news contain 22.5 minutes of editorial material on the average, of which only 15 minutes is basic news (the rest being headlines, 'bridges', announcements and so forth). The verbal contents of these fifteen minutes would easily fit on half a page or even a quarter-page of a broadsheet newspaper. That is to say: it is basically no more than an elaborate table of contents for the dailies, which often have several dozen pages of editorial material on a weekday, and often close to a hundred pages on weekends – the equivalent of a large paperback book. Interestingly enough, however, the television format is increasingly being copied by new popular newspapers (such as *USA Today*) with many colourful visuals, columns of 'news briefs' and titbits, but very little sustained documentation or analysis.

Such a quarter of an hour of television news may typically consist of a handful of larger items of one or two minutes, and then somewhere between ten and twenty smaller items of thirty seconds each or less – after which it is over. This basic schedule remains the same whether there are ten 'coups and earthquakes' on a single day, or none at all. The anchor will never open with: 'No news today, thank you, goodnight!' The evening news is always short on time, always has a hectic pace. Items will have to be compressed as much as possible and be covered in a minimum of time, which also means that they need to be stripped down to the basic so-called facts, providing little real insight.

They are of necessity extreme simplifications, catering to pre-existing stereotypes. It is physically impossible to make a plausible case for a radically different point of view within such extreme constraints. What the evening news does, basically, is recycle the dominant world-view of a society. It is a little morality play, being staged every evening in order to process the day's challenges to this world-view, and following a particular ritual.

Props and backdrops

Just as in an ordinary play, the props and backdrops are developed to convey certain meanings – but largely subliminally. There is an obvious contrast between the studio and 'out there'. In the studio, the anchors are seated in armchairs behind desks, which convey calm and authority and control. They often have a paper file at hand, which is no longer really needed (because they read from the teleprompter), but has often been maintained because it signifies documentation. On occasion, central presenters such as the weatherman or woman may stroll to, or stand in front of, a map and point to its features with a hand or a stick. They are the equivalent of the teacher and the blackboard: they educate us about scientific knowledge.

Around the central presenters, we may occasionally get an emphatic glimpse of the studio floor, particularly at the beginning and the end of the programme, or during major shifts. In the foreground there are some silhouettes of cameras and the floor manager, in the background clocks and maps, plus live monitors and computer screens, sometimes with people sitting in front of them, or busily walking back and forth. This symbolizes the ever busy news-room with its instant global connections, but often this is no more than a stage prop, since the real news-room is located elsewhere.

The television evening news anchors seem to be masters of the universe. They have the world at their fingertips. It is an 'Abracadabra' world of technical control. He or she just has to say 'we now go to . . .' and we actually find ourselves in another country, in another city, at a news location. It seems to be a modern world of flying carpets and crystal balls: the old dimensions of space and time seem to implode into one all-embracing here and now.

Correspondents in other capitals can immediately be seen against the backdrop of all-too-familiar buildings. The White House, the State Department, the Pentagon, Capitol Hill in Washington. Buckingham Palace, Downing Street, Whitehall, Westminster and Big Ben in London. The Élysée Palace, Matignon, the Quai d'Orsay, and to a lesser extent the Bourbon and Luxembourg Palaces in Paris. We vaguely know these buildings and settings: they house major institutions of major countries, which our media consider newsworthy and legitimate – the offices of the head of state, the head of government, the major ministries, the upper and lower houses of parliament.

The political symbolism for the major news-making powers (the US, Great Britain and France) is extremely rich and varied. The political symbolism for other world powers is much poorer. Moscow just had its former Red Square as a single power centre, Beijing its Tiananmen Square. The political symbolism for smaller countries is often non-existent. This also seems to imply that they themselves and their institutions are *quantitées négligeables*.

Most local television studios have various slides (or even 'live' camera shots) at hand, to use as a backdrop for correspondents, to place them on the spot. They do not limit themselves to political institutions but may cover other landmarks, which somehow tend to empower and glamorize such major news centres: the skyline by day or by night; in New York: Manhattan, the Empire State Building or the World Trade Center; in London: the City, the Thames, the Tower. All these images carry specific connotations, which one might question. In Paris there is the Arc de Triomphe (whose triumph, whose defeat?), the Champs Élysées (invariably claimed to be the longest boulevard on earth, which it is not), the Place de la Concorde (is that a French or an Egyptian obelisk?), the Louvre museum (whose ancient treasures are these, and how were they acquired?), etc. Every such landmark has a dominant reading in news symbolism, but this can always be countered by an oppositional reading.

Take the example of the Statue of Liberty, of which a small version can be found in Paris and a giant version in New York. Let us take a closer look at just this one monument. It is invariably taken to mean the freedom from exploitation and oppression which immigrants came to find in the US. Let us briefly try to deconstruct this symbol, which is routinely evoked in this sense in news films and television documentaries. First, this preferred reading glosses over the fact that there were native Americans before the immigrants came, and that they had exploitation and oppression coming to them rather than the reverse.

Second, it mostly focuses the attention on those immigrants who came through New York on their way from Europe – that is to say, almost exclusively on the whites. Third, it draws attention away from many immigrants who were processed in other Atlantic and Caribbean harbours, and who were exploited and oppressed by those very same whites: the black slaves from Africa. Fourth, it draws attention away from many immigrants who came through Pacific harbours, who were also exploited and oppressed by whites thereafter: the 'coolies' from Asia. Fifth, it draws attention away from many immigrants who came overland: field-workers from Latin America.

Though the United States is well on its way to having a majority of such minorities in a few decades from now, the media uses and abuses of the Statue of Liberty celebrate it as a country of white immigrants and ignore major symbols of red, black, yellow and other immigrants. Thus, the use of such landmarks to symbolize values, institutions and countries is never entirely innocent. Nor is the use of certain establishing shots to locate a correspondent or reporter.

The preordained script

Although (or because) the contents of the evening news are supposed to be unexpected, the form and the order of presentation are not. All items should be as short and snappy as possible, colourful and dynamic, impressive and attention-grabbing. They should be 'zap-resistant', because of the ongoing battle for ratings. Reuven Frank, the executive producer of NBC News, said in a famous phrase: 'Every news story should, without any sacrifice of probity or responsibility, display the attributes of fiction, of drama. It should have structure and conflict, problem and dénouement, rising action and falling action, a beginning, a middle and an end' (Epstein, 1974: 4). The running order of news stories also follows a preordained script.

TRAILER AND LEADER If there is major news, brief flashes and pre-announcements may already have been shown in between programmes earlier in the day, to lure and guide viewers to tune in to the evening news on that channel. The curtain-raiser of the evening news itself is often a complicated semiological hybrid of various news symbols. It may have a clock ticking away, a rotating world, the network acronym, the programme title, as well as a quick succession of almost subliminal images denoting the threat of chaos and the reassurance of order: violent demonstrators, flames and smoke, marching boots, well-known statesmen. All this may be accompanied by some vague sounds, overlaid by dramatic music – the tune. This leader sets the stage. (See Leblanc, 1987: 95 cf.; Shohat and Stam, 1994: 113 cf., and 125 cf. for the 'special styling' of Gulf war reports.)

THE OPENING PIECE Usually, there is one major headline and one major opening piece, which dominates the news of the day and often gives it an element of solemnity and singularity. It is announced by the anchor in a grave tone, with a straight face, and with a composed attitude. It is surprising how often different news media, and particularly television channels, choose the same opening subject. Many journalists take this to demonstrate that their selection criteria are clear-cut and objective. Some critics have pointed out, however, that they might just as well be considered subjective, but widely shared within a culture and subculture. If good visuals have become available on a less important event, for instance, everyone will spontaneously choose them.

NEWS SEPARATION AND CATEGORIZATION One characteristic of news is that it consists of short, self-contained and isolated items. Another characteristic is that most are usually grouped together, either implicitly or explicitly (that is to say, under a separate heading). As Fiske says (1993: 287):

> Categorization constructs a conceptual grid within which 'raw' events can be instantly located and thus inserted into a familiar set of conceptual relationships. Categories are normalizing agents . . . These groupings are part of a strategy by which news masks its social process of representation and presents itself as objective, as driven by 'the real'. Thus 'industry' and 'foreign affairs' appear to be empirical categories based in nature, yet their operation is highly ideological.

As is the division between foreign affairs and domestic affairs, or between politics, economics, social affairs, etc. (The same thing happens in academic research and education, by the way.)

This has various implications. After some time, both journalists and the public come to feel that these categories are really objective rather than subjective ones, that they exist 'out there' (in the world) rather than 'in here' (in the head). This is of course an illusion, even though the major bureaucracies are organized along the same lines. Most foreign affairs are presented from a domestic perspective, many national problems have international causes. Social affairs are both economic and political. The categorization is arbitrary but efficient. For most of these domains, furthermore, a limited number of typical frames and story-lines are readily available to pick from. Politics is about authority and challenges to it, about power rivalry between individuals. Economics is about free markets and intervention, about the greed of everyone. Social affairs are about losers who are a burden to the winners and the rest of the community. It is precisely by instantly applying these grids that news journalists are quickly able to make sense of a bewildering variety of events.

THE TAILPIECE After recurrent complaints that the evening news was too heavy and pessimistic, most channels – in both North America and Western Europe – have settled for a format whereby they have some lighter optimistic items toward the end. A funny or touching human interest story will close the show, preferably something about animals or babies or animal babies. The 'recency effect' (the psychological opposite of the 'primacy effect') guarantees that this positive note leaves a positive feeling, and thereby increases the likelihood that the viewers will stay with the channel and/or return to it on future occasions.

TAKING LEAVE The afterglow of trust and warmth is reinforced by well-scripted rituals of leave-taking by the anchors. They may use a fixed and therefore reassuring formula, such as Walter Cronkite's famous 'And that's the way it is', or Chet Huntley's and David Brinkley's 'Good-night, David; good-night Chet'. If there is more than one anchor, particularly if there is a man and a woman, they will be told to remain seated, to chat and smile to each other, while the studio sound is turned off and the credit titles start running. This leaves the image of a happy family at the network news staff, even if there is just as much competition and infighting there as anywhere else.

THE WEATHER REPORT American network television news is interrupted periodically by commercials, which are preceded by all kinds of teasers and cliff-hangers. They interrupt a piece or announce others in such a way that we become curious enough to hang on until 'after the break' rather than switch to another channel. European television is still far behind in these techniques, but one step in this direction is the insertion of commercials between the newscast itself and a separate weather report after it, since this is the only piece of information really sure to affect our ordinary life the very next day.

There are all kinds of things to be said about the hidden ideological implications of this apparently neutral item. There is its standard use of concentric maps, with our own region or country in the centre and the rest of the world in the periphery, and of world maps with a Northern and Western bias (as discussed in the Introduction to this book). There is its vision of our own country constantly being affected by intrusions from elsewhere, its look at distant continents, where conditions are often 'more extreme' than in our parts, its celebration of scientific prediction and control. It would take us too far to develop this argument here.

The casts and stages of news

The news has a well-defined cast: a limited number of central characters and roles. The anchors, correspondents and reporters in particular regulate and punctuate and mediate the input of the other players: authorities, experts and other sources. They always maintain control over the discourse of others.

THE ANCHORS In earlier days, when television had just branched off from radio, anchors were just considered news readers: people who had a handsome face, a nice voice, and who would simply read the news bulletins prepared by others. Their hairstyle, make-up and clothing would identify them as concerned and serious, well-educated and middle-class citizens. This is basically still the case, but the set-up has changed. It turned out to be important that they had authority, credibility, that they should be presented as fully-fledged journalists who had themselves played a key role in gathering the news. Even more, they were to be presented as some kind of key editors, who had supervised the entire news-gathering process throughout that day. In some cases this was hardly realistic, of course.

In American network news, therefore, anchors are often not so much journalists as actors playing journalists. Neil Postman observes that no serious journalist gets paid 3 million dollars a year, as Dan Rather of CBS does: ten times more than the president of the US and twenty times more than members of Congress. Only movie actors get that kind of money. Accordingly, Dan Rather made it his business in recent years to cover major foreign stories in local folkloric costumes. He first had himself filmed in Afghanistan, dressed as a mujahedin freedom fighter; but once the gimmick proved successful he repeated it on many other foreign trips. In doing so, he was playing an adult version of Tintin: the immortal Belgian comic-strip journalist who shuttles around the world.

It is true that the anchor looks like someone in total control. S/he hardly has to look at papers any more, since they have been replaced by the teleprompter. It thus looks as if s/he has a fabulous command of factual knowledge and analytical skill, since s/he can talk offhand about the most varied subjects. S/he has to utter only one word and other journalists immediately report from around the globe. The real situation only reveals itself whenever something goes wrong: when a 'live item' is announced which turns out to be a pre-recorded film that does not start on cue, for instance. On such occasions, it becomes clear that effective control rests elsewhere. It is the producer who weaves together all these artificial elements in a way that makes them look perfectly natural. S/he is the conductor of the TV news orchestra at this point. It is his or her task to make this carefully staged morality play appear a simple window on the world.

THE CORRESPONDENT AND THE REPORTER   The correspondent and the reporter are somewhere out in the field. S/he may do a 'stand-up': after having travelled to the scene of the action, s/he is standing up in front of it and telling the viewers what s/he has seen or heard. It may look like a terrible waste of time and money, since most often the information presented was available elsewhere and could just as well have been read elsewhere too. But that is ignoring the real ideological function of the operation. Since the reporter can actually be seen on the spot, this automatically promotes him or her to the status of eyewitness, and promotes whatever s/he says to the status of 'verified reality'. Thus the 'stand-up' is the truth-maker of what could have been said in the studio.

Another standard role of correspondents and reporters is that of 'adversarial questioning'. As Hal Himmelstein pointed out, in *Television Myth and the American Mind* (1984: 203):

> In television journalism much more than in print journalism, the symbol of truth becomes the image of the journalist himself – the aggressive advocate willing to challenge authority – rather than the story or editorial itself. Style predominates over content or context. The defender of the public's right to know satisfies the medium's insatiable demand for melodramatic personae who clearly and simplistically represent the just cause. These journalist-heroes allow viewers to vicariously watch the unapproachable bureaucrat or the arrogant general (who never answered letters of complaint or phone calls) brought to his knees by the crafty and efficient journalist – the modern-day personification of the Homeric epic hero.

STAGES The British communication scholars Fiske and Hartley first suggested that the whole cast of the TV news is in fact mobilized to claw back potentially deviant or disruptive events into the dominant value system. This is done in three stages that correspond with spaces that are both material and symbolic, they said:

> The central space is that of the studio news reader, who does not appear to be author of his/her own discourse, but who speaks the objective discourse of 'the truth'. Paradoxically, the news reader's personal traits, such as reliability or credibility, are often used to underwrite the objectivity of the discourse. Locating this discourse in the institutional studio signifies its ideological conformity: no radical, disruptive voices speak in these accents or from this space.
> Spatially positioned further away and discursively subordinated is the reporter, who signs off as both an individual and an institutional voice. Her/his function is to mediate between 'raw reality' and the final truth spoken by the news reader. Different reporters can make different contributions to the same 'truth'; they need individual signatures so that their 'truths' appear subjective, 'nominated' (Barthes) and therefore lower in the discursive hierarchy than the 'truth' of the news reader. Furthest from the studio, both geographically and discursively, is the eyewitness, the involved spokesperson, the actuality film, the voices that appear to speak the real, and that therefore need to be brought under discursive control. There is a vital contradiction here. The 'truth' exists only in the studio, yet that 'truth' depends for its authenticity upon the eyewitness and the actuality film. (quoted from Fiske, 1993: 288)

Interviews: the differential staging of 'accessed' voices

Let us take a closer look at how this whole morality play is staged. In news film and television news, for instance, journalists and 'accessed voices' are staged in different ways – which provides their statements with different qualities and truth-claims in a number of other ways. 'Accessed voices' must unconditionally obey these rules, otherwise they will be edited out. Anchors, correspondents and reporters may be seen full front on camera, and – more important – they may look directly at it, that is to say at us, the viewers. They are the only ones who are allowed to establish an open and direct relationship with us, a relation which is at the same time intimate and aloof. They are the only ones who may admit that they are aware that this is being filmed for our benefit – the audience.

The accessed voices, by contrast, are usually filmed when (or 'as if') addressing an intermediary: the journalist, a press conference, a crowd, etc. They are usually emphatically told that they may not look directly into the camera, because that is supposed to be unnatural. We all know that if bystanders look directly into the camera, and try to attract (distract) the attention of the viewers, this breaks the staging rules and disorganizes the entire piece. If possible, the journalist will make the camera stop, explain the 'rules' again, and start another take. The accessed voices are not allowed to establish an open and direct relationship with us, the viewers; they must address themselves to the intermediary. It is by insisting on this very simple staging rule that journalists succeed in promoting themselves to the role of objective observer and in downgrading others to the role of subjective players – who do not have similar claims to providing the ultimate 'truth' about 'reality'.

Interviews which are not broadcast live but have been registered beforehand are subject to other staging rules as well. The interviewee is usually told by the journalist where to stand, how to look, and even to a certain extent what to say and how. The reasons which are given are technical: 'this is how the medium operates.' But they often have a profound impact on the way the 'accessed voice' is perceived by the viewer, without either party being aware of that. When an interview is being planned and set up, the journalist will immediately scout for possible settings. The chosen background and surroundings must express the personality or role of the interviewee as perceived by the journalist in question. The intellectual is 'spontaneously' placed in front of bookshelves, the scientist in a laboratory. Similarly, a sportsman may be interviewed in a gym, and a housewife in a supermarket. On occasion people are taken to places where they have never been before. The important thing is that the journalist usually has a preconceived idea of the surroundings that suit the interviewee.

The next thing is where to look. We have already seen that the interviewee is told not to look into the camera but to pretend it is not there, to artificially act naturally. One is told to look at the interviewer, whose position is thereby both acknowledged and valorized. The text of the interview is usually carefully scripted as well, through a series of preparatory phases. It will also be emphasized that the answers need to be short and snappy. Complications and nuances should be eliminated as much as possible. If the interviewee forgets this, the journalist will stop the camera, repeat the rules, and make a second or subsequent take. I remember helping to set up a Dutch interview with a key American witness of the Iran-Contra scandal several months before the story broke. The (progressive) network threw it away because it was 'too complicated', and replaced it with a routine election speech, which was hyped to look newsworthy.

A British example: strikes, conflicts and other bad news

Reports of boycotts, pickets and demonstrations are particularly problematic. An escalating clash between police and protesters can be related in a dozen different ways. The editors will tend to ignore the slow development of the confrontation because it takes too much time. They will focus instead on the most violent images they have on film or on tape: a number of policemen getting hold of a demonstrator and beating him up in a corner; a masked demonstrator hurling Molotov cocktails and setting a police car on fire. The problem is that these images might have been shot almost simultaneously. By putting one before the other the editors tend to legitimate either police brutality or demonstrator violence. By focusing on these few strong images ('We only have thirty seconds for this item'), they may condense a huge and extended event in which the overwhelming majority of both policemen and demonstrators behaved in a very peaceful and disciplined way to a few seconds when things threatened to get out of hand – but finally did not.

One series of outspoken studies about the unreflective use of 'hidden scripts' in television news was produced by the Glasgow University Media Group, including Peter Beharrell, John Elridge, Greg Philo, Brian Winston and others. In their first study, *Bad News* (1976), they analysed newscasts on all British national channels throughout the first half of the previous year. They checked the number, length and subject of the items; the format, caste and points of view represented, etc. Their first study was followed by *More Bad News* (1980) and *Really Bad News* (1982).

Their first focus was on the way industrial disputes were covered. They claimed the underlying economics were usually presented in a very peculiar way. Long-term stagnation or deterioration of real rates of pay were often all but ignored, they said, and the focus would be on the disruption accompanying a strike. This also found expression in the words and images chosen. The causes of the conflict would be generally under-reported, and the consequences over-reported. 'Experts', government spokesmen and management representatives would be treated in different ways from trade unionists, individual strikers and their families. The former would also typically be interviewed in the calm surroundings of their offices, the latter against a noisy background in the street. This would tend to heighten or undermine their respective understandability and believability.

They said (1980: 189) that:

> unspoken assumptions, practices and perspectives are no less important than those which are made explicit, for they help constitute the 'primary framework', in Goffman's phrase, which renders the newstalk meaningful. Industrial relations news relies heavily on a few key ideological propositions which inform everything which falls into the industrial category. They include the identification and labelling of industrial disputes in terms of labour, the attribution of cause to labour and the routine reduction of workers' aspirations to cash 'demands'. The reporting of industrial news in its encoding effectively conceals the primary assumptions beneath apparent neutrality and naturalistic presentation.

One automatic comment, for instance, is that wage rises would inevitably lead to similar price increases 'for the public'. Such comments are not made when there are rises in interest rates – at least, not in the same form.

The Glasgow studies provoked much controversy, in which some channels and scholars (such as Martin Harrison) contested their methodology and conclusions. But the general argument remains valid: underneath the seeming obviousness of the scores of split-second choices made by television news editors and reporters, there are often 'hidden scripts' unrecognized as such, but which are applied time and again in similar cases. In *War and Peace News* (1985), the Glasgow group extended its analyses to coverage of the Falklands war, the Greenham Common peace demonstrations, and similar conflicts. *Getting the Message: News, Truth and Power*, edited by John Elridge (1993) includes a series of case studies of reporting ranging from AIDS to Northern Ireland, Nicaragua, the Soviet Union, Vietnam and Ethiopia.

The bardic function of TV news

But what is the overall ideological function of the TV evening news? It is a double one, says the French communication scientist Gérard Leblanc. It is a constant ritual of evoking threats to our world and our world-views, of labelling and categorizing them, of processing and mastering them – with the help of authorities, experts and other tenants of the established social order. The trustworthy anchor of the evening news is like the parent who used to come and sit at our bedside around that same time to tell us a ghastly fairy tale full of monsters and dangers, only to have them all vanquished in time for a happy ending. It is basically 'once upon a time . . . today'. It tests and renews our sense of the world, making renewed sense of our world.

In their book *Reading Television* (1992: 88), British communication scholars John Fiske and John Hartley have called this the 'bardic function' of TV. Just like the bard in ancient Celtic societies, they said, the anchors and their like perform seven essential functions in society, namely:

> 1. to articulate the main lines of the established cultural consensus about the nature of reality; 2. to implicate the individual members of the culture into its dominant value systems, by cultivating these systems and showing them working in practice; 3. to celebrate, explain, interpret, and justify the doings of the culture's individual representatives; 4. to assure the culture at large of its practical adequacy in the world by affirming and confirming its ideologies/mythologies in active engagement with the practical and potentially unpredictable world; 5. to expose, conversely, any practical inadequacies in the culture's sense of itself which might result from changed conditions in the world out there, or from pressure within the culture for a reorientation in favour of a new ideological stance; 6. to convince the audience that their status and identity as individuals is guaranteed by the culture as a whole; 7. to transmit by these means a sense of cultural membership (security and involvement). (Reformulation from Fiske, 1990: 75–6; see also Hartley, 1989: 102–6)

In order to play this role, TV news must have some kind of 'mythic adequacy': it must fit in with major presuppositions shared within a culture and group. The American communication scholar Robert Rutherford Smith investigated such 'Mythic elements in television news' (*Journal of Communication*, Winter 1979, vol. 29: 82; also see Nimmo and Combs, 1993: 28). He also concluded that television news placed an undue emphasis on the 'political spectacle' and ascribed almost magical abilities to political leaders: 'The Greek gods on Mount Olympus were no less remote and only slightly more powerful.' Of course, television news is not the only type of programme projecting such a pantheon. It is seconded by talk shows, magazines, documentaries, documentary drama and fully-fledged fiction. But together they perform a holy Mass, celebrating the same world-view, which we all hold in common.

Press pictures and television film are to a large extent scripted and staged. Many people intervene in the deployment of cameras, in the framing of shots. TV evening news in particular follows very strict rules in its successive acts: the trailer and leader, the headlines and opening piece, the order and separation of various categories of news, in the tailpiece and leave-taking formulas; in the semiological 'division of labour' among its cast: the anchormen or women, the reporters and correspondents; in their ultimate control of what guests and subjects can or cannot say or demonstrate; in the choice of backdrops and surroundings, with various implications. The overarching logic is twofold; on the one hand a vivid evocation of new threats to convention, normality and order; on the other hand their labelling, categorization and neutralization, with the help of authorities, experts and others, with exceptionally a slow and gradual reformulation of the cultural consensus.

Notes

1 26 March, 1959. Reprinted in Irving Louis Horowitz (ed.), *Power, Politics and People: The Collected Essays of C. Wright Mills* (1963), p. 405. See also Edward Said, *Covering Islam* (1981), p. 42.

Further reading

News stills: Evans; Mayes. *Television*: Fiske; Fiske and Hartley; Himmelstein. *Television news*: Altheide; Cohen, et al.; Epstein; Iyengar; Leblanc; Postman.

10 WHAT EFFECTS DO THE MEDIA HAVE?

THE PSYCHOLOGY OF COMPASSION AND MISUNDERSTANDING

....

> The most important vehicle of reality-maintenance is conversation. One may view the individual's everyday life in terms of the working away of a conversational apparatus that ongoingly maintains, modifies and reconstructs his subjective reality . . .
>
> It is important to stress, however, that the greater part of reality-maintenance in conversation is implicit, not explicit. Most conversation does not in so many words define the nature of the world. Rather, it takes place against the background of a world that is silently taken for granted.

Peter Berger and Thomas Luckmann, 'Society as subjective reality'.[1]

For a variety of reasons then, the media selectively articulate certain facts and supposed relations between facts, just as someone selects certain patterns from the chaotic centrefold of a Burda magazine for further use. But don't readers and listeners and viewers themselves do this too? What is their motivation to seek out some media formats and eschew others? What are the cognitive mechanisms regulating what they pick out from the steady media bombardment, and what do they retain? How do they make sense of this in their own cultural environment? Does the accumulation of certain types and images over the years orient their feelings and thoughts in certain directions? What is the role of the larger media environment, for instance, of Hollywood films, in this?

In the previous chapters we have discussed which are the major media in the world, where and who the major journalists and sources are, what is news and when, and how reports are framed in words and images. But do these media and messages have any effects at all? Do they contribute to our own creation of the world, to reality construction and sense-making? This question has always been at the centre of controversy, particularly in the field of communication studies.

When the field emerged, it was dominated by what we might label the 'maximum effects' theory, which has also been dubbed the 'stimulus-response', the 'magic bullet' or the 'hypodermic needle' theory. When it emerged, in the early twentieth century, it was based on a combination of several observations. On the one hand, major Western countries (particularly the US and Germany, but also

England, France and others) had gone through a period of accelerated social change, related to the industrial revolution, rapid urbanization and the rise of modern mass media. This had apparently undermined social cohesion and customs, and had apparently created a mass society of isolated individuals, who seemed to be highly vulnerable to persuasion.

On the other hand, the First World War, the rise of communism and fascism, and the Second World War appeared to demonstrate the power of propaganda. The emergence of the consumer society further seemed to underscore the power of advertising. A series of major interdisciplinary research projects in the US (just before, during and after the last war) definitely put the field of 'communication studies' on the map. Media effects were thought to be major ones at first, and there was considerable interest in various factors playing a specific role (for instance, in the famous Yale studies on persuasion by Hovland, Kelley and others).

At the same time, traditionalists periodically cried foul at the corrupting influence of the commercial media, and their exploitation of sex and violence. At one time Hollywood and the movies were blamed, at another the record industry and pop music, and at still another the comics and their 'action men' (see Lowery and DeFleur, 1983). When commercial television networks sprang up in the course of the fifties (and after a few scandals over rigged quiz shows), moral crusaders targeted them with reproaches. It was in this particular context that Klapper, the head of the research division of CBS television, published a major overview of *The Effects of Mass Communication* (1960), and concluded that very few major effects had been convincingly demonstrated. This then became known as the 'minimal effects' theory, which dominated the field for decades to come.

Since then, communication researchers have continued to struggle with media effects. Some people (for instance, those in marketing) maintained that they could be considerable, and poured billions upon billions into research on readers, listeners and viewers; on their media exposure; on advertising and marketing effectiveness. Other people (for instance, those in academia) maintained that it was all very complicated and contradictory, and that further research was needed. Over the years, a wide and bewildering variety of different approaches to media effects (and mediating influences) has been proposed.

In most textbooks, they are presented as competing theories from which we have to choose only one. I prefer to present them as complementary theories, which all shed some light on this key problem. Some of these approaches are often presented as better proved than others. The criteria for good proof applied on such occasions, however, are often highly formalistic if not completely artificial. I prefer to present the approaches here as different conceptualizations, drawing attention to different aspects of the same problem, none of which can be dismissed out of hand at the moment. Although all are ultimately related to social and individual psychology, they usually stem from different traditions (sometimes within adjacent disciplines), and I will present them as families. (For a recent overview of mainstream American research, see Bryant and Zillmann, 1994.)

Cultural reception of media contents

When we see 'scarcely clad' Africans or South American 'Indians', this often makes a libidinal and/or a sensual impression. Whenever we see Arabs or Asian Indians covered from top to toe, by contrast, this often makes a strict and puritan impression. Whenever we see houses extended with improvised material, they leave an impression of slums. Whenever we (Northern Europeans) see houses with air-conditioning, they make an impression of luxury. Yet all these snap judgments may be off the mark, because these styles of dress and building may be purely inspired by climate and other physical circumstances. Photographers and cameramen often tend to emphasize colourful markets in African capitals, not skyscrapers. Both the audience and journalists thus primarily note what is different, not what is the same, and they tend to interpret it in their own terms too. These perceptions are not imposed by the object itself, or even by its image, but by our reaction as subjects.

Similarly, it is not the media message which entirely determines audience effects, for a variety of reasons. First, one has to make a careful distinction between the overt/explicit/intended aspects of the media message, and the covert/implicit/unintended ones. In matters of culture (such as those we have been discussing throughout this book), the former are usually more visible but less important than the latter. Second, one has to make a careful distinction between the interpretation of the sender and the interpretation by the receiver. They do not necessarily coincide; often, in fact, they do not coincide at all.

The reasons and mechanisms for this have mostly been elaborated in French structuralism, linguistics and semiology. Some current English-language authors who have consistently applied such ideas in the field of communication studies and news are Fiske, Hartley, O'Sullivan and others (see the bibliography). In these fields, the message is usually called the text: this is everything that is implied in words and sounds, images and sequences. The receiver is usually called the reader: anyone who takes some kind of notice. He or she may also be a listener, a viewer – or even the sniffer of a particular perfume, for that matter.

The prime observation is that the reception of the text depends on the context supplied by the situation and the reader. This context may be multiple, layered, fractured. It usually depends on the cultural and subcultural codes activated during the reception process. It also means that the author, director, producer, performer are not the ultimate arbiters of the real meaning of a media product. There is no real meaning or essence enclosed in the message itself. A novelist or film-maker who protests that a critic has read something in, or even into, a book or film that was not there misses the point. It is ultimately the reader, listener or viewer who decides what is or is not there.

This is not to say that a message can easily be made to mean anything to anyone. The sender has conciously or unconsciously encoded certain meanings in the message, which the receiver will or will not decode as such. The repertoire of possible codes and meanings is determined by the culture of both. Within this culture or subculture of each generation, gender group, nationality, language system, class, etc. there is usually a dominant reading of such signs: a habitual reading by the most influential and/or the largest groups. This does not exclude the possibility that some groups may occasionally and/or persistently undertake alternative readings of these same signs, or even that they may undertake an oppositional, critical decoding.

This problem becomes particularly evident when a message travels from one subculture to another, from one culture to another, from one age to another. A whole system of codes which was silently implied in one may be lost on the other. The same signs may have acquired different meanings; entirely different signs may have acquired more or less the same meanings. I have previously addressed these problems in a chapter about intercultural marketing and in a book about intellectual history. In both cases, what seemed obvious to the original authors of messages and texts, was completely lost on (or distorted by) subsequent users and readers – in other places and other times.[2]

With regard to the creation of the world by the international news media, this has the following consequences. Even if Western journalists and news media did nothing else than objectively observe and neutrally report the social reality in non-Western parts of the world as they see it (as in the examples cited above of dress and housing and city centres), this would still inevitably become completely mangled and distorted in the reception process of Western culture, since many of the cultural codes implied in the text (sound, image) about the expressions and behaviour of these peoples would be lost on others. Their original meanings (to these people themselves) are not automatically available, since they are not present in the text which is accessible, but only in the original context which is not accessible to the reader (listener, viewer). He or she can do little else but decode it in his or her own terms.

Motivational sources of media uses

What was often forgotten in early discussions about media effects and mediating influences was that people have a wide range of particular motives to turn to media, and that they aim for a wide range of particular goals. This observation has been elaborated in the so-called 'uses and gratifications' tradition of media effects research. It rejects the view of media audiences as entirely passive subjects, but proposes a view of media audiences as highly active subjects instead. On the basis of earlier experiences, people develop expectations about what rewards particular media and formats will bring them, and actively seek them out (or shy away from them).

One early research project in this tradition was done by McQuail, Blumler and Brown. They submitted questionnaires to people, asking them why they watched particular types of television programmes. People give different motives for watching the evening news, for instance, than for watching a quiz show. They may also choose not to watch television at all, if there is 'nothing on', or if other alternatives prevail: reading a book, having a conversation among relatives and friends, participating in sports activities, etc. McQuail (1983: 82–3) later reorganized some two dozen psychological 'uses and gratifications' of media into the following four groups:

> I. *Information*: finding out about relevant events and conditions in immediate surroundings, society and the world; seeking advice on practical matters or opinion and decision choices; satisfying curiosity and general interest; learning, self-education; gaining a sense of security through knowledge. II. *Personal identity*: finding reinforcement for personal values; finding models of behaviour; identifying with valued others (in the media); gaining insight into one's self. III. *Integration and social interaction*: gaining insight into circumstances of others – empathy; identifying with others and gaining a sense of belonging; finding a basis for conversation and social interaction; having a substitute for real-life companionship; helping to carry out social roles; enabling one to connect with family, friends and society. IV. *Entertainment*: escaping, or being diverted, from problems; relaxing; getting intrinsic cultural or aesthetic enjoyment; filling time; emotional release; sexual arousal.

It is obvious that this inventory of possible motives for media uses and of possible gratification is a very important addition to other theories, although some advocates of this approach tend to exaggerate in the other direction, implying that there is no media power and influence at all, since people always freely choose whatever pleases them. This is forgetting that on the one hand they will have to choose from what the media have on offer, and on the other that formats are designed to have particular appeals. That is to say, they cater more to certain possible uses and gratifications and less to others. Media and formats which are highly consumption-oriented and consumption-sustaining, for instance, tend to mobilize particular human motives while ignoring others.

With relation to the creation of the world by the international news media, the 'uses and gratification' approach offers important additional insights. News (and fiction) about non-Western countries caters to various motives of Western audiences. They do not only seek information about non-Western events, but also look to bolster their own Western personal identity. They not only seek to further 'integration and interaction' with their own environment, but also 'entertainment' (for a recent overview, see Rosengren et al., 1985).

Such reflections may also help explain why information about everyday life in other cultures is under-represented, since it implicitly challenges the assumptions of one's own culture and makes one feel uneasy. Only the exceptional is highlighted, sometimes in a positive sense: in idyllic pictures of others' nature and culture, in the context of documentaries and fiction; but even more in a negative sense, in horror pictures of major disruptions. Our recurrent sense of shock at the strangeness of the situation of others continually renews our adherence to the value and the values of our own society.

Cognitive processing of media contents

News is processed by people in certain ways (Graber, 1988), as are all other forms of information. The cognitive processing of media messages basically has two aspects: selection and integration. Selection take places in four different stages. The first is selective exposure. People are selective in exposing themselves (and in paying attention) to informal and formal communication: at certain times and places, to certain media and formats, to certain voices and texts. The second stage is selective perception. People are selective in taking in messages. The third level is selective retention. People are selective in remembering certain elements and relations. The fourth stage is selective reproduction. People are selective in retrieving and rendering information in conversation. All this brings us back to the fact that communication is an ongoing and interactive process, not the unambiguous, singular, unilateral and isolated act which some researchers seem to imply.

The four stages of selection are all guided by processes of levelling, sharpening and assimilation. This brings us to the other basic aspect of cognitive processing: integration. Over the years and decades, dozens of mechanisms have been postulated with regard to integration. I will limit myself to mentioning only a few: Gestalt, field and balance, attribution theory and cognitive psychology. The first and oldest of these is Gestalt theory, which is opposed to the idea that perception, thinking and remembering are related to isolated elements, which might be individually associated with others. The Gestalt theorists claimed that such elements did in fact form meaningful configurations in the mind, in which the whole is more than the sum of the parts. Think of the well-known example of a circle with two dots in the upper half, a vertical bar descending between them, and a horizontal bar at a right angle underneath. We will 'spontaneously' see this as a face with two eyes, a nose and a mouth. Similarly, Gestalt theorists say, all our perceptions and thoughts and reminiscences are usually organized into meaningful networks.

A later relevant tradition, deriving in part from it, is that of various types of field and balance theories. Balance theories claim that we continually seek to balance our various thoughts and feelings and actions: we try to maintain some coherence. Most communication scientists are familiar with only one offshoot of this tradition: the so-called theory of cognitive dissonance, elaborated by Festinger (although in fact much older). Basically it says that when we happen to expose ourselves to 'dissonant cognitions', actually to perceive and retain them, we usually start a series of mental operations to reprocess them, to make them fit into our mental framework. This may lead either to some kind of rejection of the information or to a realignment of other ideas or actions, until balance and consonance are restored. This happens, for instance, when we are forced to do something with which we disagree.

One more recent offshoot of this tradition is so-called attribution theory, which deals with the way in which we attribute reasons and motives to the expressions and behaviours of other people and ourselves. One finding is that if an action fails we often tend to attribute it to the intrinsic characteristics of other people, whereas we tend to attribute it to external circumstances for ourselves. If an action succeeds, the reverse will be true. This tendency is found to differ somewhat between dominant and non-dominant groups, for instance, between men and women. That is to say, we tend to protect our own ego, our own self-esteem. This holds for ourselves as individuals as well as for ourselves as a group. (See also the discussion of the related concept of ethnocentrism in the concluding chapter.)

The most recent relevant tradition with regard to integration is so-called cognitive psychology. Whereas the long dominant behaviourist tradition said that psychologists should limit themselves to the analysis of external behaviour and refrain from any speculation about internal processes, the emergence of computers enabled the development of artificial intelligence and relatively sophisticated simulation models of mental functioning. 'Schemata' were postulated as 'mini-systems by which the individual internalizes, structures and makes sense of an event' (Phillips, 1981, quoted by O'Sullivan et al., 1988). 'Scripts' were postulated which organize our knowledge with regard to a certain routine course of action. When I say 'grab a seat', someone from my own culture will immediately grasp what is meant, whereas someone from another (that is, seat-less) culture may misunderstand it.

The consequences of these cognitive theories for the 'creation of the world' are wide-ranging. First: we will only expose ourselves (that is, perceive, retain and reproduce) to the information about other cultures and social systems that we can make sense of. Second: we tend to fit this information about other people and groups into configurations which are meaningful in our own group. (Think of the apocryphal reaction of Queen Marie Antoinette when she learned on the eve of the French Revolution that 'the people' didn't have bread to eat: 'Then let them eat cake'.)[3]

Third: we tend to absolve ourselves, our group, our social system of major blame for the negative conditions of others. If there is widespread poverty in the world we are quite willing to do something about it; but the idea that it is somehow related to our own wealth is unacceptable. Fourth: we will organize such ideas into coherent scripts about realistic and absurd forms of social change, for instance, about philanthropy and development aid, but not about fundamental changes in pricing and trade conditions for, say, agricultural raw materials.

Categorization and stereotyping

Long before the emergence of the computer as a major tool for mental modelling, psychologists suspected that the functioning of the mind was regulated to a high degree by principles of efficiency: simple storing, easy access, etc. Whereas the world out there is often characterized by continuities, the mind in here primarily tries to encode them as polarities. Furthermore, it tends to connect these polarities with each other in sequential or hierarchical strings. Not only are continuities such as latitude or colour somewhat artificially cut up in polarities such as West/East and white/black – as we have seen in the introduction to this volume – but they also quite easily become connected to valuations such as good/bad.

The key categorization is I/us versus them. The prevailing criterion may vary: it may be gender, age, nationality, religion, ethnicity, class, education. In fact, someone's sense of identity is to a large extent a product of the combination of dozens upon dozens of such categorizations, which have mostly been internalized through language in the course of early socialization. In that perspective, identity is also defined by something which we might label 'alternity'. That is to say, our sense of what we are is also defined by our sense of what we are not, by our sense of what we can or do not want to be, our sense of what others are. We continuously define and redefine ourselves in relation to in-groups and out-groups.

The recurrence of stereotypes, of simplified 'pictures in our heads' (as Lippmann called them), is therefore a universal phenomenon, and cannot simply be 'wished away' by moral indignation. When dealing with others, we all have a tendency to make three split-second judgments in one. The first judgment is the simple observation of difference, of different behaviour, for instance. The second judgment is the interpretation of difference, a guess at the reasons for this different behaviour. The third is a value judgment about whether this different behavior is good or bad in our eyes. The problem is that in dealing with different cultures or subcultures, these three judgments are usually combined into one.

From the simple observation of difference, we tend to jump to conclusions. We intuitively measure the behaviour of this other group against the behaviour of our own group, and tend to make a judgment as to whether it is superior or inferior. If we judge it superior or even equivalent, this automatically puts into question our own group's way of doing things and our own sense of self. If we judge it inferior, by contrast, this reaffirms our group's one best way of doing things and our own sense of self. It is obvious, therefore, that the latter alternative will generally win out over the former alternative.

Such collective judgments about other individuals and groups are made even more easily when they are identifiable by external signs – gender and age, race and nationality – which may be visible in body and dress. In such cases, we do not even have to interact with those others before we can categorize them and mobilize our stereotypes. There is a difference, though. We tend to have frequent interaction with people of other gender and age groups, at least within our own family. Therefore our stereotypes about them can never become absolute. We may very well have very little interaction with people from ethnic minorities or different nationalities. In such cases, prejudice can take on even more extreme forms.

If there is a history of confrontation between peoples, negative images may tend to perpetuate themselves and act as a self-fulfilling prophecy leading to further clashes. This is often the case between neighbouring countries, which may have a history of problems around such issues as minorities, frontiers and alliances. It is also often the case between former colonizers and the colonized, with a long heritage of mutual reproach. If the political will is strong enough, however, previous antagonisms may easily be overcome. Look at the unification of the United States of America after the Civil

War, the unification of Europe after two wars, or the reversal of alliances with Russia and Japan during the Cold War.

Meanwhile, the simultaneous cultivation of love for one's country and hatred for one's enemies are among the most fundamental mechanisms underlying a sense of collective and individual identity. They are usually spontaneously produced and reproduced within both the formal and informal communication systems (media and everyday conversation) of each country (or group of countries). These mechanisms bolster social and psychological cohesion, and permit a splitting between positive and negative feelings: the former usually reserved for one's in-group and the latter projected onto the out-group. This Manichean view of the world is intensified once real confrontations get under way (see Keene, 1991).

We seem to need enemies. This has considerable consequences for the creation of the world by the international news media. After the demise of communism, the First World has lost the Second World as a major enemy and is looking for (various groups within) the Third World to fill this role. This may be 'unfair' competitors in newly industrializing countries in East Asia, Latino drug traffickers, Arab terrorists and Islamic fundamentalists. We have seen a rapid succession of villains fitting these bills. One author even speaks of 'the monster of the month' in this regard. The point is not that certain leaders, organizations and groups are not reprehensible. It is that the different interests and views of non-Western nations are seldom seen as legitimate, and there is often a projection of surplus evil on anyone who dares to challenge the interests and views of Western nations.

Cultivation effects of media contents

Much of the research on the effects of the media has been of the traditional quantitative-empirical, one-on-one type. It assumed that the key characteristics of a message readily present themselves on the surface of a text or picture, and in unambiguous terms, that they can easily be observed by all, categorized and therefore coded by 'content analysts' belonging to one culture and/or subculture. It assumed that possible effects had to turn up in a simple comparison of measurements of audience opinions and attitudes before and after exposure to such a message. It concluded that if effects could not be registered in this way, this proved there were no such effects. And it concluded that if no media effects could be found in this way, there probably were few or none, and the opinions and attitudes of people probably derived from other sources.

The problem is, as we have noted before, that in the last instance there are no other sources for opinions and attitudes about many subjects, particularly those which are located far away in space and time. We have no direct experience about those subjects at all; we have only indirect experience of them, mediated experience; experience through science, education, media and other reality-validating domains. It is true that conversation with other people in our environment plays a major role, too. They may be parents, relatives, neighbours, friends, acquaintances, or even professionals: clergymen, politicians, colleagues. The problem is that most of them also derive their frames from mediated experience. So ultimately, our views of the world derive in large measure from mediated experience.

One way around this is to postulate that the effects of individual media messages may indeed be minimal and almost subliminal (that is to say, under an observable threshold). But the accumulated effects of such subliminal messages, which are repeated time and again, in more or less similar form, through different sources and media, may well be very significant indeed. This idea has been developed in the 'cultural indicators' and 'cultivation' approach outlined by George Gerbner in a long and continuing series of research projects, articles and chapters in books. Through a combination of content analysis of messages (mostly in network broadcasting) and audience research (mostly in the US), Gerbner and his colleagues have investigated the continuous nurture (or obliteration) of certain views of the world by the media, particularly by commercial television. They researched the presence and representation of men and women, younger and older people, the ethnic majority and ethnic minorities, white- and blue-collar workers in TV programmes, and found they were often highly stereotypical. They also researched the nature and frequency of acts of violence on TV, and the characteristics of 'goodies and baddies', of perpetrators and victims.

They compared the beliefs held by 'light' and 'heavy' viewers, and found that heavy viewers also held more stereotypical views of various gender and age groups, ethnic and professional groups. Some of the early research found that 'heavy' viewers such as poor and lonely elderly women, for instance, grossly overestimated the amount of violence in society and their chances of falling victim to it. Nancy Signorielli has reviewed evidence for the 'cultivation hypothesis' in a variety of fields in recent years, for instance, in the depiction of health problems and health solutions, as well as health professionals. There is a considerable literature on the stereotypical depiction of surgeons, doctors and nurses in novels and films.

Still, the approach of Gerbner and his associates has been challenged in a variety of ways. Some claimed they had failed to prove that the media images were the cause and the audience beliefs were the consequence of stereotyped pictures. Some claimed that the cultivation theory might hold some truth for the US with its larger (information) inequalities and more homogeneous commercial television, but not for Europe with its smaller (information) inequalities and more diverse public television (see, for example, Wober and Gunter, 1988; Bouwman, 1987). Since the rapid spread of European commercial television in recent years, and the equally rapid adaptation of European public television to these same programming styles, this criticism may have partly outlived itself. Although it is true that some of the evidence is still scattered, the cultivation approach provides a highly plausible theory of some long-term media effects (a recent overview of results was edited by Signorielli and Morgan, 1990).

The implications of the cultivation approach for the creation of the world, for reality construction and sense-making are considerable. On the one hand, we have seen throughout this book that Western reports about non-Western countries and peoples tend to be stereotypical, in a wide variety of ways; not because of a lack of energy or a lack of critical spirit of Western journalists, but because they are caught in a web of a hundred and one different 'universal' mechanisms from which it is hard to free themselves by a simple act of faith and good intentions. On the other hand, views of underdevelopment and development which are held by Western media audiences (and increasingly by non-Western media audiences too) are often stereotypical as well. There is no easy way out.

Fact and faction in Hollywood docudrama

The effects of factual news items are also to a large extent refracted and mediated by the effects of the fictional drama which surrounds it. Television news, for instance, resonates with documentaries and dramatizations concerning far-away places and long-ago times. TV films provide a major backdrop to our sense of geography and history, sociology and anthropology. Our view of most major events in world history is in fact shaped more by dramatic Hollywood depictions of it than by the dull lessons we learned in school. But these depictions are almost all heavily slanted in one direction or another.

The US is by far the largest producer of 'factual' and fictional material for television in the world (see also the Appendix to this volume). The entertainment industry is the sector which produces the largest trade surplus after the aircraft industry. Eighty per cent of the export of TV programmes in the world comes from the US (and half of it goes to Western Europe). Eighty per cent of EC movie tickets pay for American films, and 60 per cent of TV movies shown are from the US (*International Herald Tribune*, 24 February 1995). At this point, therefore, it is useful to take a closer look at the actual conditions under which such material is being produced. The US is a litigation society: there is a constant threat of major lawsuits and bad publicity.

Therefore, network lawyers guard closely a narrow range of 'least objectionable programming'. This fear of offending is limited to powerful individuals, groups and corporations from the US and its immediate overseas allies. There is no such restraint with regard to neutral or hostile Second and Third World leaders, governments or institutions. They are often caricatured at will.

This general tendency affects the major television news stories that get produced and exported. There is another field in which the retouching of images of reality is even more direct and pervasive. That is the field of faction: a varying mixture of fact and fiction, ranging from dramadoc (dramatized documentaries) to docudrama (documentary drama). It may either be an apparently painstaking reconstruction of what actually happened or a liberal interpretation of what might have been. The important thing is that this genre claims to give a more or less truthful impression of recent or historic events. It is extremely influential in further filling in our world-view, and in linking up casual news reports with our larger fantasy worlds.

The important thing to note is that the more ambitious faction productions which are continually broadcast and rebroadcast around the world were generally produced for prime-time TV on the US networks. In this case 'prime time' does not mean only that it is aimed at the largest possible (American) public, but also that it should be agreeable to the largest possible (American) range of sponsors. In the US, the sponsor does not merely pay for thirty or sixty seconds of air time during a commercial break, but is a demanding supervisor of the contents of the entire programme. If a programme is for some reason judged unacceptable by major advertisers, it will be either changed or cancelled. Thus many of the documentaries and dramas which are shown around the world as truthful depictions of real events have been censored by US advertising agencies and corporations. A few historical examples may illustrate this point.

In his study *The Sponsor*, the media expert Erik Barnouw (1978: 53–4) quotes the vice-president of a major advertising agency before the Federal Communication Commission, in the early decades of television. His client was the natural gas industry, and they were to sponsor a docudrama on the Nuremberg trials against Nazi war criminals. 'In going through the script, we noticed gas referred to in a half dozen places that had to do with the death chambers. This was just an oversight on somebody's part . . . we raised the point with CBS and they said they would remove the word "gas".' The vice-president of the even larger McCann-Erickson agency reassured the commission: 'Actually there have been very few cases where it has been necessary to exercise a veto, because the producers involved and the writers involved are normally pretty well aware of what might not be acceptable.'

In his study *The Media Monopoly*, Ben Bagdikian (1983: 158–9) quotes another FCC investigation at the time of escalating American intervention in Vietnam, and the programme guidelines of the largest American advertiser, Procter and Gamble. They said:

> 'Where it seems fitting, the characters in Procter and Gamble dramas should affect recognition and acceptance of the world situation in their thoughts and actions, although in dealing with war, our writers should minimize the "horror" aspects. The writers should be guided by the fact that any scene that contributes negatively to public morale is not acceptable. Men in uniform shall not be cast as heavy villains or portrayed as engaging in any criminal activity.' The guidelines also said: 'There will be no material on any of our programs which could in any way further the concept of business as cold, ruthless, and lacking all sentiment or spiritual motivation. If a businessman is cast in the role of villain, it must be made clear that he is not typical but as much despised by his fellow businessmen as he is by other members of society.'

In his study *Inside Prime Time*, Todd Gitlin discusses (1985: 180) the way major shows are produced today. One chapter is specifically devoted to 'movies of the week', including docudrama. It notes that most major historical and social issues have to be framed in a particularly bland way in order to be acceptable to the networks. Funny or entertaining blacks have long been acceptable, for instance, but angry blacks like Malcolm X were long considered ill-suited for prime-time TV. The woman in charge of mini-series at NBC said: 'I don't think you couldn't do a dramatic show about a black, but I think you probably wouldn't do Martin Luther King again. You would probably do the Josephine Baker story with Diana Ross, because maybe that would do better.' She added that she had contemplated 'doing' Sally Hemmings, the black slave mistress of the early American president Thomas Jefferson, but that this would probably prove impossible (see also Nederveen Pieterse, 1992; Shohat and Stam, 1994). The *Roots* series was the first time the plight of black slaves was portrayed emphatically in a prime-time TV series. The *Holocaust* series did something similar with regard to the mass killings of Jews in Nazi Germany. But both were typically sanitized Hollywood versions of major historical tragedies.

Nimmo and Combs noted about *Roots* (1993: 85):

> audiences were able to identify with it because of its fantastic assurance of the romantic triumph of values we all hold dear despite the oppressions of history. The panorama of Roots placed evil in the past and hope and justice in the present and future. It offered blacks a myth of Eden when Kunta Kinte was torn from his peaceful village in the idyllic setting of Africa. Separated from their African Dream, blacks were then unwillingly caught up in the pageant that eventually made them part of the American Dream, reassuring both black and white alike that oppression and poverty can be overcome by individual heroism and familial perseverance. By depicting

various stereotypical white racists – slavers, Klansmen – the miniseries suggested that racism was, and is, the fault of individual villains and not the system itself, thus assuaging any feelings of white guilt.

It is not only the past that gets reviewed and corrected in this way, in which certain elements are systematically highlighted and others blotted out. The same holds for present-day lifestyles. For several decades, smoking was systematically glamorized in the movies, and pertinent information on its health effects was blotted out. Barnouw (1978: 55) quoted the testimony of the vice-president of another major advertising agency, Ted Bates, before the FCC. 'One company manufactured a filter cigarette, and his policy indicated that the heavy [villain] must smoke non-filter cigarettes . . . Whereas the manufacturer of the non-filter cigarette insisted that the heavy smoked a filtered cigarette. It sounds ridiculous, but it's not at all.' Bagdikian (1983: 160) also quoted the later testimony of the vice-president of a pharmaceutical company before the FCC, saying that they refused a show 'if a scene depicted somebody committing suicide by taking a bottle of tablets'. The point of all this is a reminder that both fact and fiction on mainstream prime-time commercial TV are subject to heavy guidance and censorship.

In her book *Mediaspeak*, Donna Woolfolk Cross (1983: 89, 94) quotes a poll of the 3,000 members of the Writers Guild of America: '86 percent of the writers queried said that they had found, from personal experience, that censorship exists on "entertainment" programs.' There is a rule that generic consumer products should be glamorized in most American TV films and series, and that their possible negative sides should be systematically blotted out. Therefore, they are usually set in an upper middle-class environment of conspicuous consumption, and steer clear of lower-class characters and the average workplace. Furthermore, mainstream TV films and series should be primarily aimed at the white viewer, one of the main characters should always be a sympathetic white, and the world should preferably be presented from his or her perspective. There are exceptions, but they are usually aimed at specific target groups.

The same holds for ordinary movies. Whether dealing with colonial times or with black emancipation, there will always be a nice white whose perspective is central to the story. Otherwise, there will be no funding, since the audience groups with the most purchasing power may shun the movie. In earlier times, 'non-white' central roles were even played mostly by white actors with heavy make-up, whereas the masses of extras consisted of anonymous non-whites. This same pattern is still discernible today.[4] In his book on documentary drama *True Stories*, Derek Paget (1990: 152–61 ff.) notes that almost all major Vietnam films shown by TV networks and cinemas around the world (whether conservative or liberal) picture the conflict primarily as a major drama for young white American males – who represented only 1 per cent of the victims.[5] Elderly people, blacks and other ethnic minorities, Vietnamese and women are relegated to secondary roles – although they often carried the major burden of the war. Only very recently was the first Vietnam film made from a different perspective.

In this way, the perspective of ethnic minorities and overseas peoples is almost entirely absent from major Hollywood fiction films, and the same holds for the limited number of European blockbusters related to (de)colonization, minorities and the like (see also Nimmo and Combs, *Mediated Political Realities*, 1993).

Individual people seem to form the last link in the chain, although we should remember that sense-making is always a social activity, and that communication cannot be studied as a singular, isolated, one-sided act. Many aspects of the news system which we have identified throughout this book are in turn the result of our individual acquiescence or support. What is in our minds is also in society, and what is in society is also in our minds. Or, put differently, what is between our ears is also what is before our eyes, and vice versa. Thus if the media are pervaded by Eurocentrism, it is also because the major audiences are pervaded by Eurocentrism, and vice versa. It is not easy to liberate ourselves and others from this mental prison.

Notes

1 In *The Social Construction of Reality* (1981), p. 172.

2 Intercultural marketing: 'Luchtspiegelingen', ch. 6 in J. van Ginneken, *Rages en crashes* (Crazes and Crashes) (1993), pp. 136–66. Intellectual history: J. van Ginneken, *Crowds, Psychology and Politics* (1992), particularly the chapter on the 19th-century French social theorist G. Tarde, who pioneered many of the communication and opinion concepts discussed here.

3 The remark was certainly not made in 1789, since Rousseau already attributed it to 'a great princess' in his 1778 *Confessions*. See Paul F. Boller and John George, *They Never Said It: A Book of Fake Quotes, Misquotes and Misleading Attributions* (New York: Oxford University Press, 1989), pp. 97–8.

4 Think of worthwhile liberal 'historical' films such as *Gandhi, Cry Freedom, Mississippi Burning, Out of Africa, The Last Emperor*, and many others, but also of more openly semi-fictional films such as *City of Joy, Little Buddha, Missing, A Passage to India, Salvador, The Year of Living Dangerously* and *Under Fire*.

5 Secretary (minister) McNamara recently acknowledged during a visit to his Vietnamese counterpart Giap, that the Vietnamese had lost 3.2 million people and the US 58,000. A disproportionately large number of US combat troops, however, were recruited from 'ethnic minorities'.

Further reading

Communication studies: McQuail; McQuail and Windahl. *News processing*: Graber. *Media effects*: Bryant and Zillmann; Lowery and De Fleur. *Cultivation approach*: Signorielli and Morgan. *Fict and faction*: Gitlin (1985); Nimmo and Combs; Paget.

11 CONCLUSION: US, WE AND THEM

The making of the illusions which flood our experience has become the business of America, some of its most honest and most necessary and most respectable business. I am thinking not only of advertising and public relations and political rhetoric, but of all the activities which purport to inform and comfort and improve and educate and elevate us: the work of our best journalists, our most enterprising book publishers, our most energetic manufacturers and merchandisers, our most successful entertainers, our best guides to world travel, and our most influential leaders in foreign relations.

Daniel Boorstin, 'Extravagant expectations'.[1]

The previous chapter discussed the psychological truth that categorizations and even stereotypes are inevitable; they help us simplify the world, build and manage internal models of reality. We often jump from the observation of cultural difference, over the interpretation of cultural difference, to an evaluation of cultural difference. We protect the self-esteem of ourselves and our group by depreciating others. How does it come about that we are all ethnocentric, occicentric, Eurocentric? How does it affect our relations with others? How does it affect our ability to accept compromise, to live with ethnic minorities, to promote international understanding? What role do the news media play? And what could be done about it?

We have seen throughout this book that many mechanisms intervene to shape the news. News makes certain things explicit while leaving other things implicit; it is inevitably guided by notions of what is unexpected, extraordinary and abnormal. Small forms of cultural deviance may lead to major moral panics. Since the largest and richest transcontinental media organizations originate from the largest and richest Western countries, their selection and interpretation is primarily guided by the the preoccupations of those countries and audiences. Furthermore, their commercial orientation plays a certain role as well.

Western journalists are not only socialized by their own culture, but also by particular ideas about professionalism. Their seemingly neutral procedures, however, often have unintended side-effects. Time and other pressures, for instance, make them dependent on official and easily accessible sources. The perspectives of the structurally marginal and radically different are often silently excluded. Their focus on events rather than processes, on people rather than systems, frames reality in a very particular way. For all its emphasis on topicality, much of the news is planned and routinized.

The news net is distributed quite unevenly around the world. The centres of some cities are covered by thousands upon thousands of reporters, whereas entire continents are left to be covered by rather small numbers. This affects the forms of news-gathering and the picture of the world which results. Messages are also framed in particular ways. Language is not a mirror of reality, but rather a meaning system of its own. The choice of words, of sentences, of narratives may seem self-evident to the journalist, but it always shuns alternatives and therefore has hidden ideological implications. The same holds for the choice of images, the construction of sequences, the way in which a news photograph or a news film presents its subject and addresses the audience.

But even if all this were fundamentally different, we would still tend to normalize news in the reception process itself, by trying to fit it into our own (sub)cultural categories, by discussing it with others, by integrating it cognitively. Media images of the outside world, therefore, are mediated in many different ways: they are systematically levelled, sharpened and assimilated to our own world-views. Each of the previous chapters had half a dozen sections discussing at least a dozen different mechanisms which intervene to orient our pictures of the world. There may be a hundred and one such mechanisms or more. Even though each of them taken separately may make no more than a 1 per cent difference, all taken together make more than 100 per cent difference – particularly since most work in the same direction.

My Burda model emphasizes that the world reality we take for granted is only one of many different realities which could be distinguished and underscored. We are constantly made aware of a few (families of) patterns, and made to overlook many others. In this sense, we already live in a virtual reality which looks and feels as if it is real – but is not. The problems and solutions, our fears and hopes concerning a better world, are continually being constructed in a very peculiar way.

The media construction of the political spectacle

In his book *How Real is Real?* Paul Watzlawick (1976) argues that

> our everyday, traditional ideas of reality are delusions which we spend substantial parts of our daily lives shoring up, even at the considerable risk of trying to force facts to fit our definition of reality instead of vice versa. And the most dangerous delusion of all is that there is only one reality. What there are, in fact, are so many different versions of reality, some of which are contradictory, but all of which are the results of communication and not reflections of eternal, objective truths.

Dan Nimmo and James Combs took this observation as their point of departure for a review of numerous kinds of *Mediated Political Realities*. They said: 'the vast bulk of political reality that most of us take for granted (whether we are private citizens or public officials) consists of a combination of fantasies created and evoked by group and mass communication' (pp. 1993: 6). They then proceeded to scrutinize the underlying myths of TV news, of presidential campaigns, of Hollywood, of sports, etc. And they concluded with an inventory of some forty-three 'recurrent fantasies' underlying much of American political discourse and action.

Murray Edelman has written a brilliant and fascinating book on *Constructing the Political Spectacle* (1988). He said:

> The spectacle constituted by news reporting continuously constructs and reconstructs social problems, crises, enemies, and leaders and so creates a succession of threats and assurances . . . They also play a central role in winning support and opposition for political causes and policies. The latter role is usually masked by the assumption that citizens, journalists, and scholars are observers of 'facts' whose meanings can be accurately ascertained by those who are properly trained and motivated. That positivist view is accepted rather than defended today. We are acutely aware that observers and what they observe construct one another; that political developments are ambiguous entities that mean what concerned observers construe them to mean; and that the roles and self-concepts of the observers themselves are also constructions, created at least in part by their interpreted observations.

He added:

> The characteristic of problems, leaders, and enemies that makes them political is precisely that controversy over their meanings is not resolved. Whether poverty originates in the inadequacies of its victims or in the pathologies of social institutions, whether a leader's actions are beneficial or damaging to the polity, whether a foreign, racial, religious, or ethnic group is an enemy or a desirable ally, typify the questions that persist indefinitely and remain controversial as historical issues just as they were controversial in their time. (pp. 1-3)

He then devoted entire chapters to the dissection of the construction of political problems and solutions, leaders and enemies, etc. Chapter 2, for instance, has section headings on: problems as ideological constructions; damaging conditions that do not become problems; problems as benefits; problems as ambiguous claims; the construction of reasons for problems; the constitution of authorities; the construction of problems to justify solutions; the construction of gestures as solutions; the perpetuation of problems through policies to ameliorate them; problems as negations of other problems; the uses of invisible social problems; the definition of events as crises; audiences as creators of social problems; the devaluation of everyday experience; social problems as texts: proliferation, erasure, traces, supplements. It is clear that media and mediating processes play a huge role in the selective articulation of many of these elements every day. This is particularly true for television news.

Think of the example of the construction of the 'problem' of 'development'. Who is underdeveloped and who is overdeveloped, in what fields and based on what criteria? What are the causes and consequences of under- and overdevelopment, who is to blame and who is to be praised? Or think of the construction of the solution of 'aid': does aid lead to development, who aids whom, who hinders whom, who profits from whom, in what ways? The dominant Western discourse about 'development aid', which frames everyday media coverage of scores of related subjects, contains dozens of unproven assumptions which are usually passed over in silence and not even recognized as such.

Shanto Iyengar has done a major empirical study on *How Television Frames Political Issues* (1991) with as its main question and title: *Is Anyone Responsible?* Through a combination of content analysis, field experiments and correlational analysis, Iyengar looked at the impact of TV news framing of six contemporary political issues: international terrorism, crime, poverty, unemployment, racial inequality and the Reagan administration's Iran-Contra dealings. The conclusion was that the continuous TV news emphasis on events and personalities hampered a basic understanding of the underlying processes and the social system. It is true that:

> This 'pro-establishment effect' of television news is counter intuitive. [But] by simplifying complex issues to the level of anecdotal evidence, television news leads viewers to issue-specific attributions of responsibility, and these attributions tend to shield society and government from responsibility. Following exposure to episodic framing, Americans describe chronic problems such as poverty and crime not in terms of deep-seated social or economic conditions, but as mere idiosyncratic outcomes. (pp. 136–8)

Similar things apply to economic underdevelopment and political violence abroad.

Iyengar quoted Altheide's observation that the year-long television news coverage of the Iran hostage crisis, for instance, 'was reduced to one story – the freeing of the hostages – rather than coverage of its background and context, of the complexities of Iran, of alternative American policies, and of contemporary parochial policies in a world dominated by superpowers' (p. 15). Yet this happens time and again when there are such confrontations.

Whenever there is an armed confrontation between pro-Western and anti-Western groups anywhere in the world, the time and space pressures of television news in North America as well as in Western Europe soon tend to reduce the complicated story to a simple narrative of a mythical clash between villains and victims. This gets even worse once 'our boys' seem to get caught in the middle. But this is a misleading construction of the political spectacle. As Edelman

(1988: 5) says: 'Genocide, racial and religious persecution, and the rest of the long catalogue of political acts that have sustained human history can only come from people who are sure they are right. Only in bad novels and comic books do characters knowingly do evil and boast of it. In life, people rationalize their actions in moral terms.'

Television and education

The main character of the novel *Being There* by Jerzy Kosinsky is a simple soul named Chauncey Gardiner. His whole knowledge of the outside world stems from television: most of all from children's programmes and gardening programmes, as well as from advertising spots. Through the reproduction of their platitudes and clichés, Gardiner comes to be regarded as a wise man and a media personality. It may be seen as a parable about the media society of US (the United States) and WE (Western Europe): the West versus the rest. We are all rapidly turning into Chauncey Gardiners, as are our celebrity heroes.

The same pattern is spreading throughout the world: television is increasingly becoming the main source of information and education. Adult Japanese watch TV four hours and eleven minutes a day on average. Adult Americans watch TV four hours and one minute a day on average. Adults in Western Europe watch television three hours and sixteen minutes per day on average (according to *Television '96*, a research report by IP, the advertising sales group for the European RTL commercial TV stations).

Youngsters too get an ever larger part of their information from TV. Postman and Powers (1992: 145–6):

> In America, those between the ages of two and twelve watch an average of twenty-five hours of television per week. The young ones watch about five thousand hours before entering the first grade; and by high-school's end the average American youngster has clocked nineteen thousand hours in front of a TV set. The same youngster will have spent only thirteen thousand hours in school, assuming that he or she is in regular attendance. What it comes down to is that American children spend 30 percent of their waking hours in front of a television set. And that means exposure to roughly thirteen thousand killings, about 100,000 violent episodes, and somewhere in the neighbourhood of 650,000 commercials.

Large parts of the new generation with a 'television education' derive their basic historical and geographical frames from Hollywood films, Disney comic strips and theme parks: about the Arabian *Thousand and One Nights*, the African animal world, the American 'Indians' (or *Aladdin, The Lion King* and *Pocahontas*).

Pratkanis and Aronson (1992: 3, 11) add: 'More than half of our waking hours are spent with the mass media ... The average American will see or hear more than 7 million advertisements in his or her lifetime.' Thus we are bombarded with staggering amounts of heavily mediated information each day. The question is, of course: do we learn something from it, anything at all?

The *New York Times* recently reported that the Harris opinion polling agency had found in a survey about general education and scientific knowledge that 'A majority of American adults do not know that humans evolved from animal species or that the Sun and the Earth are in the Milky Way galaxy. And one-third think that humans and dinosaurs existed at the same time.' (Note that this was at the time of the *Jurassic Park* media hype.) The *Washington Post* recently reported that the Gallup opinion polling agency had found in a survey about historical knowledge that '60 percent of Americans are unable to name the president who ordered the nuclear attack on Japan, and 35 percent do not know that the first atomic bomb was dropped on Hiroshima,' whereas 'one out of every four people surveyed did not even know that Japan was the target of the first atomic bomb'. (Note that this was during the run-up to the widely celebrated fiftieth anniversary of the end of the Second World War.)

The knowledge level on current international affairs is equally limited. A former State Department official reported that 'Asked what percentage of the federal budget goes to foreign aid, Americans typically guess 15 percent or even more. The actual figure is less than half of 1 percent.' (This was at the time of a major push in Congress to reduce foreign aid.) (These reports come from the *International Herald Tribune*, 22 April 1994, 2 and 3 March 1995 respectively.) Even the people's representatives themselves often do not know what they are talking about. After the previous US elections, someone at *Spy* magazine pulled a little joke by calling new members of Congress and asking them about policy toward Freedonia. Some said they favoured decisive action, others pleaded for a prudent approach. The problem was, of course, that Freedonia does not exist – except in the hilarious film classic *Duck Soup* by the Marx brothers.

Similar tendencies can be noted in Western Europe. Here is just one illustration. In 1996, a Dutch historical journal submitted a questionnaire about elementary historical knowledge to parliamentarians in The Hague. Forty per cent or so reacted (probably those who considered themselves among the best-informed). They scored an average 40 per cent correct answers, and therefore miserably failed the test at an elementary school level. In spite of the advent of the often acclaimed information society, therefore, it remains to be seen how well-informed we really are, and on what we base our major foreign policy decisions.

Ethnocentrism and occicentrism of the US and WE

Within any individual and group, but also within social organizations and communication, within media systems and mediated realities, we encounter spontaneous and recurrent tendencies towards various forms of ethnocentrism. The concept of ethnocentrism was identified and defined by William Graham Sumner (quoted in LeVine and Campbell, 1972: 8), in his book *Folkways*. He said:

> Ethnocentrism is the technical name for this view of things in which one's own group is the center of everything, and all others are scaled and rated with reference to it. Folkways correspond to it to cover both the inner and the outer relation. Each group nourishes its own pride and vanity, boasts itself superior, exalts its own divinities, and looks with contempt on outsiders. Each group thinks its own folkways the only right ones, and if it observes that other groups have other folkways, these excite its scorn. Opprobrious epithets are derived from these differences.

Sumner's concept, and related ones such as the in-group and out-group, provoked a host of studies and publications over subsequent decades, which Robert LeVine and Donald Campbell later summarized and scrutinized in their overview *Ethnocentrism: Theories of Conflict, Ethnic Attitudes and Group Behavior* (1972). They identified half a dozen 'universal stereotypes', where the 'self description' of a group would contrast with a stereotype of the out-group, along the following lines: (1) We have pride, self-respect and revere the traditions of our ancestors. They are egotistical and self-centred. (2) We are loyal. They are clannish, exclude others. (3) We are honest and trustworthy among ourselves, but we are not suckers when foreigners try their tricks. They will cheat us if they can. They have no honesty or moral restraint when dealing with us. (4) We are brave and progressive. We stand up for our rights, defend what is ours, and can't be pushed around or bullied. They are aggressive and expansionistic. They want to get ahead at our expense. (5) We are peaceful, loving people, hating only our vile enemies. They are a hostile people who hate us. (6) We are moral and clean. They are immoral and unclean. Such ideas can be found at all times and places.

Some of these feelings are easy to recognize, others less so. But consider the following question. Which one of us is not thoroughly convinced, deep at heart, that our society and mores are better than those anywhere else and ever before? Who can say that this does not affect his or her value judgment of social systems elsewhere and earlier? Who is really able and willing to accept the equal value of the perspective of an African shepherd or a medieval monk? This is extremely hard to realize. We tend to be dismissive of such perspectives, and we simply do not have the information to put ourselves in their shoes. The same holds for the perspectives of the First, Second and Third Worlds, of the wide variety of countries and peoples contained within those blanket terms.

LeVine and Campbell quoted the example of earlier research by U. R. Ehrenfels on recurrent patterns in North–South stereotyping. Northerners saw themselves as: of strong character, powerful militarily, economically vigorous, good organizers, industrious, hard-working, reliable, manly, serious and thrifty. Southerners saw themselves as: eloquent, artistic, socially refined, patient, clever, intelligent, obliging, graceful, amiable and generous. By contrast, Northerners saw Southerners as: economically and militarily and generally weak, lazy, quick and fast, amiable and oily, unreliable, wasteful, optimistic, light-hearted, crafty, clever and spineless. Southerners saw Northerners as: powerful economically and militarily, hard-working, energetic, physically strong, slow and heavy, rough and dirty, egocentric, stingy, pessimistic, hard-hearted, serious, stupid and fanatic (pp. 7, 173, 162). Evidence came from twenty nations in the Northern hemisphere; there are some indications that the patterns may sometimes be reversed within or between countries of the Southern hemisphere (see also Van den Heuvel, 1992).

Throughout this book, we have seen recurrent examples of such patterns emerging from media images. Since most of the world's most influential transcontinental media are 'Northern and Western' media, it is not surprising that their dominant stereotypes are about 'Southern and Eastern' peoples. Since most of the world's most influential transcontinental media are Euro-American, it is not surprising that their dominant stereotypes are about Africans and Arabs, Asians and Latinos.

In their book *Unthinking Eurocentrism* (1994), about popular movie images of ethnic others, Ella Shohat and Robert Stam posit that

> an awareness of the intellectually debilitating effects of the Eurocentric legacy is indispensable for comprehending not only contemporary media representations but even contemporary subjectivities. Endemic in present-day thought and education, Eurocentrism is naturalized as 'common sense' . . . So embedded is Eurocentrism in everyday life, so pervasive, that it often goes unnoticed. The residual traces of centuries of axiomatic European domination inform the general culture, the everyday language, and the media, engendering a fictitious sense of the innate superiority of European-derived cultures and peoples.

They plead for multiculturalism instead, an active empowerment of marginalized voices from other cultures. And they defend themselves against criticism of such criticism: 'multiculturalism is actually an assault not on Europe or Europeans but on Eurocentrism – on the procrustean forcing of cultural heterogeneity into a single paradigmatic perspective in which Europe is seen as the unique source of meaning, as the world's center of gravity, as ontological "reality" to the rest of the world's shadow' (pp. 1–2).

Explode the Tintin myth

While writing this book, I constantly heard the inner voices of my journalistic and academic friends and colleagues resounding in my head. 'All this is sterile sophistry! What's new? It has always been like this, and it will always be like this! What else can we do? Other media systems are worse than ours!' To a certain extent they are right. It is like full democracy: the ideal itself can never be completely attained, but it is worthwhile to keep trying. It is the constant renewal of the struggle itself which is the essence of the process, not the ultimate reaching of the goal which would allow us to sit back.

At the same time, I feel a number of things can indeed be done to help improve news reporting about others. This does not necessarily demand a complete overhaul of the system, but rather a greater lucidity on the part of both producers and consumers of news and views. It demands a dismantling of the pernicious Tintin myth, for instance: that most journalists are investigative reporters with unlimited means at their individual disposal, who will not rest before they have found out the truth. Everyday media reality is much more prosaic. Here are a few suggestions.

1   Let us stop pretending that objective and neutral news reporting can easily be realized by just applying a few easy rules of thumb. Let us admit that news often implies views, and that there is often more than one truth which counts – even more so in international affairs. Let us admit that there are a hundred and one mechanisms in which a journalist is caught unwillingly, and from which he or she cannot easily extricate him- or herself. Let us make it possible to discuss these, without always seeing this as a challenge to the journalist's good faith.

2   Let us try to readjust the balance between reporting on person-alities and on social systems, on events and processes, on negativity and positivity, on sameness and otherness. Let us not limit reporting about other cultures and continents to mega-disasters, but find ways to create more understanding for and identification with ordinary people under entirely different circumstances.

3   Let us find ways to have more media material from other cultures and continents published and broadcast here. Let us promote more direct exchanges of views. Let us not always accede to the biggest and the most prestigious. Let us see to it that non-commercial media and non-commercial projects still get a chance, and that we do not have to live in an environment completely co-opted by adver-tising.

4   Let us broaden the base of recruitment of journalists, with regard to language, nationality, ethnicity, class, gender, etc. Let us not teach them that there is only one best way of doing things, but that different approaches may have equal value. Let us make practical intercultural communication a standard element in the curriculum. Encourage investigative journalism and going against the tide.

5   Let us not make ourselves overly dependent upon experts and official sources. And be alert to manipulation, particularly in situations

of armed conflict. Let us try to break out of the consensual agenda of what is topical and what is not. Let us go out of our way to hear different voices. Let us present opposite points of view completely and coherently, even if we disagree.

6   Let us not surrender to the dictatorship of the stopwatch, and of prime definitions by large-scale media organizations. Let us not squander media resources by sending crowds of reporters to the same mediatic events, particularly if it is highly improbable that they can gather alternative information. Let us be suspicious of pseudo-events which are staged to be covered and to air only one point of view. See to it that celebrations and commemorations are not only presented from one historical perspective.

7   Let us see fewer correspondents in well-covered places and more people in ill-covered places. Make more long-term investments in cultural acquaintances, rather than rotating and/or parachuting people in all the time. Be aware that being in one place and not in another always implies a certain perspective. Continually question the 'world of the news'.

8   Language is much more complicated than it seems. There is always more than one word for the same thing. Intuitively choosing one and skipping another always has implications. The same holds for sentences and narratives. Continually question the standard myths and discourses and ideologies concerning a particular subject.

9   Learn to deconstruct images: what is there and what is not, what point of view is taken, what sequence is chosen? The television evening news is not a window on the world but largely a staged play, based on fixed elements. Analyse the hidden roles and acts and scripts. Challenge the underlying logic and definitions.

10   Let us generalize media education in schools and for adults. Everybody should be able to analyse whether an item would have been reported in the same way (words, images, sequences) if the journalists, sources, dateline, etc. had been different. People should be trained to see the many different realities out there, rather than only one.

Notes

1 In *The Image: A Guide to Pseudo-events in America* (1961), p. 5.

Further reading

Problem construction: Edelman. *Ethnocentrism and enemy images*: Keene; LeVine and Campbell; Shohat and Stam. *Conflict and war reporting*: Arno and Dissanayake; Bell; J. Taylor; Knightley. *Glossary*: O'Sullivan et al.

APPENDIX: STUDYING GLOBAL MEDIA

The minor research projects described here are related to critical media analysis in the fields of international and intercultural news, media organization and content. The goal of the exercises is to heighten sensitivity to the various national and cultural perspectives embedded in news and other mediated messages surrounding us. Students should be willing to reconsider and explore their own mind-sets. This presupposes a recognition of the fact that we all live by simplified images of the world and stereotypes. Discussions should therefore be characterized by a tolerant atmosphere and the suspension of a judgmental attitude. Everyone should be bound by this contract.

General procedures

BETWEEN SIX AND TWELVE MEETINGS   The book has nine chapters, plus an introduction and a concluding chapter. It can be studied and discussed in a similar number of meetings, for instance, during weekly courses throughout a thirteen-week term. A reduced programme of six sessions might study and discuss the chapters in pairs (2 and 3, 4 and 5, 6 and 7, 8 and 9, 10 and 11 can be combined). An extended programme might study and discuss the book in combination with other books, for instance, illustrated books about advertising, popular culture, enemy images, or feature films. O'Barr, Nederveen Pieterse, Keene, Shohat and Stam are examples of such books, at ascending levels of difficulty.

INDIVIDUAL OR COLLECTIVE EXERCISES   The exercises may be carried out by individual participants or in groups, each time or in turns. It is best to have the exercises done in preparation for the next meeting, and to have participants present the results to the group as a whole. These may then be used as the basis for further discussions about which conclusions can be drawn from them (or not). The group can either work autonomously and direct its own work or be coached by a teacher or trainer. Since the exercises are presented here only in their general outline, it is important that specifics should be further filled in. That is to say, each meeting should set the exact tasks to be carried out by everyone before the next meeting, the precise categories to be used, etc.

AD HOC OR CUMULATIVE TASKS   The exercises can be done on an ad hoc basis with new and different tasks every week, and no necessary linkage between them. Or they can be done on a cumulative basis with participants collecting certain types of material throughout the programme, exchanging relevant material among themselves, and successively focusing on various different aspects of it. Participants may use identical or contrasting frames of analysis. Students of different nationalities or backgrounds, for instance, may each choose a different daily newspaper to monitor, a weekly news magazine, a radio or television news programme, and apply more or less identical frames and compare results.

CHOICE OF SUBJECTS   Individual participants or groups may choose a region of the world, a country, a group or an issue to analyse. They may do so at the beginning and stick to it for the entire course or choose one towards the end and only for a final essay. In this way they may try to apply all nine questions (as formulated in the chapter headings) to the analysis of the construction of one concrete and topical international or intercultural news subject. For instance, a crude socio-geographic subdivision may be used as a basis, with individuals or groups focusing on news coverage of ethnic minorities in North America and/or in Western Europe; on news coverage of Eastern Europe; of North Africa and West Asia; of sub-Saharan Africa; of South Asia; of East Asia, of South-east Asia and/or the Southern Pacific; of Latin America and/or the Caribbean.

MEDIA MATERIAL   Usually it is best to focus on mainstream media and the media environment of the country where the course is taught. If some participants are sufficiently familiar with a foreign language, and if examples of the foreign press are available at the news-stand, and/or foreign broadcasters available via satellite or cable, some may be encouraged to focus on the monitoring and analysis of such foreign material, so that the scope of the group (and its discussions) may be further widened. If some participants have a different nationality or background, they may contribute a different perspective if they want (but they should not have the position of the other imposed upon them, or be allowed to barricade themselves into that role).

TYPES OF MEDIA AND MATERIAL   Individual participants or groups may monitor the press, such as representative daily newspapers, weekly newspapers and/or news magazines, illustrated general interest magazines, etc. throughout the course. They may focus on certain types of editorial material (clipping, copying and/or redistributing it among themselves), such as the major intercultural front-page stories; news pictures; maps and situation sketches; editorial cartoons. Or the better equipped and more technically oriented participants may choose to monitor broadcasting: intercultural items in news programmes on radio and television, in news background programmes and talk shows, or even in advertising and clips on domestic and foreign channels. If possible, it is preferable to have adequate equipment available, which enables all to present salient examples to the group as a whole (an overhead projector screen, video recorder and monitor).

ANNOTATION Participants building files to present and analyse material (such as clippings, photocopies, tapes) should from the very start have the habit of noting the exact source of the material and, if possible, also of collecting some quantitative and qualitative information on the audience it usually reaches.

First session

MAPS EXERCISE The first session, when participants are still relatively blank about the subject, might begin with the maps exercise. The exercise is particularly revealing if participants come from contrasting national and/or cultural backgrounds. The exercise is described in the introductory chapter.

Once participants have completed drawing the maps, let them turn the papers and write on the back of each page (if they want to, for the choice should be free) not their names, but, for instance, (1) their nationality or previous nationality; (2) the nationality of their parents and/or grandparents; (3) the religion of their parents and/or grandparents; (4) the main country or countries where the participant him- or herself has lived; (5) the main country or countries which the participant has visited (on holiday, for instance).

After this, collect the sheets and redistribute them (to other participants). Ask participants to consider the specific features of the map(s), with regard to representation and non-representation, centrality, volume and detail. Ask them to take a special look at the representation of the countries mentioned. Let them keep a special eye on possibly relevant historic perspectives (for example, colonial bonds), cultural perspectives (for example, religious bonds), etc. Catholics may assign special importance to Italy and Rome, Jews to Jerusalem and Israel, Muslims to Mecca and Saudi Arabia, Hindus to Benares and India, etc. Observations may be presented to the group and discussed. The discussion should illustrate that there are various subjective cultural orientations on the same objective geographic reality. None is a priori superior to any other. The teacher or trainer may also have prepared overhead sheets of some drawn or printed maps to illustrate major points.

GEOGRAPHIC NAMES EXERCISE   Participants may think up and write down geographic names celebrating a specific historic or cultural, political or religious perspective: as many as possible, for example Columbia (Columbus), Bolivia (Simon Bolivar), El Salvador, Santo Domingo, etc. Have them report to the group in categories, for instance, for each continent. (The index of an atlas may be used as a tool.) Discuss which cultural perspectives are over- or under-represented, where and why.

Chapter 2. What is news? Philosophy

NEWS ISSUES   Try to identify one or more major international or intercultural crises under way or in the making, that is to say, those which will probably unfold further over the duration of the course. Focus some of the exercises on this or these particular crises. Return regularly to the subject during group discussions.

TRAGIC DEATH   Participants make a score card for each account of an individual or collective tragic death related in their sample of news media material. The tragic deaths may also be put in different categories, such as disease, accident, murder, suicide, etc. For each account, participants try to estimate whether the deceased apparently belonged to a specific gender, age group, nationality, ethnic group, linguistic group, etc. and try to calculate (or estimate) percentages.

Results are presented and summarized in the group, and then discussed. Is there an over-emphasis on some and an under-emphasis of others? Try, for instance, to come up with comparable instances of tragic death, which were not related at all in the samples of news media material and probably rarely will be. Why is this the case? (The teacher-trainer, or a participant, may previously try to get hold of a copy of relevant statistics, such as those referred to in the relevant section of the chapter. These may be used as a basis for comparison.)

NEWS QUIZ   Questions may be devised for a topical news quiz about intercultural subjects and frequent misconceptions (or ask participants to contribute questions themselves). Here too, answers should be quick. Numbers and proportions are particularly suitable for the exploration of gross misperceptions.

Chapter 3. Which are the media? Economics

The following exercises may be carried out by various groups.

DAILY NEWS   Take a sample of news items from the front page and foreign affairs pages of a number of dailies. Look to see if there is any indication of the news agency, syndication service or other organization which supplied the material at the beginning or the end of the items. Establish a frequency list, and discuss the results.

MAGAZINE TITLES   Go to a news-stand. Look on different shelves: those for cartoons and/or children's magazines, for fashion and/or women's magazines, men's magazines, family magazines, etc. Try to identify those titles or formats which have editions in many different countries and/or language areas. Try to identify the home country and/or language area where these titles and/or formats come from.[1]

UMFELD EFFECT   Select a number of major glossy magazines in different categories. Establish categories for different products and services. Count the number of advertisement pages in each category. Relate this to the number of editorial pages. Try to identify editorial pages with a more or less critical discussion of (the effects of) such products and services. Try to identify editorial pages with a more or less promotional discussion of (the effects of) such products and services. Discuss the extent to which the editorial content runs parallel or counter to the advertising content. Try to do the same with the items in special newspaper sections on lifestyles (books, cars, house and garden, travel, etc.).

BEST-SELLERS   Try to acquire a list of books which are currently the top ten best-sellers in fiction, non-fiction or both in the country. You can do this by going to a bookshop which has them on display, or by looking up lists in certain dailies or weeklies. Try to establish from which country and/or language area the author and/or the original edition come. You may try to do the same with a list of the top hundred 'best' fiction and/or non-fiction books, or the top hundred best-selling books of all time, which can be found in certain reference works.

TELEVISION DRAMA   Take TV guides for one week. Look at the programme listings for the main national channels. Note the major TV drama (fiction) series, regardless of the genre. See if you can gather from which country and/or language area each series comes. Establish a frequency list. Try to calculate the percentage of series originating from each country and/or language area.

FILMS   Take a sample of the weekly film listings in the newspaper. See if you can gather from which country and/or language area each film comes. Establish a frequency list. Try to calculate the percentage of films originating from each country and/or language area.

DRAMATIC PERSPECTIVE   Which countries are over-represented, which countries (or continents) are under-represented (or absent) in television drama and films? What does this imply for the views of the world, of society, of history presented to us? Focus on one socio-historic conflict between an over-represented and an under-represented foreign country, about which a number of TV films or cinema films have been made. Make a list. Do they have a certain focus and perspective in common or not?

Chapter 4. Who are journalists? Sociology

TELEVISION NEWS   Try to generate a list – as complete as possible – of all journalists contributing to the main television evening news programmes of the various channels on camera: presenters, reporters, correspondents, etc. One approach is to ask participants simply to name all people they can remember. Another approach is to ask various participants to watch, or even tape (a representative sample of) such broadcasts over the weeks. Make an index card for each journalist. Note their professional role and gender. Try to estimate the age bracket. Consider whether they apparently belong to the ethnic majority or a minority. Consider whether they have a regional or class accent. Consider whether they have a physical handicap. Calculate proportions and/or correlations between the various categories. Discuss the outcomes.

IMAGES OF JOURNALISTS   Make a list of journalist characters on overseas assignments in popular novels, comic strips (Tintin), television series, films. How 'realistic' are their adventures? How is their profession portrayed? How are their encounters with foreign cultures depicted?

EMANCIPATION   Find out to what extent relevant bodies have an intercultural policy. Does the curriculum of the major journalism schools give attention to intercultural communication? Do the major media, media interest groups and trade organizations have emancipatory policies? Try to acquire the relevant texts: multiply, distribute, analyse and discuss them.

Chapter. 5. Who is speaking? Politics

PRESS SOURCES   Take a representative sample of press news stories with an intercultural aspect (minorities, international relations, etc.). Read through them carefully. Mark every indication of a source in red. Note the labels attached to the indications of sources. Literal quotations (beginning and ending with quotation marks) may be marked in green; count or estimate the number of words in each literal quotation. Calculate proportions and/or correlations between the various categories. Discuss the outcomes.

BROADCASTING INTERVIEWEES Take a representative sample of television news interviews with an intercultural aspect. Make an index card for each interviewee. How long is the entire item and how long are their interventions? Note as well as you can whether they are presented anonymously or by their full names, by their function and the group or institution they (are supposed to) represent; also their gender, age bracket, nationality. See whether they are considered white or non-white. Calculate proportions and/or correlations between the various categories. Discuss the outcomes.

PROPORTION OF 'OFFICIALS' Try to calculate or estimate what the proportion of 'official' sources is, and their share of literal quotes. Do they speak for the government/administration of the country, its major allies, its major enemies; do they speak for business groups, public interest groups, others? Calculate proportions and/or correlations between the various categories. Discuss the outcomes.

ADVERSARY DISCOURSE Select five issues on which your government or its allies have clashed with adversarial foreign governments or adversarial cultural groups in recent times. How well-informed are you on these clashes? Would you be able to sum up the reasoning of the other party in more than one paragraph: extensively, coherently, plausibly and in more or less legitimate terms? Or can you just come up with 'bad guy' stereotypes?

Chapter 6. When does it become news? History

DISASTER Discuss a recent disaster abroad. To what extent did coverage focus on the topical incident rather than on the underlying processes? To what extent was the over- or under-coverage of certain aspects related to a cultural perspective?

NEWS RELEASE EXERCISE Take a representative sample of press news stories with an intercultural or international aspect. Read through them carefully. Mark every indication of why and how the news is reported at this point in time, for example, (press) conference, news release (report), a speech at a planned event, etc. Calculate what percentage of news is based on such planned news items.

ELEMENTARY SCHOOLBOOKS EXERCISE   Go back to your own school-books in history and similar subjects – if you still have them – or try to borrow some from children in your family, neighbours or friends for a day or two. Make photocopies of the passages dealing with certain 'delicate' themes, for instance, with explorers and conquerors, slavery and exploitation, colonialism and decolonization. See if you can identify possible examples of selective articulation in the space devoted to such subjects, the language in which they are framed, the images by which they are illustrated. Present these to the group; discuss them.

STREET-NAMES EXERCISE   Get hold of a copy of a town guidebook with street maps and names, or make a list of major street names yourself. Try to identify those street names which bear some relation to intercultural history: which mention countries or geographic places, nationalities or ethnic groups, explorers or politicians? Discuss what names might also have been used, but are absent.

TOURIST VISITOR EXERCISE   Ask participantss to go to the tourist office and collect the brochures distributed to foreign visitors. Ask them to analyse and discuss these. What landmarks are over-emphasized or under-emphasized; in what cultural perspective are they presented? (Some participants may even take the standard city tour, tape the oral presentation and analyse it.)

Chapter 7. Where does world news come from? Geography

PRESS DATELINES   Take a large sample of international relations and foreign news stories. Look at the datelines. Note the places where these stories come from, and the frequency. Check whether the country they come from is also the (only) country the stories relate to. Sometimes they come from one country, but relate to an issue between two countries. Sometimes they come from one country, but relate to another country. Is there a pattern? Do such stories more often originate from a larger country and/or a country culturally closer to us? If so, could this affect the selective articulation of voices (and perspectives) in world news?

TELEVISION CORRESPONDENTS   Refer back to the list of TV correspon-dents for news programmes on the various channels which was collected for Chapter 4 or construct a new one. Try to note or estimate the frequency and length of their reports. Which cities and countries are covered by all channels? Which cities and countries are covered only by some? Which cities and countries (or even entire continents) are hardly covered at all? What are the causes and what are the consequences of this situation? How might this affect our perspectives on the world situation, and our news thresholds for different countries and continents?

STANDARD IMAGERY What are the most frequently used stills or live backgrounds for the various neignbourhoods and cities, countries and continents (those against which correspondents sit or stand)? What are the possible implications of this standard choice of images?

Chapter 8. How are messages formulated? Linguistics

HEADLINES Build files of interesting headlines consisting of incomplete sentences. Discuss their terminology and construction, their selective articulation of certain aspects of reality.

DUAL VOCABULARY Build files of articles on ongoing forms of intercultural conflict, which involve violence or a direct threat of violence. Then focus on those conflicts, in which a party with Western or pro-Western values can be identified, and a party with non- or anti-Western values. Read carefully through the articles and underline words which imply some kind of value judgment about systems, organizations, people, actions, etc. Group them in two columns for each issue, and indicate their frequency if they return. Discuss the results.

MIND MAPPING Try to identify which terms participants associate with other terms, for instance, with French and German, white and black, Arab and Indian, desert and rainforest, oil and cotton, beach and palm-tree, etc. This may be done individually and on separate pieces of paper with the key word in the middle, a circle of first-degree associations around it, a circle of second-degree associations around that. Or it may be done collectively and on a blackboard by listing associated terms and idiomatic expressions.

MEGA-STORIES Let participants try to spell out or write out the dominant mega-stories concerning such subjects as discoverers, colonialism, slavery, development, aid, natural disasters, famine, human rights, terrorism, democracy, etc.

Chapter 9. How do images come about? Semiology

MAJOR CRISIS From the start of the teaching or training programme, keep an attentive eye on a major new crisis related to intercultural communication which may be developing and may get extensive news coverage. Ask the press group to collect news photographs and ask the broadcasting group to tape the first major television items. You may try to focus the following analyses primarily on the visual reporting of this one crisis.

PHOTOGRAPHIC IMAGES   Who is shown on news pictures with an intercultural, international or foreign news angle? Make an index card for each picture. Are some people identified by name in the byline, and do other people remain anonymous? What is their gender and age bracket; are they white or 'non-white'? Are they shown individually or in pairs, in a small or large group? Are they shown in a close, medium or long shot (total)? Is their facial expression joyous, neutral, sad?

Collections such as the 'World Press Photo' books may be useful (or compare them with non-news collections such as the famous 'Family of Man' books).

OPENING AND CLOSING   Some participants may devote particular attention to the leaders, the opening and closing images and rituals of TV evening news and topical background programmes. Tape some, edit them together and present them to the group as a whole. What do they try to convey?

CIVIL UNREST   Take a closer look at TV evening news reports of protests, strikes, demonstrations, riots. What images are not shown? What images are shown, in what sequence, with what comments? Could they have been edited and narrated in a different way? What perspective is favoured in this presentation; what perspective is blotted out?

DRAMADOC AND DOCUDRAMA   Make an inventory of cinema and television films purporting to present a well-documented and more or less correct reconstruction of real historical events. Be careful to include a number of ancient and a number of more recent examples. In what country and for what audience were they primarily produced? Is this reflected in their selective articulation of the protagonists, their acts and the facts? Would it have been possible to choose a different perspective, without obviously lying? How?

FICTION IN FILMS   Look at how cultural 'others', their actions or inaction, are presented in feature film series built around adventure abroad: Miss Marple/Hercule Poirot, James Bond, Indiana Jones. (Or even science fiction films such as *Star Trek* and *Star Wars*.)

Chapter 10. What effects do media have? Psychology

THEME PARK STEREOTYPES Whoever has visited Disneyland in Anaheim (California), Orlando (Florida) or Paris, is familiar with their subdivision into different 'lands', such as 'Pirates of the Caribbean'. Make an inventory of the elements presented. Broaden the discussion to similar elements in other theme parks and 'movie worlds' (Universal Studios). Another approach is to discuss recent Disney blockbusters such as *Aladdin* (Arabia), *The Lion King* (Africa) and *Pocahontas* (America). To what extent do they exploit existing stereotypes and to what extent do they confront them?

TOURIST BROCHURE EXERCISE Ask participants to go to travel agencies and collect brochures on specific destinations in sub-Saharan Africa; North Africa and West Asia; South Asia; South-east Asia; East Asia; the Pacific; Central and South America. Ask them to analyse the texts and pictures. What elements are over- or under-emphasized? (They may analyse them in subgroups, and prepare the discussion for the whole group.)

PHOTO ALBUM EXERCISE Ask participants to bring a photo album of visits which they and/or their immediate family members paid to one or two foreign countries or continents, the more culturally distant the better. Review and discuss these pictures. To what extent do they focus on well-identified landmarks and/or pre-existing images (the Eiffel Tower and the Sacré Coeur, palm-trees and sandy beeches, colourful markets and strange dresses). How do they depict local people, animals, plants, houses and other artefacts? What is absent from these pictures? How do these pictorial choices relate to (and reproduce) cultural stereotypes?

ETHNIC JOKES Ask participants to give examples of ethnic jokes. To what extent do such jokes promote stereotypes, deflect them, neither or both? Under what circumstances? What is the evidence pleading for or against the different points of view? What is acceptable and what is not? Why?

Chapter 11. Conclusion

EDITORIAL CARTOONS EXERCISE Participants may build a file of editorial cartoons related to international politics over time. These may then be grouped by region and/or country, by problem and/or leader(s). Those related to conflict, armed conflict, matters of life and death are usually particularly moral or moralistic in tone. To what extent do they reflect the 'us versus them' divide, enemy images, etc.?

COMIC STRIPS EXERCISE   Identify well-known classical comic strips, in which travel to distant lands and cultural 'others' play a prominent role (Tintin, Astérix and others). Analyse how these others are described and depicted. Discuss your findings. (The discussion may even be extended to the use of different kinds of animals or hybrids in some of these comic strips as a metaphor for ethnic groups.)

PROBLEM CONSTRUCTION   Select a major domestic or foreign problem. Look at the various aspects of the construction of a problem, as quoted from Edelman (see pp. 208–9). Do they apply to your case? How?

Notes

1 Examples: *Burda, Cosmo, Donald Duck, Elle, Mad, Marie Claire, Mickey Mouse, Penthouse, Playboy, Reader's Digest, Vogue,* etc.

BIBLIOGRAPHY

Abbott, Andrew (1988) *The System of Professions: An Essay on the Division of Expert Labour*. Chicago: University of Chicago Press.

Allport, G. W. and Postman, L. (1947) *The Psychology of Rumour*. New York: Holt.

Altheide, David L. (1976) *Creating Reality: How TV News Distorts Events*. Beverly Hills, CA, and London: Sage.

Ang, Ien (1985) *Watching Dallas*. London: Methuen.

Ang, Ien (1991) *Desperately Seeking the Audience*. London: Routledge.

Arno, Andrew and Dissanayake, Wimal (1984) *The News Media and International Conflict*. Boulder, CO: Westview.

Baarda, Frits (1989) *Het oog van de oorlog: Fotografen aan het front*. Den Haag: Focus/ SDU.

Bagdikian, Ben (1983) *The Media Monopoly*. Boston: Beacon.

Barnouw, Erik (1978) *The Sponsor: Notes on a Modern Potentate*. New York: Oxford University Press.

Barthes, Roland (1970) *Mythologies*. Paris: Seuil.

Bell, Martin (1995) *In Harm's Way: Reflections of a War Zone Thug*. London: Hamish Hamilton.

Benthall, Jonathan (1993) *Disasters, Relief and the Media*. London: Tauris.

Berger, Peter and Luckmann, Thomas (1981) *The Social Construction of Reality: A Treatise in the Sociology of Knowledge*. Harmondsworth: Penguin.

Boorstin, Daniel J. (1980) *The Image: A Guide to Pseudo-events in America*. New York: Atheneum.

Bouwman, Harry (1987) *Televisie als cultuurschepper*. Amsterdam: Vrije Universiteit (dissertation).

Boyd-Barrett, Oliver (1980) *The International News Agencies*. London: Constable and Beverly Hills, CA: Sage.

Boyd-Barrett, Oliver and Palmer, Michael (1981) *Trafic de nouvelles*. Paris: Moreau.

Boyd-Barrett, Oliver and Thussu, Daya Kishan (1992) *Contra-flow in Global News: International and Regional News Exchange Mechanisms*. London: Libbey.

Brand, Stewart (1988) *The Media Lab: Inventing the Future at MIT*. New York: Viking Penguin.

Brants, C. H. and Brants, K. L. K. (1991) *De sociale constructie van fraude*. Arnhem: Gouda Quint (dissertation).

Breed, Warren (1960) 'Social control in the newsroom: a functional analysis', in Schramm, W. (ed.), *Mass Communications*. Urbana, IL: University of Illinois Press. pp. 178–94.

Broder, David (1987) *Behind the Front Page: A Candid Look at How the News is Made*. New York: Simon and Schuster.

Brucker, Herbert (1951) *Freedom of Information*. New York: Macmillan.

Brunsdon, Charlotte and Morley, David (1978) *Everyday Television: Nationwide*. London: British Film Institute.

Bryant, Jennings and Zillmann, Dolf (1994) *Media Effects: Advances in Theory and Research*. Hillsdale, NJ: Erlbaum.

Cerf, Christopher and Navasky, Victor (1984) *The Experts Speak: The Definitive Compendium of Authoritative Misinformation*. New York: Pantheon.

Chamorro, Edgar (1987) *Packaging the Contras: A Case of CIA Disinformation.* New York: Institute for Media Analysis.

Cohen, Akiba A., Adoni, Hanna and Bantz, Charles R. (1990) *Social Conflict and Television News.* Newbury Park, CA: Sage.

Cohen, Bernard (1963) *The Press and Foreign Policy.* Princeton, NJ: Princeton University Press.

Cohen, Jeff and Solomon, Norman (1993) *Adventures in Medialand: Behind the News, Beyond the Pundits.* Monroe (Maine): Common Courage.

Cohen, Stanley (1993) *Folk Devils and Moral Panics: The Creation of the Mods and Rockers.* Oxford: Blackwell.

Cohen, Stanley and Young, Jock (eds) (1973) *The Manufacture of News: Social Problems, Deviance and the Mass Media.* London: Constable.

Cole, J. P. (1983) *Geography of World Affairs.* London: Butterworth Heinemann.

Compaine, Benjamin (ed.) (1979) *Who Owns the Media? Concentration and Ownership in the Mass Communications Industry.* New York: Harmony.

Cross, Donna W. (1983) *Mediaspeak: How Television Makes up your Mind.* New York: Mentor/New American Library.

Crouse, Timothy (1973) *The Boys on the Bus.* New York: Random House.

Cuilenburg, J. J. van, Scholten, O. and Noomen, G. W. (1992) *Communicatiewetenschap.* Muiderberg: Coutinho.

De Landtsheer, Christ'l (1987) *De politieke taal in de Vlaamse media.* Antwerpen: Kluwer.

DeMause, Lloyd (1982) *Foundations of Psychohistory.* New York: Creative Roots.

DeMause, Lloyd (1984) *Reagan's America.* New York: Creative Roots.

Downing, John, Mohammadi, Ali and Sreberny-Mohammadi, Annabelle (1990) *Questioning the Media: A Critical Introduction.* Newbury Park, CA: Sage.

Edelman, Murray (1988) *Constructing the Political Spectacle.* Chicago: University of Chicago Press.

Elridge, John (ed.) (1993) *Getting the Message: News, Truth and Power.* London: Routledge.

Epstein, Edward Jay (1974) *News from Nowhere: Television and the News.* New York: Vintage/Random House.

Ericson, Richard V., Baranek, Patricia M. and Chan, Janet B. L. (1987) *Visualizing Deviance: A Study of News Organization.* Milton Keynes: Open University.

Eudes, Yves (1982) *La conquête des esprits: L'appareil d'exportation culturelle du gouvernement américain vers le tiers monde.* Paris: Maspéro.

Evans, Harold (1978) *Pictures on a Page: Photo-journalism, Graphics and Picture Editing.* London: Heinemann.

Fauconnier, Guido (1973) *Massamedia en samenleving: Inleiding tot de wetenschappelijke studie van de massacommunicatie.* Antwerpen: Nederlandse Boekhandel.

Fiske, John (1990) *Introduction to Communication Studies.* London and New York: Routledge.

Fiske, John (1993) *Television Culture.* London: Routledge.

Fiske, John and Hartley, John (1992) *Reading Television.* London and New York: Routledge.

Foot, Paul (1990) *Who Framed Colin Wallace?* New edn. London: Pan.

Fowler, Roger (1991) *Language in the News: Discourse and Ideology in the Press.* London and New York: Routledge.

Fowler, R., Hodge, B., Kress, G. and Trew, T. (1979) *Language and Control.* London: Routledge & Kegan Paul.

Frederick, Howard H. (1993) *Global Communication and International Relations.* Belmont, CA: Wadworth.

Freidson, Eliot (1994) *Professionalism Reborn: Theory, Prophecy and Policy.* Cambridge: Polity.

Fulbright, William (1970) *The Pentagon Propaganda Machine.* New York: H. Liveright.

Galtung, J. and Ruge, M. H. (1965) 'The structure of foreign news', *Journal of Peace Research*, 2: 64–91.

Gans, Herbert J. (1980) *Deciding What's News: A Study of CBS Evening News, NBC Nightly News, Newsweek and Time*. New York: Vintage/Random House.

Gerbner, George and Márványi, George (1977) 'The many worlds of the world's press', *Journal of Communication*, 26: 173–99.

Gerbner, George and Siefert, Martha (eds) (1984) *World Communications: A Handbook*. New York and London: Longman.

Gerbner, George, Mowlana, Hamid and Nordenstreng, Kaarle (1993) *The Global Media Debate: Its Rise, Fall and Renewal*. Norwood, NJ: Ablex.

Gervasi, Tom (1988) *Soviet Military Power: The Pentagon's Propaganda Document, Annotated and Corrected*. New York: Vintage/Random House.

Gitlin, Todd (1980) *The Whole World is Watching: Mass Media in the Making and Unmaking of the New Left*. Berkeley, CA: University of California Press.

Gitlin, Todd (1985) *Inside Prime Time*. New York: Pantheon.

Glasgow University Media Group (1976) *Bad News*. London: Routledge and Kegan Paul.

Glasgow University Media Group (1980) *More Bad News*. London: Routledge and Kegan Paul.

Goffman, Erving (1986) *Frame Analysis: An Essay on the Organization of Experience*. Boston: Northeastern University Press.

Goode, Erich and Ben-Yehuda, Nachman (1994) *Moral Panics: The Social Construction of Deviance*. Oxford: Blackwell.

Graber, Doris A. (1988) *Processing the News: How People Tame the Information Tide*. 2nd edn. New York: Longman.

Gudykunst, William B. and Kim, Young Yun (1992) *Communicating with Strangers: An Approach to Intercultural Communication*. New York: McGraw Hill.

Hall, Stuart, et al. (eds) (1978) *Policing the Crisis: Mugging, the State, and Law and Order*. London: Macmillan.

Hamelink, Cees J. (1983) *Cultural Autonomy in Global Communications*. New York: Longman (repr. London: Centre for the Study of Communication and Culture 1988).

Hamelink, Cees J. (1994) *Trends in World Communication: On Disempowerment and Self-empowerment*. Penang (Malaysia): Southbound/Third World Network.

Hamelink, Cees (1994) *The Politics of World Communication: A Human Rights Perspective*. London: Sage.

Hamelink, Cees and Linné, Olga (eds) (1994) *Mass Communication Research, on Problems and Policies: The Art of Asking the Right Questions* (in honour of James D. Halloran). Norwood, NJ: Ablex.

Harrison, Paul and Palmer, Robin (1986) *News Out of Africa: Biafra to Band Aid*. London: Hilary Stripman.

Hartley, John (1989) *Understanding News*. London and New York: Routledge.

Herman, Edward S. and Chomsky, Noam (1988) *Manufacturing Consent: The Political Economy of the Mass Media*. New York: Pantheon.

Himmelstein, Hal (1984) *Television Myth and the American Mind*. New York: Praeger.

Hofstede, Geert (1980) *Culture's Consequences: International Differences in Work-related Values*. Beverly Hills, CA: Sage.

Hofstede, Geert (1991) *Cultures and Organizations: Software of the Mind*. London: McGraw Hill.

Hughes, H. Stuart (1975) *The Sea Change: The Migration of Social Thought*. New York: Harper and Row.

Huxley, Aldous (1969) *Brave New World*. New York: Perennial/Harper and Row. (First published in 1932).

Iyengar, Shanto (1991) *Is Anyone Responsible? How Television News Frames Political Issues*. Chicago: University of Chicago Press.

Janis, I. L. (1972) *Victims of Groupthink*. Boston: Houghton Mifflin.

Jay, Martin (1973) *The Dialectical Imagination: A History of the Frankfurt School.* Boston: Little Brown.

Johnson, Terence (1993) *Professions and Power.* London: Macmillan.

Jowett, Garth S. and O'Donnell, Victoria (1986) *Propaganda and Persuasion.* Newbury Park, CA: Sage.

Julien, Claude (ed.) (1988) *La communication victime des marchands.* Paris: Le Monde Diplomatique/Série 'Manière de voir', no. 3.

Keene, Sam (1991) *Faces of the Enemy: Reflections of the Hostile Imagination.* San Francisco: Harper Collins.

Keesing, Roger M. (1981) *Cultural Anthropology: A Contemporary Perspective.* New York: Holt, Rinehart and Winston.

Klapper, Joseph (1960) *The Effects of Mass Communication.* New York: Free Press.

Knightley, Philip (1989) *The First Casualty, from the Crimea to the Falklands: The War correspondent as Hero, Propagandist and Myth Maker.* London: Pan.

Kolakowski, Leszek (1981) *Main Currents of Marxism.* Oxford: Oxford University Press.

Kundera, Milan (1982) *The Book of Laughter and Forgetting.* London: Faber & Faber.

Leblanc, Gérard (1987) *Treize heures, vingt heures: Le monde en suspens.* Marburg: Hitzeroth.

Lee, Martin A. and Solomon, Norman (1990) *Unreliable Sources: A Guide to Detecting Bias in News Media.* New York: Lyle Stuart/Carol.

LeVine, Robert and Campbell, Donald (1972) *Ethnocentrism: Theories of Conflict, Ethnic Attitudes and Group Behavior.* New York: Wiley.

Lippmann, Walter (1947) *Public Opinion.* New York: Macmillan.

Lorenz, Chris (1987) *De constructie van het verleden: Een inleiding in de theorie van de geschiedenis.* Amsterdam: Boom.

Lowery, Shearon and DeFleur, Melvin (1983) *Milestones in Mass Communication Research: Media Effects.* New York: Longman.

Lull, James (1995) *Media, Communications, Culture: A Global Approach.* Cambridge: Polity.

Lutz, William (1989) *Doublespeak.* New York: Harper Perennial.

MacBride, Sean (1983) *Many Voices, One World: Towards a New More Just and More Efficient World Information and Communication Order.* London: Kogan Page; New York: Unipub; Paris: Unesco.

Mander, Jerry (1978) *Four Arguments for the Elimination of Television.* New York: Quill.

Manoff, Robert Karl and Schudson, Michael (eds) (1987) *Reading the News.* New York: Pantheon.

Margolis, Michael and Mauser, Gary A. (1989) *Manipulating Public Opinion: Essays on Public Opinion as a Dependent Variable.* Pacific Grove, CA: Brooks Cole.

Marx, Gary and McAdam, Douglas (1994) *Collective Behavior and Social Movements: Process and Structure.* Englewood Cliffs, NJ: Prentice Hall.

Marx, Karl (1970) *Selected Writings in Sociology and Social Philosophy.* Harmondsworth: Penguin.

Mattelart, Armand (1979) *Multinational Corporations and the Control of Culture.* Brighton: Harvester.

Mayes, Stephen (1995) *Dit kritisch weerzien: 40 jaar World Press Photo.* Den Haag: SDU.

McCombs, M. E. and Shaw, D. L. (1972) 'The agenda-setting function of the mass media', *Public Opinion Quarterly,* 36: 176–87.

McPhail, Thomas (1987) *Electronic Colonialism: The Future of International Broadcasting and Communication.* Newbury Park, CA: Sage.

McQuail, Denis (1983) *Mass Communication Theory: An Introduction.* London: Sage (2nd edn 1987, 3rd edn 1994).

McQuail, Denis and Windahl, Sven (1993) *Communication Models for the Study of Mass Communication.* London and New York: Longman.

Melkote, Srinivas (1991) *Communication for Development in the Third World: Theory and Practice.* New Delhi: Sage.

Middleton, David and Edwards, Derek (1990) *Collective Remembering.* London: Sage.

Mills, C. Wright (1963) *Power, Politics and People: The Collected Essays*, ed. I. L. Horowitz. New York: Oxford University Press.

Monmonier, Mark (1989) *Maps with the News: The Development of American Journalistic Cartography*. Chicago: University of Chicago Press.

Monmonier, Mark (1991) *How to Lie with Maps*. Chicago: University of Chicago Press.

Mowlana, Hamid (1986) *Global Information and World Communication*. New York and London: Longman.

Muzik, Peter (1989) *Die Medienmultis*. Wien: Jahrbuch Neue Medien.

Nederveen Pieterse, Jan (1990) *Empire and Emancipation: Power and Liberation on a World Scale*. London: Pluto.

Nederveen Pieterse, Jan (1992) *White on Black: Images of Africa and Blacks in Western Popular Culture*. New Haven: Yale University Press.

Neibuhr, Reinhold (1963) 'The role of newspapers in America's function as a great power', in Casey, Ralph D. (ed.), *The Press in Perspective*. Baton Rouge, LA: Louisiana State University Press.

Nimmo, Dan and Combs, James E. (1993) *Mediated Political Realities*. New York and London: Longman.

Noelle-Neumann, Elisabeth (1984) *The Spiral of Silence: Public Opinion, Our Social Skin*. Chicago: University of Chicago Press.

O'Barr, William M. (1994) *Culture and the Ad: Exploring Otherness in the World of Advertising*. Boulder, CO: Westview.

Orwell, George (1981) *Nineteen Eighty-four*. Harmondsworth: Penguin. (First published in 1949.)

O'Sullivan, Tim, et al. (1988) *Key Concepts in Communication*. London and New York: Routledge.

Paget, Derek (1990) *True Stories? Documentary Drama on Radio, Screen and Stage*. Manchester: Manchester University Press; New York: St Martin's.

Parenti, Michael (1986) *Inventing Reality: The Politics of the Mass Media*. New York: St. Martin's.

Paulos, John Allen (1993) *A Mathematician Reads the Newspaper*. New York: Basic Books.

Phillips, J. L. (1981) *Piaget's Theory: A Primer*. San Francisco: Freeman.

Philo, Greg (1993) 'From Buerk to Band Aid', in Elridge, J. (ed.), *Getting the Message*. London: Routledge.

Postman, Neil (1985) *Amusing Ourselves to Death*. New York: Viking Penguin.

Postman, Neil and Powers, Steve (1992) *How to Watch TV News*. New York: Viking Penguin.

Pratkanis, Anthony and Aronson, Elliot (1992) *The Age of Propaganda: The Everyday Use and Abuse of Persuasion*. New York: Freeman.

Price, Stuart (1993) *Media Studies*. London: Pitman.

Price, Vincent (1992) *Public Opinion*. Newbury Park, CA: Sage.

Protess, D. L. and McCombs, M. E. (eds) (1991) *Agenda Setting: Readings on Media, Public Opinion and Policy Making*. Hillsdale, NJ: Erlbaum.

Ramonet, Ignacio (ed.) (1992) *Médias, mensonges et démocratie*. Paris: Le Monde Diplomatique/Série 'Manière de voir', no. 14.

Ramonet, Ignacio (ed.) (1993) *L'agonie de la culture?* Paris: Le Monde Diplomatique/Série 'Manière de voir', no. 19.

Ramonet, Ignacio and Halimi, Serge (eds) (1995) *Médias et contrôle des esprits*. Paris: Le Monde Diplomatique/Série 'Manière de Voir', no. 27.

Reeves, Geoffrey (1993) *Communications and the 'Third World'*. London and New York: Routledge.

Rietman, L. (1988) *Over objectiviteit, betonrot en de pijlers van de democratie: De westeuropese pers en het nieuws over Midden Amerika*. Nijmegen: Katholieke Universiteit/Institut voor Massacommunicatie (MA thesis).

Roloff, Michael E. and Berger, Charles R. (eds) (1982) *Social Cognition and Communication*. Beverly Hills, CA: Sage.

Romano, Carlin (1987) 'The grisly truth about bare facts', in Manoff, Robert Karl and Schudson, Michael (eds), *Reading the News*. New York: Pantheon.

Rosenblum, Mort (1981) *Coups and Earthquakes: Reporting the World to America*. New York: Harper Colophon.

Rosenblum, Mort (1993) *Who Stole the News? Why we Can't Keep up with What Happens in the World and What we Can Do About It*. New York: Wiley.

Rosengren, Karl Erik, et al. (eds) (1985) *Media Gratifications Research: Current Perspectives*. Beverly Hills, CA: Sage.

Ryan, Charlotte (1991) *Prime Time Activism: Media Strategies for Grassroots Organizing*. Boston: South End.

Said, Edward (1978) *Orientalism: Western Conceptions of the Orient*. London: Penguin.

Said, Edward (1981) *Covering Islam: How the Media and the Experts Determine how we see the Rest of the World*. London: Routledge and Kegan Paul.

Schiller, Herbert (1969) *Mass Communication and American Empire*. New York: Kelley.

Schiller, Herbert (1973) *The Mind Managers*. Boston: Beacon.

Schiller, Herbert (1976) *Communication and Cultural Domination*. White Plains, NY: Sharpe.

Schlesinger, Philip (1987) *Putting 'Reality' Together: BBC News*. London and New York: Methuen.

Schudson, Michael (1978) *Discovering the News: A Social History of American Newspapers*. New York: Basic Books.

Schulz, Winfried (1976) *Die Konstruktion von Realität in den Nachrichtenmedien: Analyse der aktuellen Berichterstattung*. Freiburg and München: Alber.

Seiter, Ellen, et al. (eds) (1989) *Remote Control: Television Audiences and Cultural Power*. London: Routledge.

Servaes, Jan and Tonnaer, Clement (1992) *De nieuwsmarkt*. Groningen: Wolters Noordhoff.

Shoemaker, Pamela J. (1991) *Gatekeeping*. Newbury Park, CA: Sage.

Shoemaker, Pamela and Reese, Stephen D. (1991) *Mediating the Message: Theories of Influences on Mass Media Content*. New York: Longman.

Shohat, Ella and Stam, Robert (1994) *Unthinking Eurocentrism: Multiculturalism and the Media*. London: Routledge.

Sigal, Leon V. (1973) *Reporters and Officials: The Organization and Politics of Newsmaking*. Lexington, MA: Heath.

Signorielli, Nancy and Morgan, Michael (1990) *Cultivation Analysis: New Directions in Media Effects Research*. Newbury Park, CA: Sage.

Siune, Karen and Truetzschler (eds) (1992) *Dynamics of Media Politics: Broadcast and Electronic Media in Western Europe*. London: Sage.

Smith, Hedrick (1988) *The Power Game: How Washington Works*. New York: Random House.

Smith, R. C. (1978) 'The magazines' smoking habit', *Columbia Journalism Review*, January/February: 29–31.

Stevenson, Robert L. and Shaw, Donald Lewis (1984) *Foreign News and the World Information Order*. Ames: Iowa State University Press.

Stone, William and Schaffner, Paul (1988) *The Psychology of Politics*. 2nd edn. New York: Springer.

Taylor, John (1991) *War Photography: Realism in the British Press*. London: Routledge; New York: Comedia.

Taylor, Peter (1984) *The Smoke Ring: Tobacco, Money and Multinational Politics*. London: Sphere.

't Hart, Paul (1990) *Groupthink in Government: A Study of Small Groups and Political Failure*. Leiden: Rijksuniversiteit (dissertation).

Trowler, Paul (1991) *Investigating the Media*. London: Harper Collins.

Tuchman, Gaye (1978) *Making News: A Study in the Construction of Reality*. New York: Free Press; London: Collier Macmillan.

Tunstall, Jeremy (1994) *The Media are American: Anglo-American Media in the World.* 2nd edn. London: Constable.

Tunstall, Jeremy (ed.) (1970) *Media Sociology.* London: Constable.

Tunstall, Jeremy and Palmer, Michael (1991) *Media Moguls.* London and New York: Routledge.

Van den Heuvel, Henriëtte (1992) *Us and Them: The Influence of Ethnicity and Gender on Stereotyping, Attitudes and Explanations of Behaviour.* Amsterdam University Faculty of Psychology (dissertation).

Van der Krogt, Th. P. W. M. (1981) *Professionalisering en collectieve macht: Een conceptueel kader.* Den Haag: Vuga (dissertation).

Van Dijk, Teun A. (1988a) *News as Discourse.* Hillsdale, NJ: Erlbaum.

Van Dijk, Teun A. (1988b) *News Analysis.* Hillsdale, NJ: Erlbaum.

Van Dijk, Teun (1991) *Racism and the Press.* London: Routledge.

Van Ginneken, Jaap (1992) *Crowds, Psychology and Politics.* New York: Cambridge University Press.

Van Ginneken, Jaap (1993a) *De uitvinding van het publiek: De opkomst van het opinie- en marktonderzoek in Nederland.* Amsterdam: Cramwinckel.

Van Ginneken, Jaap (1993b) *Rages en crashes: De onvoorspelbaarheid van de economie.* Bloemendaal: Aramith.

Van Ginneken, Jaap (1994) *Den Haag op de divan: Een psychologische analyse van onze politieke top.* Haarlem: Aramith.

Vasterman, Peter and Aerden, Onno (1995) *De context van het nieuws.* Groningen: Wolters Noordhoff.

Vink, Nico (1988) *The Telenovela and Emancipation: A Study on Television and Social Change in Brazil.* Amsterdam University (dissertation).

Wallis, Roger and Baran, Stanley (1990) *The Known World of Broadcast News: International News and the Electronic Media.* London: Routledge and Comedia.

Watzlawick, Paul (1976) *How Real is Real?* New York: Vintage Books.

Waugh, Evelyn (1943) *Scoop: A Novel about Journalists.* London: Penguin. (First published in 1938.)

Weaver, D. H. and Wilhoit, G. C. (1986) *The American Journalist: A Portrait of US Newspeople and Their Work.* Bloomington, IN: Indiana University Press.

Wesselius, Jacqueline (ed.) (1994) *Het mijnenveld: Over journalistiek en moraal.* Amsterdam: Nijgh and Van Ditmar.

Williams, Raymond (1983) *Keywords: A Vocabulary of Culture and Society.* London: Flamingo (Fontana).

Willis, Jim (1991) *The Shadow World: Life Between the News Media and Reality.* New York: Praeger.

Wober, Mallory and Gunter, Barrie (1988) *Television and Social Control.* Aldershot: Avebury.

Wombell, Paul (1991) *PhotoVideo: Photography in the Age of the Computer.* London: Rivers Oram.

Statistical data

Cordellier, Serge and Didiot, Béatrice (eds) (1995) *L'état du monde.* Paris: Éditions la Découverte.

Council of Europe (1995) *Statistical Yearbook.* Brussels: Council of Europe.

Famighetti, Robert, et al. (eds) (1995) *The World Almanac and Book of Facts.* Mahwah, NJ: Funk and Wagnalls.

Frémy, Dominique and Frémy, Michèle (ed.) (1995) *Quid.* Paris: Laffont.

Mermet, Gérard (1991) *Euroscopie.* Paris: Larousse.

UNESCO (1992) *Statistical Yearbook.* Paris: Unesco.

UNESCO (1989) *World Communication Report.* Paris: Unesco.

INDEX

....